D1271896

HOLY GHOST FATHERS
FERNDALE
NORWALK, CONN.

JESUS CHRIST, LORD OF HISTORY

HOLY GHOST FATHERS
FERNDALE
NORWALK, CONN.

"I am the light of the world." JO. 9:5. PHOTOGRAPH BY ED LETTAU.

LORD AND KING SERIES

JESUS CHRIST
LORD OF HISTORY

A FIRST-YEAR RELIGION COURSE

by

Vincent M. Novak, S. J.

HOLT, RINEHART AND WINSTON

NEW YORK

TO MY FATHER
NOW WITH GOD

BX 1970
N62 x
cop. 2

Imprimi potest
John J. McGinty, S.J.
Provincial of the New York Province
April 28, 1964

Nihil obstat
James F. Rigney, S.T.D.
Censor Librum
May 18, 1964

Imprimatur
✠ Francis Cardinal Spellman
Archbishop of New York
May 18, 1964

Copyright © 1964, Holt, Rinehart and Winston, Inc.
All rights reserved
Printed in the United States of America
56127–0114

TO THE TEACHERS OF GOD'S WORD

To proclaim the mystery of salvation, to "present" Jesus Christ, Lord and King, this is the true mission of religious education. To help us communicate this living *message* to the youth of today, the Lord Himself has provided a most effective language. He has left us four *signs* which in striking unity point to the same reality, the Mystery of Christ. They are the *history* of salvation in which the mystery has been accomplished, the *liturgy* where the mystery is made present, the *witness* by which the mystery is lived, and the *teaching* of the Church which expresses the mystery in more precise and well ordered terms.

Father Vincent M. Novak, S.J., Father John S. Nelson, S.J., and Father Joseph A. Novak, S.J., together with the teachers who helped to pilot their "Lord and King" series, have achieved signal success in presenting the Christian Message in its fullest light. They have placed Jesus Christ at the center of their program so that in the Holy Spirit He may lead each student to the Father. It was for this purpose that the three authors have built their courses around four *signs* of revelation noted above. But in addition, thanks to their own vigorous study and five years of classroom experience, they have accomplished something more valuable still: not content with their own employment of these signs, they have guided their students to experience the language of God's Message for themselves.

The International Institute of Lumen Vitae takes great pleasure in extending warmest congratulations to its three alumni. They have taken advantage in a most felicitous way of the coursework and the projects which are part of the total formation at Lumen Vitae, and furthermore, have not ceased to grow in their own development as they adapt their study to the needs of American students.

G. DELCUVE, S.J.

FEB 23 1984

AUTHOR'S PREFACE

I would like, first of all, to express my gratitude to the recent Fathers Provincial of the New York Province of the Society for having assigned me to this work and for offering their continued encouragement. Special thanks are due to Rev. Lorenzo K. Reed, S.J., at present the Director of Higher Education for the New York Province. Without Father Reed's invaluable assistance the experimental versions of this work would never have reached our classrooms in their attractive pilot editions. Brother Daniel J. Dempsey, S.J., Father Reed's assistant, labored with energy and patience for the same objective.

To Rev. Francis A. Fahey, S.J., one of my associates at the Fordham Preparatory School, I am indebted for wise pedagogical counsel both while he and I taught the course in its earliest form and during the years of constant revision. The Lumen Vitae faculty under the direction of Rev. Georges Delcuve, S.J., generously shared its catechetical knowledge, while the theological specialists from Woodstock reviewed the manuscript and made excellent suggestions for improving the text.

Finally, I am grateful to the members of the class of 1963 at the Fordham Preparatory School, and to the principals and faculty of this our first pilot school. The latter encouraged my work in every way, while the students of this graduating class pioneered the new program for each of the four years. The gratifying response of these young men together with the positive criticisms and the constructive suggestions they made helped considerably to shape the course in its final form.

The texts quoted from Holy Scripture have been taken from the new Confraternity of Christian Doctrine translation for those books of the Old Testament which have been translated and for all the books of the New Testament. Other scriptural quotations are from the Douai Version.

I wish to express my grateful appreciation to Abbe Henri Viot, Director of the Oeuvre de Diffusion de l'Evangile, Paris, for permission to reproduce the line drawings of Pierre Joubert and to Claude Ponsot for the symbolic liturgical drawings designed specifically for this text.

Contents

FOREWORD

FOR THE STUDENT

For the first time in your lives you are going to leave your question-and-answer catechism behind you. As befits your present age, you will study your Catholic faith more as an adult and less as a child. You must prove to yourselves as well as to your teachers that you are mature enough to reach this new understanding of your faith, and it should inspire the rest of your lives in God's service. Both you and your teachers are pledged to that objective.

The first things a good quarterback wants to know when he takes over a team in mid-game are the facts of the game situation: What's the score right now? What weaknesses and strengths shaped the game so far? What strategy looks best from here on in? In order to measure up to your vocation in the serious business of life, you should look for much the same information from your religion course:

1. Where do *you* fit into God's Plan right now?
2. What past events shaped man's and therefore *your* present relationship to God?
3. What strategy, with the above knowledge, should guide *your* future?

The title of this book for your freshman year is *Jesus Christ, Lord of History*. You will follow the history of man right from the beginning, and above all you will see how the Son of God reigns as Lord and King over every period of mankind's existence. True, you have been born into only one of these periods, but you will see that men of the past have helped to shape your life: Abraham formed the beginnings of a people who would bring you God's truth; Moses signed a friendship pact with God which you keep by observing the commandments; Christ Himself breathed life into the mystical body of the Church by which you stay spiritually healthy and strong. This "past" is really *your present*. You are what you are today because of these great men who lived before you. *You must know them to know yourself.* You will learn of them in your course this year.

INTRODUCTION

St. John sat at his writing table all aglow with the wonder of his Lord. As the only surviving apostle, he looked back over the long years, and the memories of the Savior were vivid and fresh. How clearly he could picture the lone, majestic figure whom he had first encountered at the Jordan (John 1:35-39). What a thrill it was to remember the day on the mountain, to see again the transfigured King before whose radiance he had fallen in awe and fear (Mark 9:1-7). And most vividly of all, the resplendent vision of the Risen Lord never ceased to stir his heart. John thrilled again to the glory of Easter, to the empty tomb on Easter morning (John 20:3-10), to the Master's dramatic appearance on Easter night (John 20:19-23), to the final farewell as Christ ascended to the Father in triumph (Acts 1:9-12).

Among these and other striking memories of Jesus, his friend, three episodes lingered in John's memory with special significance. John never tired of recounting each of them to his friends. That was why these episodes were recorded so prominently in the Gospel that bears his name. They helped capture the true wonder of his Lord.

I. IT IS THE LORD

John could still feel the chill of that morning on the lake so many years before. With Peter and the others he had been fishing all the night through. Could he ever forget the vision of the man on the shore? As their boat neared its place of mooring, the majestic figure spoke, and the timbre of his voice even in recollection stirred John's heart as he wrote. As so often before, it was through a miracle, this time a miraculous catch of fish, that the apostles recognized their Lord. "It is the Lord," shouted John, and the words rang out with the thrill of the Resurrection. The Savior had returned again to share His glory with His friends.

1

- READ John 21:1-14 for the full account of this meeting at the lakeshore.

From this incident John intends that we never forget this truth: **Jesus Christ is our all-powerful, triumphant Lord.**

II. I AM A KING

At the climax of Jesus' trial before Pontius Pilate, the Gospel of St. John records a highly significant exchange that had taken place between Christ and the Roman procurator:

> *"Thou art then a king?" asked Pilate.*
> *Jesus answered: "Thou sayest it; I am a king."* ... *(John 18:37)*

The confidence of tone and the majesty of presence impressed Pilate. Even in rags and spattered with blood Jesus looked like a king. Truly He seemed more the judge than the judged. His judgment would indeed fall upon men, not just upon the guilty Jews and Romans, but upon all sinful men. The Gospel is careful to record Pilate's reaction to Jesus. Just a few minutes later he addressed the Jews:

> *"Behold your king . . . Shall I crucify your king?" (John 19:15)*

In this account of the Roman trial St. John implicitly but clearly proclaims to men of all time: **Jesus Christ is the King and Judge of all men.**

III. I AM THE LIGHT OF THE WORLD

Earlier in Jesus' life a third incident had left a deep impression upon St. John. The scene was the Temple courtyard during the feast of Tabernacles, a holy day commemorating the wandering in the desert after the Hebrews under Moses had escaped from slavery in Egypt. One evening during a discussion with the crowds our Lord gestured toward a flaming torch mounted on a candelabrum nearby which the Jews reserved for use in liturgical processions. When everybody's eyes had turned to the brilliant flame, our Lord spoke these meaningful words: "I am the Light of the World." (John 8:12) .

What did our Lord mean when He said that He was "the Light of the World"? It is important for us to find out. Fortunately, another episode which is recorded by St. John helps us to discover His meaning.

One day as our Lord was leaving the Temple He caught sight of a man groping his way along the street. The man was blind, — blind from birth. The disciples noticed our Lord's interest and out of curiosity they asked: "Master, who has sinned, this man or his parents, that he should be born blind?" To the Hebrew mind of those days there was no third possibility. Imagine how dumbstruck they were, therefore, when our Lord replied: "Neither has this man sinned nor his parents, but the works of God were to be made manifest in him." Many in the crowd wrinkled their faces in confusion, and their puzzlement was not eased by the further words of Christ's reply. Yet these are the words which should mean a great deal to us in our Religion course this year:

"As long as I am in the world I am the light of the world." (John 9:5)

- READ about the miraculous cure of the man born blind with its interesting sequel in John 9:6-34.

As you see from reading the full story, the incident was not closed with the cure of the young man born blind or with his reprimand by the Pharisees. When Jesus heard of all the trouble the young man was having, He went out of His way to find him. In the meeting that followed the real meaning of the miracle recorded by the evangelist is highlighted, and we all receive a new and deeper insight into the role of Christ as the Light of the World:

(Jesus) said to him, "Dost thou believe in the Son of God?" He (the young man) answered and said, "Who is he, Lord, that I may believe in him?" And Jesus said to him, "Thou hast both seen him, and he it is who speaks with thee." And he said, "I believe, Lord." And falling down, he worshipped him. (John 9:35-38)

You should be able to appreciate at this point that the gift of physical sight was not really the big thing that Christ did for this young man. Physical sight was a symbol of a much greater gift, the gift of religious faith for the eyes of the soul. Through the eyes of faith the young man now recognized Christ for whom He was.

What St. John is telling all of us who are already blessed with this faith in our Lord is this: **Jesus Christ is the Light of the World.**

CONCLUSION

It will really be the work of our entire course to try to understand the full significance of faith in Jesus Christ as **Lord** and **King, and the Light of the World.** But even at this early stage we can put our faith into a meaningful perspective. The drawing that follows represents one artist's effort to capture the ideas that we shall be discussing for the rest of the year.

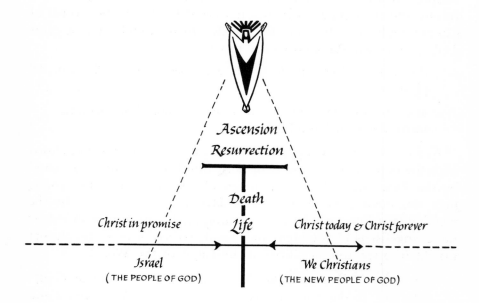

The horizontal line represents the passage of time in the history of mankind. The dotted lines at the beginning and end represent eternity both before the world began and after the world as we know it will come to an end. Jesus Christ is the focal point of all mankind's history. Risen from the dead and ascended to glory He throws His light all the way back over the left half of the history-line, the part of history which we call the Old Testament. Recall how Christ explained all this to the two discouraged disciples on their way to Emmaus after the shattering experience of Good Friday:

"O foolish ones and slow of heart to believe in all that the prophets have spoken! Did not the Christ have to suffer these things before entering into his glory?" **And beginning then with Moses and with all the Prophets, he interpreted to them in all the Scriptures the things referring to himself.** *(Luke 24:25-27)*

But light from the Glorious Christ also beams out across the right half of the line, the part of history which we call the New Testament. Christ illumines the future as well as the past. "As long as I am in the world I am the Light of the World," He told the crowds when He cured the young man born blind. But He did not mean that He would only continue to work and to preach as long as He lived on earth as man. He would **live on** in the world so that He could work and preach till the end of time. Recall how He put this promise to the apostles when He founded the Church and made the apostles the Church's first bishops:

"Go, therefore, and make disciples of all nations, baptizing them in the name of the Father, and of the Son, and of the Holy Spirit, teaching them to observe all that I have commanded you; and behold, I am with you all days, even unto the consummation of the world." (Mt. 28:19-20)

And when Christ said "unto the consummation of the world," He meant that He would be present then, too. The fact is that it will be this triumphant coming of Christ in glory on the last day that will mark the true culmination of God's Plan in history. Our Lord and King will take full and final possession of His Kingdom, and we who are heirs of the Kingdom will take possession of it, too. Christ our brother, the "firstborn" in our family, will lead the way:

*For those whom he (God) has foreknown he has also predestined to become conformed to the image of his Son, that he should be **the firstborn among many brethren.** (Rom. 8:29)*

*. . . you have received a spirit of adoption as sons, by virtue of which we cry, "Abba! Father!" The Spirit himself gives testimony to our spirit that **we are sons of God.** But if we are sons, we are heirs also: **heirs indeed of God and joint heirs with Christ,** provided, however, we suffer with him that we may also be glorified with him. (Rom. 8:15-17)*

In the book which is called the Apocalypse, St. John pictures

Christ riding a white horse, a mighty warrior-king doing battle for his kingdom. Upon his garment is written the claim to his power and authority: "King of kings, and Lord of lords" (Apoc. 19:16). And John fills out the picture further still:

> *And the armies of heaven, clothed in fine linen, white and pure, were following him on white horses. (Apoc. 19:14)*

In the imaginative language so typical of the Apocalypse John is telling us that we too are meant to ride at the Savior's side on that glorious day of triumph.

We can sum up the significance of this artist's drawing depicting God's Plan in history by saying that Jesus Christ, our **Lord and King,** is the **Light of the World.** He dominates and illumines every era of mankind's history. And most encouraging of all, the glorious Christ reigns and is present to each of us **today.** Our Lord and King searches us out as friend to friend so that His Easter glory may light up our souls. Day by day He transforms our lives and makes us more like Himself, as long as we open our hearts to His presence within us.

As the year's work progresses, you will reach fuller understanding of the wonderful truths this drawing conveys. For now, here are the three most important points you should try to grasp and retain:

1. In God's Plan Jesus Christ is at the center of history. History both before and after Christ takes its meaning from Him, from His death, His resurrection, and His ascension to glory, that is, from His Redemptive Mission.

2. Jesus Christ will come again in glory, and on that last day complete His triumph into eternity.

3. But Christ reigns in glory today, too, and by His presence within us shares His victory **even now.**

A precious truth comes home to us here. If Christ is the key to history, then Christ is the key to the history and purpose of our lives, too. Life without Him can have no meaning. With Him everything falls into place within God's Plan. A Christian is a confirmed optimist; nothing can shake his faith in the present or future. He is a man of vision, a man with a glorious destiny. St. Paul, and we with him, can exult with full confidence in the Lord:

> *For I am sure that neither death, nor life, nor angels, nor principalities, nor things present, nor things to come, nor*

powers, nor height, nor depth, nor any other creature will be able to separate us from the love of God which is in Christ Jesus our Lord. (Rom. 8:38-39)

But knowing that Christ is the key to history and the center of our lives is one thing; living according to this knowledge is another. When each of us was baptized, our godparents in our name gave a solemn pledge of faith. They promised loyalty to our Lord and King for all of our lives. What does that pledge mean to us now? This is an honest question, and if we are honest, we will ask it of ourselves often as we study about our Lord and King during the coming year.

- READ Mt. 5:14-16 and discuss how Americans of the 1960's could live up to these challenges from Christ.

  Choose any career that you wish and write up your ideas in a short essay. What about a Christian as a doctor? as a lawyer? as a politician? as a businessman? as a priest?

In summary form our first-year Religion course will take up these four stages of God's Christ-centered plan of history:

A. **Christ Promised**

This first section of our course covers the era before Christ's coming; therefore, from creation to the Incarnation. The promise to Adam of a redeemer was the first plank in a vast bridge of prophecy that spanned what we call the Old Testament. Christ is coming, but no one knows exactly how or when. Adam, Abraham, Moses, David and the prophets wait in hope.

B. **Christ on Earth**

The Christ is come. His life on earth holds our attention from Bethlehem through Calvary to Olivet and His ascension to glory.

C. **Christ Living On**

It is in the Church, His mystical body, that Christ lives on among men. This section explores the historical beginnings of Christ's Church and reveals the mystery of union with Christ that the Mass and the sacraments achieve.

D. **Christ Triumphant**

The final section projects us into mankind's future destiny. On Christ's day of total victory He will call men to share His glory or pass the judgment that will separate sinners from the People of God forever.

- LOOK UP the following quotations in the Bible and make your judgment as to which of the four stages of God's Plan each text best applies. Could some apply to more than one?
  a. Ex. 13:21; b. Is. 42:9; c. Jo. 1:1-5; d. Jo. 12:35-36; e. 1 Jo. 2:8-11

Note how well the psalmist sums up what our attitude toward the Plan of God should be:

*"The Lord is **my light and my salvation;** whom should I fear?" (Psalm 26)*

In the chapter that follows we shall learn to look for "light" from the Lord of History as we open the book of salvation which we reverently call the Word of God, the Bible. As St. Jerome, the great father of biblical studies, said many centuries ago: "To be ignorant of the Bible is to be ignorant of Christ." And to be ignorant of Christ is to be ignorant of the meaning of our lives and the plan that God has formed for our vocations in life.

QUESTIONS

1. What ideas would you highlight in St. John's reports of the incident at the lakeshore after Christ's Resurrection and the trial before Pontius Pilate?

2. What greater gift than physical sight was given to the young man who was born blind? What connection is there between this greater gift and the sight restored?

3. Explain how Jesus Christ is present in the Old Testament.

4. In what ways is Christ present in the future till the end of time?

5. Why is Christ's presence today so significant to us?

6. Sum up the three big points to note from your sketch of God's Plan in history.

7. What honest question might we well ask ourselves frequently during our course?

8. Name and sum up briefly the four main divisions of our first-year course.

CHAPTER I

A Searchlight on the Bible

A science-fiction story once built its plot around a fascinating machine which could bring all sound waves from outer space back into the earth's orbit; radio antennas could then pick them up. Think of it! It would be possible to play back the face-to-face conversations of history's great personalities including the prophets, the apostles, and even Christ Himself. Some young people mistakenly think that the Bible is just such a word-for-word recorded radio script. They are in for a few surprises.

I. THE BIBLE: BOOK OR BOOKS?

At the very beginning it is important to understand clearly the true nature of what we call the Bible. The Bible is really a library, not one book. Also, even though the Bible was composed in the ordinary human ways of authorship, still there is a fundamental difference which sets it apart from all merely human production. The fact is that there are so many special things to say about the Bible that the sooner we realize that it is in a class all by itself, the sooner we shall begin to understand just what God has done here. Therefore, keep the following ideas in your mind when you read the Bible. They will solve many a problem about what we find there.

A. God speaks to us through the Bible.

B. Both God and man are its authors.

C. God does not change the human author's background and personality.

D. God guarantees biblical truth.

E. The Church alone can tell us with certainty which books God inspired and what God meant to say.

9

A. God Speaks to Us Through the Bible

The tremendous fact of human history is that God chose to be part of it. Now this may not seem so much to us because we Catholics take it for granted; all Catholics know that the Son of God became man. But God entered history long before the Incarnation, and in various ways. Instead of abandoning man after the fall of Adam and Eve, God patiently guided Adam's descendants on the long road back to Himself. Not all at once, but little by little He worked through different men and women who, in fits and starts through many centuries, led His people home. God spoke with these chosen leaders and directed them, as we shall see later. In working with them and through them, God became a force in our human history. **The Bible is the record of these dealings of God with man,** a record of the exchange of word and action between the Creator of the world and His struggling subjects, between a loving Father and His wayward children.

B. Both God and Man Are Authors of the Bible

1. THE HEBREW PEOPLE

The Hebrew people have a significant place in history because God chose them to be the carriers of His revelation, that is, the religious truths He graciously made known to them. It certainly was not because of their political prestige or power in the ancient world that God singled out the Hebrews. In fact, the real powers of that age could smile with contempt at these backward herdsmen and religious fanatics. That is what they thought of the Hebrews. But God does not do things the way that shortsighted men would think best; He raised up these unknown and weak people to be His spokesmen to mankind.

These Hebrew spokesmen, some of whom were herdsmen, others farmers, fishermen, and later on even a tentmaker, cooperated with God's grace and recorded all that they felt God wanted men to know. Sometimes their way of recording God's messages for posterity was by word of mouth. This is called **oral tradition.** With the development of writing materials, however, a little library of manuscripts took shape, forming **a written tradition.** At the time Nabuchodonosor of Babylon dragged the Hebrew people into slavery this famous remark was literally true: "The future of the human race was packed to the back of a camel." These documents were so precious that the world today would be a very different place, had they been lost or destroyed. But who was it that recorded God's revelation in these documents? In His own way God did; but man did too. This needs explanation.

2. INSPIRATION

To guide men in producing the books in which God's revelations were to be recorded, God gave them a special grace which we call **inspiration.** Inspiration is the directing influence of the Holy Spirit under which the human authors recorded **all** that God wanted them to record and **only** what God wanted them to record. Because God thus directed with His grace the recording of every sentence of the inspired text, we may say correctly that the Bible is the "Word of God." And yet the men who thought out the ideas passed them on or put them down on the equivalent of paper, were truly the authors, too. How can that be? There will always be some mystery here, since who can fully explain God's special powers? But this much we can say:

C. God Does Not Change the Human Author's Background and Personality

In other words, God took the author the way he was. God allowed him to think out what he wanted to say in his own mind and to express his thoughts in his own way. Any man chosen by God could put the stamp of his own individuality on all that he composed. If a biblical author was an educated man, education colored every part; if he was a herdsman, the simplicity of nature with pictures of herds and pasture lands showed up in his section of the text. Now when a man composes in his own way freely, then we can say rightly that he is an author in the fullest sense.

1. Inspiration was **not** God's dictation to a prophet-secretary.

2. Inspiration was **not** a division of labor, God taking some parts of the work and assigning other parts to men.

3. Inspiration was **not** a means of forcing authors against their free will to record what God wanted recorded.

BUT: Inspiration was a divine influence causing the human authors to record **all** that God wanted them to record and **only** what God wanted them to record. And they did work **freely** and **in their own way.**

THEREFORE: Both God and man were authors, each of the **entire** Bible, but each in his own special way.

D. **God Guarantees Biblical Truth**

This is something that you know already. God can neither deceive nor be deceived. If He Himself is truly the author of the Bible through His directing grace, then it follows as night the day that when the human authors under God's inspiration intend to teach us anything, they cannot lead us into error. To give a name to this idea we say: Because of God's inspiration the Bible enjoys the privilege of **inerrancy.**

E. **The Church Alone Can Tell Us With Certainty What Books God Inspired, and What God Meant to Say**

Perhaps you remember some Sunday at Mass when a sentence or two in the Gospel puzzled you and made you wonder what was meant. Reading the Scriptures is not always easy, and the problem becomes even more involved when reading the Old Testament. One of the biblical authors saw this difficulty arising a long time ago, so he warned the first Christians against attempting to interpret for themselves the prophecies which were written under the inspiration of the Holy Spirit.

> *This, then, you must understand first of all, that no prophecy of Scripture is made by private interpretation. For not by the will of man was prophecy brought at any time; but holy men of God spoke as they were moved by the Holy Spirit. (2 Peter 1:20-21)*

The Church of Christ, therefore, has been appointed by God to supervise the interpretation of Scripture. But how does the Church under the guidance of the Holy Spirit go about discovering God's truth in the Bible? The first approach the Church employs is to search out truths of God's revelation through a deceptively simple process: finding out **what the inspired author intended to say.** The Scripture scholars who do the work of the Church will generally follow these three steps, which are in reality very complex, in order to get at the human author's meaning:

1. Fill in the background of the author, if he is known, and his times.

2. Identify the type of writing the author employs.

3. Uncover the meaning the author intends.

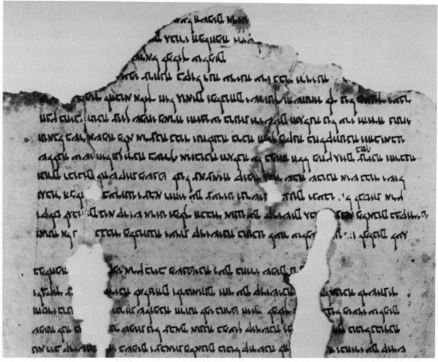

The Dead Sea Scrolls, a close-up section from an early bible manuscript. THE MATSON PHOTO SERVICE

1. THE AUTHOR AND HIS TIMES

To find out everything possible about the authors, the Church depends heavily upon human scholarship and science: the history of ancient civilizations, the deciphering of languages, especially the very early cuneiform found in time-worn records, and the fascinating findings of archaeology. This last-mentioned science of archaeology actually digs up from beneath layers and layers of earth and debris many of the ancient cities which have lain there camouflaged for centuries. This is certainly true: the more the scientists can find out about the individual author and the times in which he lived, the more they can help the Church determine his true message.

2. THE LITERARY FORM

Identifying the type of writing is the next step. Is the author writing the scientific history of documented facts which we expect today? Is his contribution perhaps make-believe, a fictional short story? What were the literary norms and customs for those different types of writing? We are not interested here in what they might be in our modern times; what were they when **this** author lived and wrote **this** section of the sacred text? We are interested in the literary norms of his times. Perhaps we shall see the critical importance of these discoveries better by making a comparison with a parallel case from modern times.

Take the case of television: How foolish we would be to accept everything we see on television in the same way! In a couple of hours of TV viewing we might see a news program, a western movie about Sitting Bull, and a Mickey Mouse cartoon. In the news program we see history being made before our eyes. As we view the western, we know and believe that Sitting Bull really lived and that he fought Indian wars. But we do not feel obliged to accept all the details which the Hollywood producer imaginatively builds into the story. Finally, as the cartoon plays on, we are sharp enough to catch the writer's point in playing up the heroism of Mickey Mouse defending Minnie. Though we stand for heroism as something true and noble, we do not mistake for reality the fantasy of little animals speaking and acting like human beings.

Now we must be sensible in the same way when we talk about the Bible. Just as there are different kinds of programs on television, so there are different kinds of writing in the Bible. We can see this when we compare the Scripture with other literature of biblical times. These different kinds of writing are called "literary forms."

A literary form is the kind of writing freely chosen by the author for a particular purpose.

In the Bible you will find historical data similar to what we expect in our history books today, i.e., as close to the facts as possible, but you will also come across stories mixed in with factual data, or poems or fanciful descriptions to give reading pleasure or to inspire noble sentiments, and you will even find what we would call clear-cut fiction (remember the parables told by our Lord?). If anybody reads all these different kinds of writing in the same way with the same kind of belief, he is bound to arrive at ridiculous conclusions;

just as much as he would, were he to accept all television programs in the same way.

3. THE AUTHOR'S MEANING

Once the Scripture scholars have as complete an idea as possible of the author and his background, once they identify correctly the literary form he employs, then they are getting close to the meaning the human author intends, and which of course God intends through him. This understanding of the human author's words is called the **"literal sense."** * The literal sense is very important because the biblical author is the one inspired with God's truth, not the readers.

There are now only two final questions that must be answered in order to determine the human author's meaning, i.e., the literal sense, in any given passage:

    a. Does the author in this passage **intend to teach?**

    b. In the passages where he clearly intends to teach, **what truths does he communicate?**

Consider each question separately

a. IS THE AUTHOR TEACHING?

It would be a difficult world to live in if everybody intended to teach every time he put ink to paper. You could never find a good detective story to read or an amusing comic strip. Life would be like studying out of textbooks most of our ordinary day, and that means weekends, too. The library of books we call the Bible does not always teach, either. Often it does teach, and of course these are the most precious passages since in them we have God's truth reaching us. But the biblical authors also may try in some passages to bring comfort and consolation to people who are suffering, or to give a vision of beauty to people who must live amid ugly surroundings, or just to offer spiritual refreshment to the tired and weary. The Scripture scholars must find out what **this** author intends as his purpose in **this** passage of the sacred text, or, as with non-literal meanings which we shall leave for later on, what God Himself may

---

* Biblical scholars also speak of other senses of Scripture which are "non-literal," in that God as the author of Scripture may have intended more significance to persons, events and things described in the Scriptures or to the words themselves than even the human author at the time may have been aware. We shall investigate these other God-intended meanings of Scripture later on. They are usually called *"the typical sense"* and *"the fuller sense."*

have intended, with or without the knowledge of the human author at the time he worked on the passage.

b. WHAT DOES THE AUTHOR TEACH?

The final step is the most sought after of all: when intending to teach, what truths does the author communicate? This last step is best understood by turning to the Bible itself for examples to illustrate the abstract principle. We shall do exactly that in the next chapter, where we shall take up the story of Creation. We shall draw from the Book of Genesis **the religious truths which God and the biblical authors intend to teach us.**

SUMMARY

Three rules of thumb for reading the Bible correctly

1. Take the author for what he was, a man of his times living among and writing for a certain class of people.

2. Identify the type of writing he employed in any particular section, "the literary form."

3. Accept his purpose to teach or not to teach, and accept the religious truths which God and he intended to communicate. BUT NOTE WELL: The only source of absolute certainty is the Holy Spirit speaking in the Church.

QUESTIONS

1. What is a meaningful description of the Bible?
2. In what two ways were the Hebrew traditions preserved?
3. What is "inspiration" of the Bible?
4. When under inspiration from God, why did the sacred authors of the Scriptures remain true authors of what they wrote?
5. What do you mean by the term "inerrancy"?
6. How does the Church go about finding out what God wants us to know through the revelation of the Scriptures?
7. How does the Church find out about the biblical author's background?
8. What is a "literary form" in the Bible and why is it so important to recognize the different literary forms?
9. Do the authors of the Bible always intend to teach some religious truth?
10. What is the last and final step in the study of the Bible?

Part One
CHRIST PROMISED

Earliest Preparations in God's Plan

CHAPTER II

GOD OFFERS HIS GIFTS: CREATION

We live in the day of astronauts and skindivers exploring the unknown; man has always been anxious to conquer new worlds. With the progress of modern science he is even more curious to discover the origins of the world in which he lives. In this respect the Hebrew people of ancient times who command our interest in biblical history were no different from modern man. Living close to nature as herdsmen and in later centuries farmers, they stood in awe and wonderment before nature and nature's secrets. They wanted to know **how** and **why**.

Picture Hebrew families sitting outside their tents at the end of a hard day's labor with the herds and flocks. They loved to join their friends beneath starry skies and recount to one another the fascinating stories passed down from their fathers by word-of-mouth tradition. Some of the stories were original and uniquely Hebrew; others they had collected from foreign peoples, from the Babylonians, from the Egyptians, and from the Chanaanites. It is not surprising, therefore, that simple herdsmen and farmers like themselves would become so confused that they would not know what to believe.

They did not have a written history or book of fables; some of the stories passed down by oral tradition were a mixture of fact and fiction.

Section 1. THE HEBREW STORY OF CREATION

It was about the year 1290 B.C. that God raised up the great Hebrew leader, Moses. In his long association with the Chosen People during the Exodus years Moses was inspired by God to put some order and clarification into the beliefs of the people. The Israelites were bewildered by the jumble of stories which they had heard from their own past and from the pagan peoples around them to explain the most basic things in life, like the origin of life itself, the creation of the world, and the true destiny of men.

Moses gradually instructed his people in God's truth. He did not have all the answers to their questions, but he could put their minds at ease about the most fundamental of the religious truths that God wanted man to know. Moses could tell the puzzled inquirers that it was the same Yahweh who had delivered them out of Egypt who also had made the heavens and the earth and everything else, including man himself. It was Yahweh who had made man the lord of creation, the lord of the fields and of the flocks.

After Moses' death we can be sure that faithful Hebrews cherished all the revelations from Yahweh which Moses had bequeathed to them and their children. Conscientious parents to be sure took great pains to teach them to their children and vigilant leaders of clans were ever alert to oversee the accurate transmission of the faith of their fathers. Furthermore, in times like these which are not blessed with so much knowledge in print as in our age, poets and folk-singers helped to preserve the heritage of Israel in poem and song. Only many centuries later would these traditions of Hebrew faith be recorded in the form familiar to us from the book of Genesis.

In this and the chapter to follow we shall listen to the testimony of these inspired traditions, especially as they touch the creation of the world and man's first sin. In a succeeding chapter we shall follow the origins of the Hebrew nation from the time God called a prosperous herdsman named Abram.

I. GENESIS AND CREATION

To read the book of Genesis, therefore, is to open a window into Israel's past. The first eleven chapters form an introduction or a

prologue to the recorded history of the Hebrew people as it began
with Abraham. In this prologue's inspired lines the saga of Israel's
link to man's most distant past is told. The authors had no documents
from creation times to go by, no unbroken line of communication
with man's first parents to guide them. All they had were the written
and oral traditions that had come down since Moses' time, the kind
of simple stories that parents had taught their children and poets
had immortalized in folk songs. But most of all, they were inspired
by the Holy Spirit as they transmitted their traditions. And yet,
through poetic descriptions such as these God had intended that
the religious message of creation should be preserved for all time.

- WOULD it be reasonable to expect a newspaper report of the
  world's creation from the biblical authors? Would it be reasonable to criticize the authors for their unscientific approach to
  the world's creation? In reply discuss what the authors intended
  by their accounts of creation and what they did not intend.

When were the creation stories strung together into our present
version of the book of Genesis? We cannot be absolutely certain,
but the research of biblical scholars points to the era of the Babylonian Captivity as the most probable time for the editing of Genesis
in its present form. In the anguished soul-searching that followed
the fall of Jerusalem, the priests of Juda, some as captives in Babylon,
began the great work of shaping and ordering traditions from the
Hebrew past. They assembled both oral and written traditions,
especially important written materials that were blocked together
during the reign of Solomon in the tenth century B.C. Their work
came to be known as the Pentateuch, i.e. the first five books of the
Bible. They hoped through this compilation of the Word of God
that they would keep the fires of faith aglow in the hearts of the
Chosen People.

It is very interesting to note the hand of these dedicated priests
so clearly in evidence as we read the book of Genesis which they
helped to transmit. Do you remember in the first chapter of Genesis
how the account of creation divides God's labors into a week con-
sisting of seven days? This is clearly the effort of the biblical writers
to impress the people with the sacredness of the Sabbath. God
Himself is pictured as keeping the Sabbath after six days of a work
week that would be normal to any Hebrew. The seventh day was a
day of rest.

Let us now with all reverence listen to the creation accounts and look for the religious truths that they were intended to convey:

THE FIRST DAY: God separated the light from the darkness, day from night.

> . . . God said, "Let there be light," and there was light. God saw that the light was good. God separated the light from the darkness, calling the light Day and the darkness Night. And there was evening and morning, the first day. (Gen. 1:3-5)

THE SECOND DAY: God separated the upper from the lower waters, the waters above the heavens from the earthly waters below.

> Then God said, "Let there be a firmament in the midst of the waters to divide the waters." And so it was. God made the firmament, dividing the waters that were below the firmament from those that were above it. God called the firmament Heaven. And there was evening and morning, the second day. (Gen. 1:6-8)

How the Hebrews Pictured the World.

THE THIRD DAY: God separated dry land from the earthly waters below, the earth from the seas.

> Then God said, "Let the waters below the heavens be gathered into one place and let dry land appear." And so it was. God called the dry land Earth and the assembled waters Seas. (Gen. 1:9-10)

And God saw that it was good. Then God said, "Let the earth bring forth vegetation: seed-bearing plants and all kinds of fruit trees that bear fruit containing their seed." And so it was. The earth brought forth vegetation, every kind of seed-bearing plant and all kinds of trees that bear fruit containing their seed. God saw that it was good. And there was evening and morning, the third day. (Gen. 1:11-13)

THE FOURTH DAY: God filled the firmament with lights in the skies, especially the sun by day and the moon by night.

And God said, "Let there be lights in the firmament of the heavens to separate day from night; let them serve as signs and for the fixing of seasons, days and years; let them serve as lights in the firmament of the heavens to shed light upon the earth." So it was. God made the two great lights, the greater light to rule the day and the smaller one to rule the night, and he made the stars. God set them in the firmament of the heavens to shed light upon the earth, to rule the day and the night and to separate the light from the darkness. God saw that it was good. And there was evening and morning, the fourth day. (Gen. 1:14-19)

THE FIFTH DAY: God brought fish to life in the earthly waters below and filled the heavens below the firmament with birds.

Then God said, "Let the waters abound with life, and above the earth let winged creatures fly below the firmament of the heavens." And so it was. God created the great sea monsters, all kinds of living, swimming creatures with which the waters abound and all kinds of winged birds. God saw that it was good, and God blessed them, saying, "Be fruitful, multiply, and fill the waters of the seas; and let the birds multiply on the earth." And there was evening and morning, the fifth day. (Gen. 1:20-23)

THE SIXTH DAY: God brought every kind of animal to life and they inhabited the earth.

God said, "Let the earth bring forth all kinds of living creatures: cattle, crawling creatures and wild animals." And so it was. God made all kinds of wild beasts, every kind of cattle, and every kind of creature crawling on the ground. And God saw that it was good. (Gen. 1:24-25)

God crowned His work with the creation of man made in the very image of God. God made man the lord of all His creation.

God said, "Let us make mankind in our image and likeness, and let him have dominion over the fish of the sea, the birds of the air, the cattle, over all the wild animals and every creature that crawls on the earth."

God created man in his image. In the image of God he created him. Male and female he created them.

Then God blessed them and said to them, "Be fruitful and multiply; fill the earth and subdue it. Have dominion over the fish of the sea, the birds of the air, the cattle and all the animals that crawl on the earth." God also said, "See I give you every seed-bearing plant on the earth and every tree which has seed-bearing fruit to be your food. To every wild animal of the earth, to every bird of the air, and to every creature that crawls on the earth and has the breath of life, I give the green plants for food." And so it was. God saw that all he had made was very good. And there was evening and morning, the sixth day. (Gen. 1:26-31)

THE SEVENTH DAY: God rested, having completed His work of creation. *. . . On the sixth day God finished the work he had been doing. And he rested on the seventh day from all the work he had done. (Gen. 2:2-3)*

And so it was that the sacred author made these religious truths clear:

1. The one true God made the world and everything in it. Everything God made was good.

2. God made man and woman in His own image, and blessing them with special powers made them lords of His creation so that they might work it and thus continue His own creative act.

3. God intends that man set aside one day of rest each week in order formally to worship and honor his Creator.

- READ Genesis 2:7 for another poetic description of God creating the first man. Why should we not be surprised at a second allusion to man's creation or at the different mode of description?

- RECALL what you learned about the different traditions that were handed down among the Hebrew people, the different kinds of stories to convey the same ideas.

The story of creation must have buoyed up the spirits of the people of Israel, especially through the trying years of the Exodus from Egypt and the years of exile in Babylon. When crushed with suffering, man dreams of a happier past and hopes for a happier future. Surely amid their troubles the Israelites of Moses' day and the exiled Hebrews in Babylon must have wondered whether God ever intended a life of peace and contentment for man. Age-old traditions which were finally recorded in Genesis centuries later assured them of God's designs for the happiness of man.

> *The Lord God planted a garden in Eden, to the east, and he put there the man he had formed.*
>
> *The Lord God made to grow out of the ground all kinds of trees pleasant to the sight and good for food, the tree of life also in the midst of the garden . . . ,*
>
> *The Lord God took man and placed him in the garden of Eden to till it and to keep it. (Gen. 2:8-9, 15.)*

NOTE: The image of a "garden" as a symbol of happiness is probably taken from the lavish estates that oriental princes used to beautify for their own and their choicest friends' enjoyment.

As another touching indication of God's concern for the happiness of man, the decision was made to bless the first man with a companion "like himself." God created Eve and gave her to Adam as a wife to share his joys.

> *Then the Lord God said, "It is not good that man is alone; I will make him a helper like himself . . . ." (Gen. 2:18)*

To add to the happiness of the first man and woman God is recorded as visiting the Garden of Eden and meeting with Adam and Eve. He was their loving father and friend.

> *. . . they (Adam and Eve) heard the sound of the Lord God walking in the garden in the cool of the day . . . the Lord called the man and said to him, "Where are you?" (Gen. 3:8-9)*

NOTE: This description of God "walking" in the garden is a good illustration of the sacred author's attempt to make God more real for his simple readers. He knew very well that God was above and beyond anything merely human like walking. Two big words fit these ideas:

1. *Anthropomorphism:* a picturing of God in human terms.

2. *Transcendence:* a state completely above men, beyond human understanding.

It is because God is transcendent that just as the biblical authors we too must speak of God in anthropomorphisms.

- REREAD Gen. 2:7 for another anthropomorphism by which God is pictured as a potter working with clay and then literally breathing life into the face of His masterpiece. Can you find other examples of anthropomorphism in Gen. 2 and 3?

It was through poetic pictures such as these that the authors of Genesis made these further religious truths clear:

4. Man was made for a life of happiness as he worked the garden for his creator and friend.

5. Woman, made equal to man in the image of God, was appointed man's helpmate, his devoted companion in marriage.

6. And lastly, the all-powerful God is a personal God, someone who cares a great deal about man, creating him by His own initiative and blessing him with wonderful gifts.

- CLASS DISCUSSION: We are living in an age of spectacular scientific advance, the Nuclear and the Space Age. From what you have seen of God's design for the first man and woman, what would you say about such technological progress in God's plan for modern man:

  1. Does God approve of splitting the atom, of nuclear energy?
  2. Does God object to astronaut exploration of outer space?
  3. Are there any limits to the scientific progress which God permits to man? Any responsibilities?

  Form your judgments from the revelation given in Genesis, especially the "garden" symbolism and God's instructions to "work in the garden." Do you see any new dignity here for all kinds of work in the world? For the work of a scientist, of an engineer, of a carpenter?

A SUMMARY

It was Moses who under the inspiration of God first tried to give the unlettered Hebrews a theologically correct account of creation to offset the theologically false accounts current among pagan people of those times. Hebrew tradition, both oral and written, transmitted the teachings of Moses over the centuries; but it was probably only in the sixth and fifth centuries B.C. that a group of priests framed the traditions into the seven-day workweek so familiar to us from the book of Genesis. These priestly authors were interested as well as Moses in general religious truths concerning creation, not in its detailed reporting or scientific explanation.

By God's design the Church of Christ, also inspired by the Holy Spirit, is meant to develop the original revelation from the Scriptures. We learn from the Church a more technical definition of creation, God's purposes in creating, God's special gifts to Adam and Eve, especially the gift of God's own presence within them.

Man responds to God's goodness through worship and service. This is the virtue of religion which is best energized by sincere love of God.

Section 2. THE HOLY SPIRIT SPEAKS THROUGH THE CHURCH

Thus far we have seen some general truths that the Scriptures have taught us about God and His creation of the world. The Bible is a precious source of such revelation. But we may ask, does our reading of the Bible as it was given us by the biblical authors tell us all we can learn about God and the world in which we live? In other words, did God intend some fuller developments to this original revelation from Scripture? Surely the answer is already familiar to you; it is a solid truth of our Catholic faith:

God intended that Christ's Church should carry on His Revelation through the Holy Spirit.

As we shall see more fully later, **the Church is Christ living on in our midst.** We live our Christian lives in union with Christ in His Church and we learn more and more of God's revelation through the voice of Christ's spokesman in the world, the Church. Just as the Holy Spirit inspired the authors and editors of Scripture, so too in a similar fashion He is ever at work in the Church. As a consequence of this work of the Spirit we Christians can come to know and understand more about God than we ever could from just reading the Scriptures on our own.

I. WHAT THE CHURCH TEACHES ABOUT CREATION

We shall study a great deal more about the Church's teaching when we take up the Ecumenical Councils in the third year of our Religion program. However, it would be helpful at this point to sum up some of the truths that the Spirit has made more precise through the Church's teaching on creation:

A. The Meaning of Creation
The Hebrew people who produced the Bible never went in for definitions the way other civilizations, particularly the Greeks, were so fond of doing. It was through the study and reflection of the Church's theologians who were much influenced by the Greeks in later centuries, therefore, that a more technical notion of creation was elaborated:

Creation is making something out of nothing.

When a man builds something, he uses material already in existence, as wood for a chair or steel for an auto. God made the world without any such material with which to start.

B. God's Purpose in Creating the World
In her divinely inspired teaching the Church sees two principal purposes for God's creating the world:

1. to manifest His goodness
2. for man's use and benefit

In His desire to reveal Himself to man God intended to show by the world's magnificence how truly powerful, good and beautiful is its Creator. With his special powers of intellect man alone among God's creatures on earth can give due recognition to God's accomplishments. Struck with awe and wonder before God and His creation, man in a most natural way reacts by giving glory to God. In a word, man **worships** God. In what is truly one of the most striking aspects of God's magnanimous designs, man can give this glory to God in the very use and enjoyment of the gifts which God has so bountifully bestowed. In using these gifts in keeping with God's design man honors God. For example, a father gives honor to God in raising his family and enjoying its pleasures just as he pleases God by participating in Mass on Sunday.

C. How God Created Man

God never revealed to us the exact way He went about creating man and the other creatures of this world. We have already seen that the book of Genesis must not be misinterpreted as a scientific explanation of God's mode of creation. God rather permits us to seek answers to these fascinating questions in the scientific data of nature itself. In a true sense it can be said that God is speaking to us in scientific truth, in that He is the designer of all the wonders discovered by science. It is impossible, therefore, since God is the creator of science, that scientific knowledge contradict the true understanding of God's revelation.

NOTE: The Church encourages all men of science and awaits with great interest any of their findings that may explain the origin and development of man. The numerous resemblances which scientists have discovered between the human body and certain animals, together with the testimony of many fossil remains discovered in modern times, have led many scientists to believe that God took the body of the first man from a certain line of animals specially prepared by Him for that purpose. The human soul, however, was created in the strict sense of creation by an act of God Himself.

D. God's Gifts to the First Man and Woman

Besides the purely natural gifts of body, of soul and of life itself, God showed His boundless love for the first man and woman by a number of special gifts which were not part of their ordinary human nature nor in any way due to them as human beings.*

---

* Theologians at times distinguish these gifts still further as either preternatural gifts (beyond nature at least for human beings, though not for superior creatures like angels) or supernatural gifts (completely above the nature of any and every creature). The distinction, however, is not important for our purposes here.

These extraordinary gifts to Adam and Eve were:

1. FREEDOM FROM DEATH

Without a special gift the body by its very nature is doomed to die. Adam and Eve were not meant to die.

2. FREEDOM FROM SUFFERING

Since they were free from death, the first parents were free from the causes of death: sickness, accidents, and weakness from old age. They were also free from pain and discomfort, to which as human beings they would otherwise have been subject.

3. PERFECT CONTROL OF THE SENSE APPETITES

The appetite or desire for sense pleasure, as for example the anticipation of delicious food, is really intended by God as something good, and is not evil at all. But when desires such as these are no longer controlled by man's higher powers of reason and will, they can lead to evil, as to the sin of overeating or gluttony. In Adam's case all of the appetites whether for food, for drink, or for the pleasures of sex were under the perfect control of Adam's intellect and free will. His appetites could never run away with him and rebel against his will, as happens in the tragically human sins since Adam's time, like gluttony, drunkenness, and the sins against the sacredness of sex.

4. SPECIAL INTELLIGENCE AND KNOWLEDGE

Without the labor of study Adam and Eve enjoyed the rewards of brilliant minds. They could understand the wonders of nature with a clarity that we never approach in our study of astronomy, physics, biology and subjects like those; nor could they forget all that they knew, as we so often do in our school work.

To anyone studying the story of creation thus far, these four special gifts give striking testimony to God's generosity. If God had gifted man with nothing else but life itself as a human being, how grateful man should have been. But how much more did He give man with these extraordinary gifts! Our human minds which are so used to man's selfishness cannot help but be amazed at the goodness of God.

We might wonder whether there was any other gift that God could have bestowed upon His favored creatures. Yes, there was, but only a person who has known what it is to love can appreciate this final gift. Love seeks to give of itself. God, as the source of all love, planned to give of Himself to His children, Adam and Eve.

God shared some of His own Life with man.

E. God's Gift of Himself

By His master plan God intended that all men should share the happiness of His kingdom. To anyone but God Himself such a plan would have been completely unreal and impossible. Why?

This was the problem: To live with God was unthinkable for human beings. A tree cannot hope to grow into a pony, nor a pony into a man; neither could man rise to the level of God and live with God in the same kingdom of heaven.

This was God's solution: God's love found a way, through a kind of adoption. But this adoption was much more than the legal "as if" that we associate by modern customs with adoption of a child into a foster family. Divine adoption effects a participation in the very life of God, **a living by the same principle of life by which He lives.** Since this sharing in the life of God is totally God's free gift, we call it just that, a "gratia," the Latin word for gift or grace. And since this gift makes us like God Himself, holy, we call it **sanctifying grace.**

This is the tremendous fact: Adam and Eve became God's children in a very real sense, life of His life. Now they could live with God, because as God's children they were heirs to His Kingdom, too. Remember again how St. Paul exulted in God's goodness:

> *For whoever are led by the Spirit of God, they are the sons of God. Now you have not received a spirit of bondage so as to be again in fear, but you have received **a spirit of adoption as sons, by virtue of which we cry, "Abba! Father!"** The Spirit himself gives testimony to our spirit that we are sons of God. But if we are sons, we are heirs also; heirs indeed of God and joint heirs with Christ, provided, however, we suffer with him that we may also be glorified with him. (Rom. 8:14-17)*

- WRITE a letter to a non-Catholic friend who out of interest in the Catholic faith inquires about the meaning of sanctifying grace. You would do well to follow St. Paul's ideas in the preceding passage point by point.

II. MAN'S RESPONSE TO GOD'S GIFTS

With his special intelligence, Adam certainly realized his favored position. He who should be a servant had become a son. For a time he and his wife, Eve, tried their best to show God all the appreciation that God deserved for His goodness. With a full and grateful heart they offered God the loyalty, service, and worship that would be expected of children of God.

In much the same manner the way we Christians serve God, the way we pray, the way we offer Mass are all part of our personal response to God and His gifts. God certainly does not need our worship or our service; they add nothing to His happiness or to His power. But at least the worship we give and our attempts at loyal service demonstrate our gratitude. We call this response of worship and this response of service the virtue of **religion.**

Religion is man's response to God in worship and service.

In thus recognizing God's dominion over himself and all the world, man is true to his own nature as a child of God and thus finds his happiness. He becomes the spokesman for all of mute creation. The mountains in their majesty, the trees in their splendor, the flowers in their delicate beauty all give honor to God in their own silent way by just being what they are; but only man can offer the worship of a mind and a heart.

Behind these acts of religion, much as the energy that feeds the thrust of rockets into space, is another virtue, that of **charity.** Charity gives man's acts of religion, whether internal or external, their most genuine meaning. Without love acts of religion never attain to their true worth. What a difference there is between the man who goes to Mass on Sunday for fear of God's punishment should he fail to go, and the loyal son who out of gratitude for his Father's generous gifts never misses the chance to show his love in worship.

Recall how we express this gratitude in the liturgy of the Mass:

> *How shall I make a return to the Lord for all the good he has done for me? The cup of salvation I will take up, and I will call upon the name of the Lord.* (Psalm 115, prayed each day at the priest's Communion)

SUMMARY

1. Everything in the world was made by God and everything is good.

2. God made man and woman in His own image, and blessing them with special powers, put them at the head of creation to work it and so to continue His creation.

3. God wishes that man set aside a day of rest each week in order formally to honor and worship his Creator.

4. God created man for the perfect happiness to be found in His service and friendship.

5. And lastly, the all-powerful God is a personal being, Some One, who out of goodness took the initiative in blessing man with wonderful gifts.

QUESTIONS

1. What was the purpose of the authors of the Bible in writing about the origin of the world?

2. How did the creation of man differ from the creation of everything else in the world?

3. Why is it that man can plan and make decisions and animals cannot?

4. Why does man resemble God?

5. Why is it necessary to rest from work on the Sabbath?

6. How does the sacred writer show that man is the friend of God?

7. What does it mean to create?

8. Why did God create?

9. Does the theory of evolution contradict what we learn about the origin of man in the Bible?

10. Explain each of the extraordinary gifts of God to Adam and Eve. Which was the greatest of all the gifts and why?

11. What do you mean by the response to God in religion? What is the connection between religion and charity?

CHAPTER III

GOD'S GIFTS ARE REJECTED: SIN

If any of you ever lost a brother in war or know what it is to have a close friend come down with polio, then you will better understand a problem that vexed the Hebrews of every generation, and really all of mankind ever since. Since the Scriptures revealed that Adam and Eve were supposed to live in happiness with God, their friend, **why is there so much suffering in the world?**

For example, in Moses' time the Hebrews became weary of the day-by-day struggle for existence which dogged their steps in the wilderness ever since they had fled from Egypt.

> *"Would that we had died at the Lord's hand in the land of Egypt, as we sat by our fleshpots and ate our fill of bread!" (Ex. 16:3)*

When at a later stage of their hard journey an armed band of hostile warriors blocked their northward passage to the Promised Land, in fear for their lives they circled deep into the south again. More delay and more suffering! Imagine what this setback meant to a young Hebrew and his family. "Why is the Lord bringing us into this land only to have us fall by the sword?" (Num. 14:3), they grumbled. Suffering hounded them on every side.

It was not too different at the fall of the kingdom of Juda. In the sixth century B.C. Nabuchodonosor's pagan horde overran the holy city, Jerusalem, and desecrated the sacred Temple of Yahweh. Juda's citizens were forced to stand by while the hated foreigners demolished the city, leaving the Temple itself a shamble of toppled stone and burnt-out timber. Evil in its starkest form had overwhelmed the People of God. They were helpless as the cream of their youth were marched off to Babylon's slave marts.

Beset themselves with experience of suffering, men of all time have tried to probe the mystery:

How did evil come to wield such power in God's world?

34

Section 1. SIN ENTERS THE WORLD

The traditions of Hebrew faith which we discussed in connection with creation could never have evaded the problem of suffering. Suffering was too much a part of human experience. Moses, under God's inspiration, tried to explain the presence of evil and each successive generation pondered over the biblical tradition of sin's entrance into the world. It is probable that these traditions concerning the first sin and its terrible consequences took the shape familiar to us from the Bible during the reign of King Solomon in the tenth century B.C. This is the account which the priest-editors of the sixth century were careful to insert into their edition of the Pentateuch.

I. GENESIS AND SIN

The Genesis account records the first sin in simple, but symbolic terms.

A. God had asked a son's obedience of Adam

Adam and Eve were his privileged children; He was their Father and Lord. One particular command the sacred writer records for posterity:

> And the Lord God commanded the man thus, "From every tree of the garden you may eat; but from the tree of the knowledge of good and evil you must not eat; for the day you eat of it, you must die." (Gen. 2:16-17)

What does this command mean?

The key to correct understanding is the idea of "symbol." **A symbol is something which stands for something else,** usually a material thing for some spiritual idea. Thus, a heart stands for love on St. Valentine's Day and a lion stands for courage in King Richard's nickname, "the lion-hearted."

Study the symbols used in Genesis:

Symbol	*Meaning*
1. The Garden of Eden — modeled on an ancient royal estate.	the condition or state of perfect happiness.
2. Eating the fruit of a tree — an ancient way of speaking.	participating in some action.
3. The tree of knowledge of good and evil — a Hebrew expression.	not just a knowing, but an experiencing something, here clearly evil; our notion of "sin."

THEREFORE: The command from God meant, "Do not commit sin; if you do, you will die."

4. The tree of life—from Assyrian and Babylonian mythology.	immortality, like a "fountain of youth."
5. The serpent — probably chosen to show contempt for Chanaanite and Egyptian snake-gods.	Satan, identified later by our Lord as the fallen angel Lucifer. (Luke 10:17-19)
6. The cherubim to guard the way to the tree of life—the figure of a winged bull often found on Assyrian and Babylonian monuments to protect sacred places.	the denial to man of any return to the state of perfect happiness he had lost because of Adam's sin.

B. After giving His command God would not force the loyalty of Adam and Eve

He allowed them full liberty to choose between good and evil, between fidelity to Him or treason. The stage was now set for what we have come to call "temptation," **a choice to be made between obedience to God or to one's own will.** Note how authentic and true to life is the experience of the temptation recorded in the third chapter of Genesis.

SO RUNS THE DRAMA

1. Enter the tempter uninvited:

He (the serpent) said to the woman, "Did God say 'You shall not eat of any tree of the garden'?" (Gen. 3:1)

2. Eve makes her first mistake when she elects to match discussion with the tempter instead of telling him to go away:

The woman answered the serpent, "Of the fruit of all the trees in the garden we may eat; but 'Of the fruit of the tree in the middle of the garden,' God said, 'you shall not eat, neither shall you touch it, lest you die.' " (Gen. 3:2-3)

3. With Eve's attention won, the tempter makes his deceitful promises:

But the serpent said to the woman, "No, you shall not die; for God knows that when you eat of it, your eyes will be opened and you will be like God, knowing good and evil." (Gen. 3:4-5)

4. Allured by the promises Eve feels strongly attracted to the object of the temptation:

Now the woman saw that the tree was good for food, pleasing to the eyes, and desirable for the knowledge it would give. (Gen. 3:6)

5. Eve surrenders to temptation and sins, then coaxes Adam to join her. With tragic weakness Adam complies. The life of God is killed within them both.

She took of its fruit and ate it, and also gave some to her husband and he ate. (Gen. 3:6)

6. Both experience the evil consequences of sin; with the loss of God's extraordinary gift of perfect control they become conscious of their nakedness:

Then the eyes of both were opened, and they realized that they were naked; so they sewed fig-leaves together and made themselves coverings. (Gen. 3:7)

7. Shame at their sin set in, together with the first pangs of remorse. They could not bear to face the Lord, their friend:

When they heard the sound of the Lord God walking in the garden in the cool of the day, the man and his wife hid themselves from the Lord God among the trees in the garden. (Gen. 3:8)

8. How human the sinners show themselves to be! They make lame excuses for their fall:

The man said, "The woman you placed at my side gave me fruit from the tree and I ate." Then the Lord God said to the woman, "Why have you done this?" The woman said, "The serpent deceived me and I ate."

C. God's Punishment

God could not tolerate the open rebellion against His clear-cut command. His justice demanded the punishment which He had promised, should the first man and woman disobey His precept: ". . . for the day you eat of it, you must die." (Gen. 2:17.) Of his own will, man had thrown away the perfect happiness that had been God's gracious gift.

THUS GOD SPOKE:

— to Adam:

"Because you have listened to your wife, and have eaten of the tree of which I commanded you not to eat: Cursed be the ground because of you; in toil shall you eat of it all the days of your life; thorns and thistles shall it bring forth to you, and you shall eat the plants of the field. In the sweat of your brow you shall eat bread, till you return to the ground, since out of it were taken; for dust you are and unto dust you shall return." (Gen. 3:17-19)

— to Eve:

"I will make great your distress in childbearing; in pain shall you bring forth children;" . . . (Gen. 3:16)

— to all the descendants of Adam and Eve, though indirectly through His actions and not the words:

He (God) drove out the man; and at the east of the garden of Eden he placed the Cherubim, and the flaming sword, which turned every way, to guard the way to the tree of life. (Gen. 3:24)

CONCLUSION

And so because of the sin of their first parents, all men were kept from the Garden of Eden, the state of perfect happiness. For a long time the pre-eminent gift of sonship in the family was lost.

D. But there was one ray of hope: a Redeemer was promised to win back God's friendship

. . . God said to the serpent: ". . . I will put enmity between you and the woman, between your seed and her seed; He shall crush your head, and you shall lie in wait for his heel." (Gen. 3:15)

The picture is of a man grinding the head of a serpent into the earth, but the serpent's fangs are buried in the heel of his conqueror.

The Church has traditionally seen in this promise of God the first prophecy of the Savior who was to come. That is why these lines of Genesis are called the **Protoevangelium,** the first announcement of the "good news" of our redemption. Christ and Satan are joined in an all-out combat. The total victory will be Christ's as He stamps the serpent's head into the earth. In the victory Christ represents all mankind. In the struggle He will suffer, as is symbolized by the serpent's fangs buried in His heel.

When in the light of fuller revelation within God's unfolding plan a broader meaning is seen in the words of Holy Scripture, we have what is called by biblical scholars "the fuller sense" of Scripture. Because the biblical authors themselves at their early stage of the History of Salvation would not have been able to see all that God intended these words to convey, this is a "non-literal" sense of Scripture (review the footnote in the chapter "A Searchlight on the Bible," page 15).

The fuller sense is a further meaning seen in the words of a biblical passage over and above the literal meaning of the human authors.

It should be noted that only the Holy Spirit speaking definitively through the Church could fill out the meaning and the fuller sense of any passage of Scripture with absolute certainty. Nevertheless, even when such a definitive statement has not been made by the Church, the Church encourages her biblical scholars to advance the understanding of the Bible whenever possible.

- COMPARE Genesis 3:15 with St. Paul's teaching in Romans 5:17-18. Writing after the completion of Christ's redemptive mission St. Paul shows the significance of Adam's fall in relation to the salvation brought by Christ. Why is Christ called the "second Adam?"

CONCLUSION

Suffering will always dog the steps of men in this life, because by the original sin and all the actual sins thereafter man has chosen unfaithfulness to his God; the sinner has **preferred himself to his Creator and Lord.**

E. Sin fed on sin

The sacred writers unmask some of evil's many faces. Fill out the details by the readings suggested below.

1. VENGEANCE AND MURDER

Murder enters the world among the descendants of Adam and Eve.

- READ Genesis 4:1-16.

2. MORAL CORRUPTION ON A MASS SCALE

The sacred authors present God as regretting that He had ever made man. He would remove all traces of man from the earth by a terrible flood. The just man Noe alone He would spare with his family.

- READ Genesis 6:5-14.

3. PRIDE AND ARROGANT INDEPENDENCE FROM GOD

Descendants of Noe built a tremendous tower, a monument to human pride. (This was probably one of the pagan temples called "ziggurats" which have been unearthed by archaeologists.)

- READ Genesis 11:1-9.

4. ABANDONMENT OF THE ONE, TRUE GOD

Archaeologists have uncovered evidence of a horrible polytheism with human sacrifice. Man reached the depths of degradation with worship of creatures ranging from the sun and the moon down to the level of cats and snakes.

- CONSULT a book of historical data on the religious situation just before Abraham's time. Give some specific examples of how the one true God was abandoned. A recommended source book is: RELIGIONS OF THE ANCIENT EAST, in the "Twentieth Century Series."

A Mesopotamian Ziggurat.

CONCLUSION

Sin had run its evil course. Man forgot his God. With his spiritual sense dulled by sin, he became more and more incapable of cooperating with God's Plan for his happiness.

BUT GOD DID NOT FORGET MAN: He went to great lengths to form a chosen people with this double vocation:

1. To safeguard faith in the one, true God.

2. To prepare the way for the coming of the promised Savior, the one bright hope for mankind.

This is the story of Abraham in the chapter to follow.

Section 2. THE HOLY SPIRIT SPEAKS THROUGH THE CHURCH

As was pointed out in the previous chapter, we can learn still more of God's revelation by the Church's theological reflection upon the original data from Holy Scripture. In the course of her history the Church under the guidance of the Holy Spirit has thought a great deal about the sin of Adam and Eve, and its consequences for all mankind.

I. WHAT THE CHURCH TEACHES ABOUT SIN

The original sin of our first parents set the pattern for the sins of all mankind.

Adam and Eve committed serious sin because in a moment of temptation they deliberately chose to act against their conscience.
You will note three elements in this pattern for sin, each of which should be carefully understood:

A. Conscience

Conscience is the judgment of a man's intellect counseling him to do something good or avoid something evil. By God's design for man's decisions in life, man must always follow the bidding of his conscience. He has the added obligation, of course, to keep his conscience well informed. In some ways conscience is like an alarm clock; if set correctly, it will not fail to jolt us awake to any danger we may be in. The ideal conscience is so well formed in judging right and wrong and so values God's friendship that it would run no risk of separation from God which is the price of every serious sin.

- WITH THE HELP of your teacher, diagnose the various illnesses of a disordered conscience: the scrupulous, the doubtful, the lax, and the erroneous.

B. Temptation

Temptation is the attraction to something evil. It can be particularly potent because of the weaknesses as a result of original sin. Because of original sin man lost extraordinary gifts: control of his appetites and superior intelligence. Temptation feeds on weakness. But temptation in itself is not always a bad thing for the person tempted. Temptation can influence a person either of two ways:

1. It can lead to sin.

2. It can prove one's loyalty under fire.

THEREFORE: The mere fact of temptation, no matter how strong it may be, never spells S-I-N. Temptation can be turned into a blessing or a curse. The decision rests with the person tempted, aided by God's grace. The man of courage under fire proves himself a loyal son of God.

C. Mortal Sin

Mortal sin is a serious offense against God. "Mortal" means the "death-sin" because it kills the God-life in the soul, sanctifying grace. The servant who like Adam had become a son through baptism becomes a servant again, but to Satan, not to God. A man in mortal sin is fully deserving of hellfire.

Why such a terrible punishment for even one mortal sin?

Because in justice the punishment must match this triple evil that attends every serious sin:

1. Rebellion against the Creator.

2. Contempt for the Law-giver.

3. Ingratitude and disrepect to a Father.

In view of the dire consequences it should be evident that there can be no such thing as half-way mortal sins. Mortal sin is a rejection of Him whom one realizes to be Creator, Law-giver, and Father. Each of three conditions must be fulfilled in a strict mortal sin and all must be present **simultaneously:**

a. Serious matter.

b. Sufficient knowledge and reflection.

c. Full consent of the will.

● DISCUSS with your teacher's help different cases in which some condition for a full mortal sin was lacking; for example, in a sin of theft, of impurity, of uncharitableness, or the like.

A PRACTICAL RULE: The act of infidelity called mortal sin scars the sinner's soul deeply. In the case of a person who usually proves loyal amid temptations, **a sincere doubt** most often means that one of the three strict conditions was not fully present. The sin, if it was a sin at all, may be confessed as "doubtful," though even this is not absolutely required by the laws for confession. Since in this case the state of grace may be presumed, Holy Communion may be received even before confession.

II. THE TRAGIC CONSEQUENCES OF ADAM'S SIN

The sin of the first man in God's creation seemed to shatter the beautiful plan that God had intended to be operative for all mankind. **Adam forfeited all the extraordinary gifts so generously bestowed.** A double column will point up the tragic consequences:

The Gift	*The Loss*
1. Freedom from death.	death to every man.
2. Freedom from suffering.	sickness and pain enter the world.
3. Control of the appetites.	constant rebellion of the appetites against man's will.
4. Advanced intelligence and effortless knowledge.	slowness of mind and ignorance, or limited knowledge after laborious effort.
5. Sonship in God's family with a sharing in God's own life, plus heaven for an inheritance.	sonship forfeited and God-life lost, with man's supernatural destiny with God unattainable.

And so it was that Adam labored "by the sweat of his brow" in sorrow and repentance, and longed for Him who would deliver the human race, Adam's entire family, from the curse of original sin.

In a similar fashion actual sin, the willful sins of men since Adam's time, inflicts parallel consequences. The sinner forfeits the gifts of God rewon for men by Jesus Christ. The privilege of sonship in God's family, rewon by Christ, is rejected. The unrepentant sinner casts his lot with the father of evil, Satan, and he can blame only himself for the consequences of his tragic decision. In place of heaven the sinner's inheritance is hell.

- IN A written assignment compare the ordinary sinner of our times with Adam. Does he have more reason to hope for God's mercy? Why?

CONCLUSION: Some Practical Attitudes.

The man who is honest with himself and realistic in life will guide himself with these useful principles for spiritual combat:

A. Recognize His Weakness

He knows that the special gift of complete self-control over man's appetites was lost and never regained. He rightly fears as formidable enemies the spirit of evil which he meets at work in "the world," and the fifth column which he encounters in concupiscence, i.e., the rebellious desires of "the flesh." In "the world" and "the flesh" the devil finds strong allies (see the Epistle of 1 John 2:15-17).

B. Put His Confidence in Christ

He never fights alone. Christ his Lord is present within him through grace. Together they are invincible, and Satan knows it.

C. Cooperate in His Own Defense

Like a determined athlete he trains himself for the combat. He will be master of his appetites, not their slave. There is no substitute for manly self-discipline in order to cooperate with the grace of God to resist temptation.

D. Take the Offensive

Since a good offense is the best defense, he sets his spiritual sights high. The higher his ideals soar, the closer he gets to Christ in whom sin never won a foothold.

- INVESTIGATE the lives of some sinners turned saints. What incident gave new directions to their lives? What happened to St. Augustine, St. Mary Magdalene, St. Paul?

In times of stress from temptation the psalmists can be effective spokesmen for struggling Christians and Jews:

1. IN TEMPTATION
   *Be not far from me, for I am in distress; be near, for I have no
   one to help me. (Ps. 21:12)*

2. IN SORROW FOR SIN
   *Turn away your face from my sins, and blot out all my guilt.
   A clean heart create for me, O God. . . . (Ps. 50:11-12)*

3. IN FULLEST CONFIDENCE
   The Lord is my shepherd; I shall not want. (Ps. 22:1)

SUMMARY

The traditions of Israel's faith explained the presence of evil
existing from the entrance of sin into the world. This is the story
that came down through the ages. God in effect had said to Adam
and Eve, "Do not commit sin; if you do, you will die." But our
first parents listened to the tempter and because of their sin were
kept from the Garden of Eden, the state of perfect happiness. The
gift of sonship in the family of God as well as the other extraordinary
gifts were also lost. The one ray of hope was the promise of a
Redeemer. But because of the sin of Adam and Eve, suffering and
evil and sin entered into this world.

QUESTIONS

1. What is a symbol? Give some examples.
2. What did the command of God to Adam and Eve really mean?
3. Did the command of God to Adam and Eve take away their full
liberty?
4. What was lost to man by the sin of Adam and Eve?
5. After their sin, was there any ray of hope given to Adam and Eve?
6. Why will there always be suffering in the world?
7. Mention some of the "evils" or "suffering" which afflicted the world
after the sin of Adam and Eve.
8. What is conscience? Can a person follow his conscience in what he
thinks is correct and still commit sin?
9. What is temptation? How can it be either a blessing or a curse?
10. What is mortal sin? What are the three conditions required for
mortal sin? Must all three conditions be simultaneously present? Why is
such a terrible punishment given to mortal sin?
11. What practical attitudes toward temptation and confidence in God
should one adopt after studying this chapter?

Later Preparations in God's Plan

CHAPTER IV

AN EARLY COVENANT: ABRAHAM AND THE PATRIARCHS

Even third and fourth generation Americans look back with pride and affection upon the foreign land of their ancestors. We admire the grandparents and great-grandparents who first ventured to this new land in the hope of a better future.

One of the interesting things about this man Abram (God changed his name to Abraham later) was that his bright future seemed behind him when he followed the call of a God who up to this point probably meant little if anything to him and his family. This God who called him was just one more deity among all the others in the polytheism of his times. And yet this God made exacting demands upon Abram, asking him to give up a prosperous life with his kinfolk, and head into the unpredictable future of life in a strange land.

We can be grateful to the authors of the Pentateuch with its Mosaic traditions, about whom we have spoken in the preceding chapters, for preserving the data handed down from ancient times. The story of Abraham and the other patriarchs is recorded in the latter part of the book of Genesis.

BLACK SEA

HITTITE

Carchemish

Ha...

Ugarit

CYPRUS

Hamath

EUPHRA...

Byblos

Palmyr...

MEDITERRANEAN SEA

Damascus

PALESTINE

Sichem

Jerusalem

Tanis

ARABIA

Memphis

Sinai

EGYPT

NILE RIVER

RED SEA

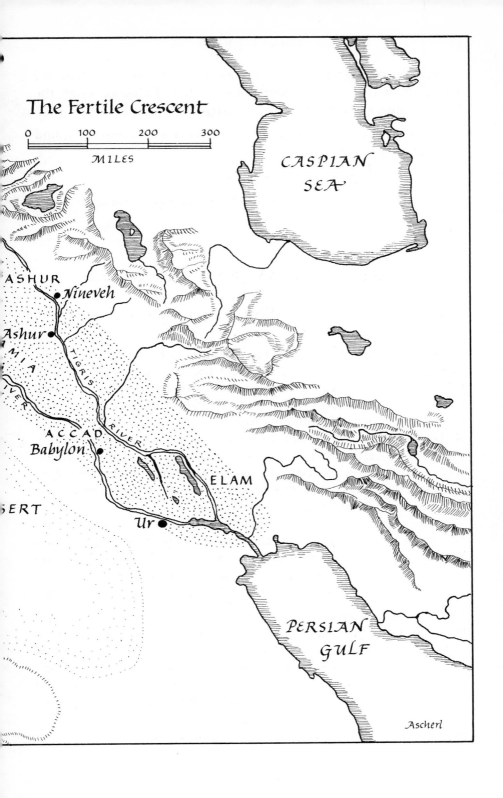

The Fertile Crescent

0   100   200   300
MILES

CASPIAN
SEA

ASHUR

●Nineveh

Ashur●

TIGRIS

MIA

RIVER

RIVER

ACCAD
Babylon●

ELAM

Ur●

ERT

PERSIAN
GULF

Ascherl

Three particular questions interest us here, and we shall see how each of the answers exerted tremendous influence upon the religious history of man:

1. What were the currents of civilization which moved around this chosen man of God?

2. In what spirit did Abram listen to God's call?

3. To what special mission did Abram's cooperation lead?

Section 1. ABRAM AND HIS TIMES

I. THE FERTILE CRESCENT: Ur of the Chaldees, Haran, Sichem

Sometime after the year 1850 B.C. in an area known as the Fertile Crescent, a migration took place from the once prosperous city of Ur in lower Mesopotamia between the Tigris and Euphrates rivers. Under pressure of invasion from several sides the power of Ur was shaken and many of its inhabitants headed north for the sister-town of Haran which was much like itself in culture and influence. Biblical scholars number among these migrants the herdsman sheik, Thare, with his entire clan. Following their age-old livelihood in the desert country, they settled in a semi-nomadic style of life outside of the prosperous city of Haran.

Thare numbered among his rugged sons a man named Abram. Just as his father, Abram was taught to worship and serve the many gods of those pagan times (see Josue 24:2), especially the moon-god Sin and his queen, Nin-gal. Thare and Abram prospered in their new environment and seemed to be blessed by their pagan gods.

NOTE: Perhaps some may wonder how such knowledge of civilizations four thousand years old is available to us. In the great adventure called archaeology, cities like Ur and Haran are literally dug out of the earth. Thousands of crockery pieces, carved jewels, and tablets inscribed with ancient writing have been found within the battered remains of what once were the homes and buildings of a prosperous community. By a painstaking process the inscriptions have been deciphered and the light they throw upon the civilizations of the

*Archeological remains of the ancient city, Ur of the Chaldees,
the birthplace of Abraham.* EWING GALLOWAY, N. Y.

ancient past enable us to reconstruct the world which moved around
the man with whom God chose to deal at this stage of human
history. For it was to this herdsman sheik named Abram that God
revealed Himself as the one, true God.

II.   THE CALL OF ABRAM

We do not know exactly by what kind of religious experience
God revealed Himself to Abram. It matters little, however, since
we have the important thing, God's message, in the sacred text:

> *The Lord said to Abram: "Leave your country, your kinsfolk
> and your father's house, for the land which I will show you;
> . . . I will bless you, and make your name great, so that you
> shall be a blessing. I will bless them that bless you, and curse
> them that curse you. In you shall all the nations of the earth be
> blessed." (Gen. 12:1-3)*

So went God's promise. Note well that, though delivered especially to the Hebrews as the Chosen People, the promise was to reach all mankind, "all nations." Abram and his people were delivered from idolatry and pagan error **in order that from his nation might spring forth the Savior promised long ago in the Garden of Eden.**

Abram had to make a big decision. His fortunes had fared well. Why throw everything over now for what many men of his time would judge the whim of some fickle god? But his response was unquestioning; not with mere words and empty promises, but **in action.** He revealed God's message to Sara, his wife, and then took his share of servants, herds and flocks and began the trek southward "to the land the Lord would show." The heroic faith of Abram will live in Hebrew and Christian memory.

- READ in Genesis 14:1-20 how Abram's faith and confidence in the Lord were vindicated in the battle with some petty chieftains.

- IN GENESIS 14:18-20 read about Abram's meeting with another king from the neighboring area of Jerusalem. This other king was Melchisedec, respected also as a priest, who gives the victorious Abram a special blessing. Can you explain the close connection of this passage with St. Paul's letter to the Hebrews 7:1-3?

III. ABRAM'S FAITH REWARDED: Making a Covenant with God.

The one sadness of Abram's life was Sara's inability to conceive a child. As the years passed, all hope seemed lost for any offspring, any heir. Always on familiar terms with God, Abram did not hesitate to express his sorrow. He was puzzled, too, because God seemed to be teasing him with riddles:

> *"I will make your posterity as the dust of the earth; if anyone can count the grains of dust, your posterity can also be counted." (Gen. 13:16)*

> *"Look at the heavens and, if you can, count the stars . . . So shall your posterity be." (Gen. 15:5)*

The sacred text speaks of Abram as an old man when God showed him how to put together the scattered pieces of the puzzle. This prophecy gave Abram a clearer picture of his destiny:

> *"I am God the Almighty. Walk in my presence and be perfect. I will make my covenant between you and me, and will multiply you exceedingly . . . This is my covenant with you: You shall be the father of a multitude of nations; you shall no longer be called Abram, but your name shall be Abraham; for I will make you the father of a multitude of nations. I will make you exceedingly fruitful; I will make nations of you, and kings shall descend from you.* **I will establish my covenant between you and me and your descendants after you throughout their generations, as a perpetual covenant, that I may be a God to you and to your descendants after you.** *I will give you and your descendants after you this land in which you are immigrants, all the land of Chanaan as a perpetual possession, and I will be their God." (Gen. 17:1-8)*

And then shortly afterward, as if to clear away the final trace of any doubt in Abram's mind, God added:

> *"I will bless her (Sara), and will also give you a son by her; yes, I will bless her, and she shall be the mother of nations; kings of peoples shall descend from her." (Gen. 17:16)*

With the changed name as a symbol of his special mission from God, Abraham stood amazed at the grandeur of God's plans. And yet he could not even suspect the true magnificence of his destiny. In looking back it is much easier for us to see the full meaning of God's design. Through this man of unwavering faith God set into motion His Divine Plan in history, decided long before in eternity:

God would send His Son to be born as one of the people of Abraham.

But in His promise God also made clear that the horizons of the Incarnation would stretch far beyond the borders of Chanaan. Abraham was destined to be the spiritual father of a people far more vast.

> *The Lord said, ". . . For Abraham shall surely become a great and powerful nation, and all the nations of the earth shall be blessed in him." (Gen. 18:18)*

In the "people of Abraham," therefore, we have a preparation that looks forward to the Church that Christ would come to found.

IV. THE FINAL TEST OF GREATNESS

It happens in life frequently enough that God will raise a man to dizzy heights of success and then put him to the acid test of true greatness of soul. Is he willing for the love of God to give up human greatness? Since Abraham had pleased God in so many things, he was ready for this final test of his holiness.

> *God said, "Take your only son Isaac whom you love and go into the district of Moria, and there offer him as a holocaust on the hill which I shall point out to you." (Gen. 22:2)*

Even if we remember that human sacrifice to a man of Abraham's time was taken for granted and not considered the horrible abomination that it is to us, still we have no difficulty in reading Abraham's gloomy thoughts as he dismissed his servants near the deserted hill. What had he done to bring God's anger upon him? Everything was lost now, but **he would obey.** In a flash the poised sacrificial knife was struck from his hand by an angel. By his obedience of intention Abraham had proved his loyalty to God. By this incident God also showed His displeasure at the pagan practice of human sacrifice.

Because of this episode as well as for other reasons Abraham's son, Isaac, is considered "a type" of Jesus Christ. This means that the faithful in the early Church, acquainted as they were with the saving events of God's Plan as they took place with Christ's death and resurrection, saw in the person of Isaac a foreshadowing of Jesus Christ. As one similarity, though not an exact parallel, Christ too was a victim of sacrifice, and even Christ's resurrection from the dead can be seen as foreshadowed in Isaac's deliverance from death by the intervention of God.

As we continue to read the Bible we shall find added examples of these similarities or parallels in what is called "typology." God thus uses persons, events or things from the Old Testament to help fuller understanding of the key persons, events or things in the Redemptive Mission of Jesus Christ. The person, event or thing in the New Testament is called the "anti-type."

- READ Hebrews 11:17-19 and explain the type and the anti-type. We shall see other examples as they come up in the History of Salvation.

A type is a person, event or thing from the Old Testament which in the light of the New Testament is seen to have foreshadowed like persons, events or things in God's Plan for our Salvation.

Whether the Old Testament authors were aware of God's intentions for typology, we cannot be sure (see the footnote of the non-literal senses of Scripture on page 15 in the earlier chapter, "A Searchlight on the Bible").

Typical nomad with a camel caravan on the Mount of Olives.
THE MATSON PHOTO SERVICE

V. A BIRD'S-EYE VIEW OF PATRIARCHAL HISTORY: like Father, like Son

A. Isaac

When the Hebrews ran up against the prevalent polytheism in the centuries following Abraham, they were careful to protect their sacred traditions of monotheism by giving their worship only to "the God of Abraham, Isaac, and Jacob." Thus the Hebrew descendants of Abraham remained loyal to "the one, true God."

Little is told us about Isaac other than that he took command of the clan at his father's death in keeping with the age-old Bedouin customs of patriarchal society. As sheik, he directed the wanderings of their semi-nomadic life as they dwelt in Bedouin tents on the outskirts of prosperous towns and lived off their flocks and herds.

B. Jacob (also called Israel)

The more sharply etched personality of Jacob dominates the last sections of Genesis. Like his father and his father's father before him, he ruled the clan with a strong hand. Jacob's trickery had at an early date snatched the birthright from his elder brother, the dull-witted Esau. Certainly God did not approve of the trick Jacob and his mother, Rebecca, had played upon the aged Isaac; a lie is a lie and not to be justified by good intentions. God, however, permitted this deceit and thereby gave us a good insight into some of His ways in dealing with men. He does not direct the personalities of history by puppet-strings; even the weaknesses and sins of men He uses to carry out His own designs.

- CAN you think of any other examples in biblical history where God in similar fashion allows evil to further His own plans?

The Chosen People continued to multiply rapidly, but we can hardly call this wandering tribe of semi-nomads a nation. After Jacob's time, in his honor they called themselves "the sons of Israel." They remained just another tribe until the great famine in Chanaan swept them south and west into the fertile valleys of the Nile. Here God had already years before raised up one of their number to receive them with hospitality and thus gradually prepare His people for their role in His Master Plan for the human race.

C. Joseph

It was the spiteful jealousy of his brothers which set off the chain of events that brought Joseph to his position of influence in Egypt. Again we see God making use of human weakness.

Perhaps we may wonder at the quick rise to power of this young Hebrew in a foreign land. The scattered findings of archaeology, however, give strong support to the biblical facts in this manner: About the year 1730 B.C. marauding bands of Asiatics known as the Hyksos invaded the highly cultured but weakening empire of Egypt. The invaders from the northeast conquered this ancient land, per-

An Egyptian pyramid seen at sunset during flood time of the Nile.
THE MATSON PHOTO SERVICE

haps because of the horse-drawn warrior's chariot which they seem to have introduced into Egypt. Thus a new line of pharaohs came into power, not Egyptian at all, but Asiatic or even Semite, just like the young Joseph who was sold into their midst as a slave. Among racial kinsmen such as these it was possible that a bright young man could rise quickly up the ladder of success, and finally become a power in the realm answerable to the pharaoh alone.

- READ Chapters 37-50 in which are recorded the different events in Joseph's life.

  In parallel columns list the similarities by which Joseph fore-shadows the Savior, Jesus Christ, of whom he is "a type."

VI. MESSAGES OF HOPE

The Holy Scriptures depict Jacob and Joseph at their deaths leaving to their people encouraging messages of hope:

Jacob prophesied:

*"The sceptre shall not depart from Juda, nor the staff from between his feet, **until he comes to whom it belongs.***" (Gen. 49:10)

Joseph promised:

*". . . God will certainly come to you and lead you up from this land **to the land which he promised on oath to Abraham, Isaac and Jacob.**" (Gen. 50:24)*

"The sceptre" and "the staff" are symbols of authority and power. The message of Jacob, therefore, meant that the nation's authority and power were destined to pass to the family of Jacob's son, Juda. An offspring from the family of Juda "to whom this power belongs" by God's design would one day ascend the Hebrew throne and all the nations of the world would bow down before him.

It is not always possible in prophecies like these of Jacob and Joseph to tell exactly what the biblical authors had in mind. Biblical scholars tell us, however, that since this passage was probably recorded during the era of the Monarchy, the immediate reference in Jacob's prophecy is probably to King David, the nation's greatest monarch, born indeed of the house of Juda. But since even the power of King David was limited in many ways and was certainly restricted to the borders of the Kingdom of Juda, this prophecy must still look to a greater era in order to fulfill the people's grander expectations. David, therefore, is only **a type** of the great Messiah-King who at the end of time will take possession of a kingdom that will know no bounds, the kingdom of Yahweh. This day of triumph will be the great "Day of Yahweh" for which all faithful Hebrews hoped and prayed. We Christians also look to this day of final victory because it will mean that we too will triumph at the side of our Lord and King, as we saw earlier in the introduction to this course.

In view of the prophecy of Jacob, which is reinforced by other prophecies like that of Joseph, how much better we can understand what the Angel Gabriel's announcement to Mary really meant.

Gabriel was telling Mary that in her son the prophecy of Jacob would find its true fulfillment. The Messiah would indeed be born to the house of David and he would ascend David's throne, but his rule would far surpass the limited kingdom of Juda. The Christ to whom Mary would give birth would rule over all men and "of his kingdom there shall be no end." Gabriel's message went like this:

> "... *Behold, thou shalt conceive in thy womb and shalt bring forth a son; and thou shalt call his name Jesus; ... and the Lord God will* **give him the throne of David his father, and he shall be king over the house of Jacob forever; and of his kingdom there shall be no end.**" *(Luke 1:31-33)*

VII. DARKNESS BEFORE THE DAWN

But a long night awaited the Hebrews before they saw the dawn of their Savior's coming. After close to two centuries of friendly cooperation from the Asiatic pharaohs, a hostile monarch took power who was determined to humble the Hebrew foreigners. Bitter years of suppression and slavery followed. The stage was set for a sudden turn in Hebrew history. The Lord of History slowly plotted the road which would lead toward the final fulfillment of Jewish destiny.

This new turn of events will fill out the next chapter, where we shall see how the proud Hebrew clans bent beneath the yoke of slavery and cried to God for deliverance and a Savior.

Section 2. THE DEEPER MEANING OF ABRAHAM AND THE PATRIARCHS

People interested in history are never really satisfied with the mere record of facts. They try to get below the surface, down to the underlying ideas which give life to human events. It is easy to look up and memorize the date Lincoln freed the slaves, but what was the spiritual ideal behind his historic decision? You are catching on fast if some of you answer, "Because he believed all men are equal in the sight of God." Ideals like this move nations and trigger great events.

Now if we look at the Abraham story as if it were an X-ray picture with all the minor details blacked out and the principal ideas showing up strong and clear, we can make out these three ideas most sharply etched of all:

1. THE CALL, THE VOCATION: GOD ACTED FIRST. God took the initiative in choosing Abraham for a job designed just for him. Man has no right to expect such personal attention, but God in His goodness gives it anyway.

2. THE RESPONSE OF FAITH. God called Abraham, but He would not force Abraham's cooperation. The invitation to collaborate with God is freely given, but the invitation must be freely accepted, too. Abraham could have said no to God but his response was a determined **yes.** We call this kind of positive response to God "faith."

3. THE COVENANT. Abraham never wavered in this **pact of friendship** made with God. Abraham knew he could count on God to be true to His word. Result: a total confidence by Abraham, no matter what.

Some memory helps

1. VOCATION is the personal call to a particular mission within God's Plan for men, e.g., the call of Abraham or the call of Joseph.

2. FAITH is the supernatural virtue by which
   a. we freely accept God's truth since God Himself is witness;
   b. and pledge our total cooperation in response to God's call, e.g., the response of Abraham and Joseph.

3. A COVENANT was the pact freely entered into by God and man whereby Israel accepted Yahweh as its Lord and pledged obedience to His will. God in His turn pledged favor and protection, e.g., the Covenant with Abraham.

Something to think over

In the vocation offered to man personally by God and in the active response of faith is found **the total meaning of life.**

- AS A COOPERATIVE CLASS PROJECT, put out a series of studies on the lives of saints. Build each study around the three themes exemplified in Abraham of Vocation, Faith, Covenant. How did each saint make his or her impact upon the world?

Abraham in the Church's Liturgy

1. Look up the rites for the sacrament of baptism and find one section toward the beginning that is in the finest tradition of Abraham.

2. What reference can you find to Abraham in the liturgy of Matrimony?

3. Consult your Missals and focus your attention on these words in the Canon of the Mass:

> . . . accept (these offerings) as You were pleased to accept the offerings of Your servant Abel the just, the sacrifice of our father Abraham, and that of Melchisedec, Your high priest, a holy sacrifice, a spotless victim.

- WRITE a paragraph explaining what these three incidents mentioned in this quote from the Canon have in common, especially in this context of the Sacrifice of the Mass.
  Clue: review the meaning of "type."

St. Paul conveys the message of the Abraham story very well:

> . . . remain perfect and completely in accord with all the will of God. (Col. 4:12)

SUMMARY

The Messiah, or Redeemer, promised to Adam and Eve centuries earlier would be born in the line of Abraham, Isaac, Jacob, and then through Juda's branch of the family. This preparation for the coming of the Messiah would take centuries.

Abram received a call from God to which he responded with tremendous faith. God made a covenant with him. This covenant with God and promise of a Redeemer was kept alive by the descendants of Abraham.

QUESTIONS

1. How do we get our knowledge of the ancient cities of Abram's time? Is our knowledge guesswork? Explain.

2. How did God call Abram? What did God mean when He said, "In you shall all nations of the earth be blessed?"

3. What is a covenant? What was the covenant between God and Abram?

4. "Abraham" is the new name given by God. Why did God give Abram this new name?

5. What is the outstanding characteristic of Abraham? How was it severely tested?

6. What is a type? Is Isaac a type of Christ? Explain.

7. Who were the descendants of Abraham? Give a brief sketch of each.

8. Is our vocation to serve God as revealed to us by our particular talents or inclinations similar to the vocation of Abraham? Explain in what way.

CHAPTER V

THE COVENANT OF SINAI: MOSES

The plight of political prisoners in Communist Siberia today would be a parallel to the enslavement of the Hebrews in Egypt. Just as thousands are pressed into slave labor in Siberian industry, so after the fall of the Asiatic pharaohs the rulers of Egypt tyrannized the defenseless Hebrews. They were herded into work gangs in order to build the cities of the new Egypt. As mute testimony to their labors, cities of more than three thousand years ago have been unearthed in recent times from beneath layers of Egyptian sand.

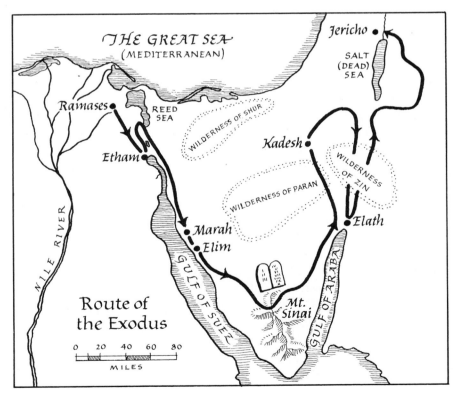

To many of the dehumanized workers God seemed to have abandoned His people. But in reality God's Plan for mankind did not stall or jump its tracks as it gradually and steadily moved along in human history. An important truth emerges: God does not do everything at once. Taking men as they are, He puts up with ignorance, sinfulness, and infidelity for His own good purposes. He allows the decisions of free men to have their full play in history. Time and time again we shall see that even sinful decisions will not block His goals. We just saw how God made providential use of Joseph after he had been sold into slavery by his own brothers. Now we shall study the sad plight of the Hebrews in Egypt around the year 1290 B.C., about 600 years after Abraham, as God prepared the deliverer who would lead them out of bondage.

Section 1. MOSES AND HIS TIMES
(circa 1290 B.C. on)

I. GOD CALLS MOSES: the First Challenge

A. A Leader is Born

Moses enjoyed the education and upbringing of the finest Egyptian aristocracy. The story of his escape from early death through the kindness of an Egyptian princess is well known. In the middle of the luxuries of life at the palace Moses did not forget his fellow Hebrews. Once when he saw an Egyptian maltreating a Hebrew, he slew the Egyptian in a flash of anger. The discovery of the slaying drove him into hiding in the nearby desert country of Madian. There he later married and fully intended to spend the rest of his life as a herdsman, when God stepped in.

Through the flame of a bush which burned without being consumed by the fire, God appeared to Moses one day near Mount Horeb. Just as He had done with Abraham, God gave Moses a special kind of message, a call to an extraordinary mission:

> *"Moses! Moses!" He answered, "Here I am." God said, "Come no nearer! Remove the sandals from your feet, for the place where you stand is holy ground. I am the God of your father,"*
> *he continued, "the God of Abraham, the God of Isaac, the God of Jacob . . . I have witnessed the affliction of my people in*

Egypt and have heard their cry of complaint against their slave drivers, so I know well what they are suffering. Therefore I have come down to rescue them from the hands of the Egyptians and lead them out of that land into a good and spacious land, a land flowing with milk and honey . . . Come now! I will send you to Pharaoh to lead my people, the Israelites, out of Egypt." (Ex. 3:4-10)

Moses shrank with fear from the responsibility God laid upon his shoulders, but God assured him of assistance and protection.

"Thus shall you say to the Israelites: The Lord, the God of your fathers, the God of Abraham, the God of Isaac, the God of Jacob, has sent me to you." (Ex. 3:15)

When Moses pressed further for God's name as an added guarantee, the reply thundered back:

"I am who am." (The Hebrew form Yahweh is the third person of the simple declarative form of the verb to be and means "He is.")

God did not wish to reveal His name more clearly to Moses. The reason was probably due to the ancient belief that knowing a person's name gave the knower a special power over the person. No one can hold any power over God. God from this time onward always remained for the Hebrews the great Lord of all, mysterious beyond all human understanding.

- COMPARE this Hebrew sense of God with our Christian point of view. Perhaps John 1:18 will help you understand the reason for the difference.

B. Moses Before Pharaoh

Moses made the trek back to Egypt with his brother, Aaron, at his side. Together they boldly approached the Pharaoh to announce God's message. By one amazing feat after another Moses attempted to convince the Egyptian of God's power, but he refused to yield to God's command that the Hebrews be set free. Even when brought to his knees by a series of horrible plagues and threatened still further with the death of each Egyptian first-born son, the stubborn Pharaoh held firm.

- READ Exodus 7:14 to 11:1.

Discuss the miraculous nature of the plagues inflicted upon the Egyptians. What would you say about the style of description in these passages? Concerned only with facts? Highly imaginative? Contrast the modern "scientific" history with this different type of history common in earlier centuries. This is a "literary form," but note that *it is still history,* an account of something that actually happened, although not exactly in the same imaginative details. The writers felt free to embellish the core of facts so that they might point up the religious message more enthusiastically.

C. The Night of the Passover

The moment was now at hand for great events.

Then the Lord told Moses, "One more plague will I bring upon Pharaoh and upon Egypt. After that he will let you depart. In fact, he will not merely let you go; he will drive you away." (Ex. 11:1)

This is what happened on this night of nights in Jewish history. God ordered the Hebrews to prepare a special ritualistic meal, something like the ceremony which shepherd peoples used in springtime for dedicating their flocks to their pagan gods. As an added part of the ritual Moses commanded each family to smear the blood of the lamb on the doorposts outside. This was to signal to the exterminating angel that faithful Hebrews lived within, and thus their first-born children would be spared from the death blow.

And so it happened. The avenging angel slew the first-born of each Egyptian family, but spared the Hebrew households. It took little time for the Pharaoh at long last to see the hopelessness of his situation. He called for Moses and charged him to clear out of his land all of the hated Hebrew foreigners. At a prearranged signal the Hebrew people emerged from their homes with all the equipment needed for a long journey. The Exodus had begun.

D. The Reliving of History

A nation commemorates great events. It was God Himself who instructed the Hebrews never to forget this glorious night in their history. The generations to follow should share in the great events of the Exodus by "reliving" its history in liturgical rite. From this time on, the Hebrews faithfully celebrated this liturgy of Passover, the "keeping alive" of their finest hour.

- PIECE together these basic ideas of liturgy from God's instructions in Exodus 12:1-32, especially vs. 26-27:

  "When your children ask you, 'What does this rite of yours mean?' you shall reply, 'This is the Passover sacrifice of the Lord, who passed over the houses of the Israelites in Egypt; when he struck down the Egyptians, he spared our houses.' "

NOTE: It is at the Easter Vigil that Christians commemorate Christianity's finest hour, the glorious resurrection of Jesus Christ, our Redeemer. We shall see afterward how the Jewish Passover is only a pale "type" of God's liturgical masterpiece, **the Mass.**

II. FORMING A NATION: Moses' Second Challenge

A. **To Form Them Politically**

It was noted earlier that the wandering clans of Hebrew herdsmen or transplanted communities in Egypt could hardly be called a nation. Nevertheless, the four hundred years of exile in Egypt saw the tiny clans multiply so in number that they could at least be considered a people in the making. But it takes more than numbers to form a nation as a political unit; **it takes a strong sense of community and dedication to a common goal, with dynamic leadership.** Moses provided that leadership; his was the difficult mission of welding scattered, self-seeking tribes into a political unity, into a people united in spirit, willing to sacrifice for the good of the nation as a whole.

B. **To Form Them Spiritually**

In God's fuller design, however, there was a still greater challenge to be faced. The Hebrews were the chosen people of God. Besides political unity God expected of them a spiritual maturity which would enable them to proclaim His revelation to the pagan world. Again the responsibility fell upon Moses to make of the Hebrews a religious people worthy of their spiritual heritage. In the glory of their exodus and in the spiritual trials of their desert march he was to bring to birth a spiritual community which would mature in the centuries to come.

C. Some Triumphs, Some Setbacks Along the Way

1. MIRACULOUS CROSSING OF THE REED SEA

This was a glorious triumph as God delivered them from the pursuing Egyptians. Confidence in God was at a new high.

- READ the Canticle of Moses, Exodus 15:1-18. What would you say about the literary form of this passage?

2. DESPAIR IN THE DESERT

The hardships of desert life made even Egypt a happy memory. *"Would that we had died at the Lord's hand in the land of Egypt, as we sat by our fleshpots and ate our fill of bread!" (Ex. 16:3)*

3. THE QUAIL, THE MANNA, AND THE WATER

God fed His people with a flock of quail for meat, and a strange kind of bread that appeared on the ground each morning; He empowered Moses to strike water from a rock. But the renewal of courage was shortlived; grumbling against Moses started up again.

- READ Exodus 16:4-36 and 17:1-7.

4. BATTLE WITH THE ARMY OF AMALEC

A victory for the Hebrews by God's help in answer to Moses' prayer, as symbolized by his upraised arms.

- READ Exodus 17:8-16.

5. THE MEETING WITH GOD ON MOUNT SINAI

The Covenant of Sinai was established. The Hebrews are to be God's People, but they must remain faithful to Yahweh's commandments.

- READ Exodus 22:1-21.

6. VIOLATION OF THE COVENANT BY THE WORSHIP OF THE GOLDEN CALF

Moses shattered the tablets of the Law in disgust with his people; then he ordered punishment of the guilty.

- READ Exodus 32:1-29.

7. CONSTRUCTION OF THE SACRED TENT

The Ark of the Covenant was housed within. The cloud which settled over the tent showed that God was present in the tent.

- READ Exodus 34:42-43 and 40:34.

8. DEATH OF MOSES

Moses' mission was accomplished. Josue led the people in the attack upon Jericho. The Israelites entered the Promised Land with the fall of Jericho.

- READ Deuteronomy 34:1-12 and Josue 6:1-21.

Mount Sinai. THE MATSON PHOTO SERVICE

III. MOSES' LEGACY TO THE WORLD: the Covenant of Sinai

A. The Covenant Before Sinai

When you come right down to it, outside of a few striking instances in Abraham's life little was actually asked of Abraham and his descendants in their everyday moral life. There was no immediate and total revolution from their pagan ways. In fact, many of their failings rivaled the sins of their Chanaanite neighbors: they married several wives, they lied, they quarreled, they stole.

The creeping pace of their moral improvement would have discouraged anybody but God.

What was their notion of God and morality?

In a word, the Hebrew clans in patriarchal times looked to God with the same awe and respect owed to their clan chieftains on earth. By their age-old traditions they pledged unswerving allegiance to the sheik who was their father in all things. This bond was sacred in Bedouin culture, and to this day still is sacred in the Bedouin lands of the Near East. The early faithful of Yahweh envisioned their God and themselves in a similar relationship of mutual love and fidelity. They prided themselves on their loyalty, worshiped Yahweh alone among all the gods of their times, and put their trust and confidence in Him as the great father of their clans. But that was about the sum total of their religious concern for what we call morality.

B. The Sinai Covenant Prepared

Therefore, with Moses as His middleman, God continued to purify His wayward children, and in the desert of Sinai He put His people through the hard training school of suffering. The time was drawing near when God would bring their side of the sacred pact into a sharper focus.

What was this sharper focus?

Let Moses relay the message to us as he did for the Hebrews:

"Hear, O Israel! The Lord is our God, the Lord alone! Therefore, you shall love the Lord, your God, with all your heart, and with all your soul, and with all your strength. Take to heart these words which I enjoin on you today." (Deut. 6:4-6)

What God asked, therefore, of the Hebrews was simply a return of love for love. God loved them first by electing them His Chosen People and promising them a share in a glorious Kingdom. In the same spirit of fatherly love and concern God pointed out the paths which alone could direct their steps to this goal of perfect happiness. These paths in their quest were mapped out by God's Eternal Will. They could never deviate the slightest nor switch direction from one generation of Hebrews to the next. God would not be God if He did not always love the good and hate evil. The Hebrews who loved God and who would gratefully accept God's gifts must do no less.

These paths were "the commandments," and God gave them to Moses at this epoch of history on Mount Sinai.

IV. THE COVENANT OF SINAI SPELLED OUT

In a fateful hour for mankind God thus declared His will (Deut. 5:6-21) :

FIRST COMMANDMENT

"I, the Lord, am your God, who brought you out of the land of Egypt, that place of slavery. You shall not have other gods besides me."

The Hebrews knew well that other peoples in Chanaan, Egypt, and Babylonia worshiped many gods: the god of the flocks, the god of the crops, the god of the winds, the gods of the sun and the moon. As followers of Yahweh they had to turn their backs on pagan worship. Yahweh alone was the one, true God. Neither might they use carved images to represent Him. The head of a vulture on the body of an ox or a human head on the body of a snake would not bring the power of God into their midst as the pagans believed.

SECOND COMMANDMENT

"You shall not take the name of the Lord, your God in vain. For the Lord will not leave unpunished him who takes his name in vain."

At the meeting with God near the burning bush God had told Moses that the Hebrews should call Him "He who is," the Hebrew **Yahweh.** At God's command Moses would work miracles by this mysterious name, but no one was to usurp its use for his own selfish designs, nor pronounce it irreverently, nor expect to hold God under his power in any way.

THIRD COMMANDMENT

"Take care to keep holy the Sabbath day . . . Six days you may labor and do all your work, but the seventh day is the Sabbath of the Lord, your God."

The Hebrews worked hard in tending their flocks and herds in the heat of the desert. Always on the march, they expended much energy in pitching camp and then breaking it again as they set out anew on their arduous trek over rocky hills and barren plains. But the Sabbath must be different. The Sabbath was the day of rest; but what is more, it was also the day reserved for ritual worship, ill suited to the busy schedule of their ordinary working day. Let them always keep this day sacred.

FOURTH COMMANDMENT

"Honor your father and your mother . . . that you may have a long life and prosperity in the land which the Lord, your God, is giving you."

Family life in their tightly knit clans was always sacred to the Hebrews. Children owed obedience to their parents who in turn owed allegiance to the patriarch of the clan. Authority was essential to community life.

FIFTH COMMANDMENT

"You shall not kill."

Life itself was precious. If life was cheap in the eyes of many pagans, it must not be so for God's People. The murderer must answer with his life. Human sacrifice was also an abomination before God.

SIXTH COMMANDMENT

"You shall not commit adultery."

A sin against marriage was a sin against the clan. The clan would punish the culprits. But what is more, impurity of all types breaks the Covenant with Yahweh. Let them beware of mingling with pagan peoples already corrupt from sins of the flesh.

SEVENTH COMMANDMENT

"You shall not steal."

No one might take to himself what belonged to another. God in good time would punish the prowling bandits who harassed their desert march. The right of property was God-given.

EIGHTH COMMANDMENT

"You shall not bear dishonest witness against your neighbor."

God abhors lies and deceits. Though some of their own ancestors gave notorious bad example, the Hebrews were bound to purify themselves of double-dealing.

NINTH COMMANDMENT

> *"You shall not covet your neighbor's wife."*

The man of evil desires is already a man of sin. Yahweh knows the heart of man.

TENTH COMMANDMENT

> *"You shall not desire your neighbor's house . . . nor anything that belongs to him."*

It was all too easy to envy the man with a better tent, fatter herds, richer jewels and trinkets from Egypt. Every man was to look to himself and trust in the Lord for the material things he needs.

Thus God had spoken. It was clear to all that they must change many of their ways. These were the paths God wanted them to follow, because this was the only map of life which could lead them to happiness, and God wanted them to be happy. In following the will of their Creator they could reach the ultimate goal of life. But what is more, in the loyal response to the Covenant they were to prove themselves faithful "sons of God."

V. THE COVENANT OF SINAI SEALED AND RATIFIED

Moses proclaimed to the Hebrews all that God had told him. As with any pact, they must now seal the solemn agreement with their pledged word. They shouted approvingly:

> *"We will do everything that the Lord has told us." (Ex. 24:3)*

Moses sent some young men for a pair of young bulls as victims for sacrifice, thus confirming the Covenant by a solemn religious rite. Moses read the text of the Covenant and again all replied enthusiastically:

> *"All that the Lord has said, we will heed and do." (Ex. 24:7)*

Employing a gesture sanctified by tradition, Moses next sprinkled the blood over the people saying:

> *"This is the blood of the Covenant which the Lord has made with you in accordance with all these words of his." (Ex. 24:8)*

As his people thus sealed their pact of fidelity to his God, surely this must have been Moses' greatest hour.

- WHAT is the Christian parallel to the ratification of the Covenant with God? Look up a Christian's baptismal vows.

- HOW does a Catholic seal his pact with God in the similar liturgical manner?
  A clue: Compare Exodus 24:8 with Matthew 26:27-28.

Centuries later the Psalmist put to song the spiritual experience of this Covenant with God:

> *Oh, that I might be firm in the ways of keeping thy statutes! Teach me wisdom and knowledge, for in your commands I trust. With all my heart I seek you; let me not stray from your commands. (Ps. 118:5, 66, 10)*

VI. MOSES AND JESUS CHRIST: the Covenants, Old and New

Do you remember the time our Lord gave Peter, James, and John a preview of His resurrected glory to come? Moses, the hero of this chapter in our course, was on that occasion close by Christ's side. The apostles saw the two talking with one another. In the interchange of conversation, therefore, we see the perfect symbol of the beautiful interlocking of the Old Testament with the New.

What is this interlocking of the Old and the New?

The Old Testament is the foreshadowing of the New and the New is the fulfillment of the Old.

The Old Testament, therefore, is a land of mystery where we must learn to discover the different roads that lead to Christ, the Light of the World.

Moses and Christ are two focal points of interest **because Moses is a "type" of Christ.** (Review your understanding of typology from the discussion earlier about Isaac as a type of Christ.)

- DISCUSS and then memorize this typology:

Old Covenant	*New Covenant*
Under the liberator, Moses, a united Israel was delivered from slavery and led through the desert into the Promised Land.	Under the Savior, Jesus Christ, a united Church was redeemed from sin and guided through life into the Kingdom of Heaven.

- SHARPEN your sense of typology with the following:
  1. the paschal lamb;
  2. crossing the Reed Sea;
  3. the manna in the desert;
  4. the brazen serpent (Numbers 21:8-9) ;
  5. crossing the Jordan into the Promised Land.

Section 2. THE COMMANDMENTS IN CHRISTIAN LIFE

In the perspective of God's Plan for men, the Covenant plays a key role in the life of every Christian. The commandments are **the charter of this Covenant between God and man.** With every man God takes the initiative by extending the invitation to join a solemn pact of friendship. It was from Moses in the Old Testament and Christ in the New Testament that man has learned what his personal response to the invitation should be, what God justly expects from him as his share in the pact.

What is a Christian's share in the pact with God?
  1. To love God in the manner of a loyal son.
     "As the Father has loved me, I also have loved you. Abide in my love." (John 15:9)

  2. To prove this love in deeds, by living the Covenant charter.
     "If you love me, keep my commandments." (John 14:15)

As biblical history makes clear from Eden to the time of Christ into the era of the Church, God has magnificent plans for His children. The loyal Christian's cooperation with these designs is measured by his fidelity to God's commandments.

- READ Chapters 14 and 15 of St. John and underscore the passages which give a true focus to the Covenant and its charter.

Some Memory Helps
  1. **The Commandments** are the charter of the Covenant, i.e., God's standards of life which spell out a Christian's loyalty.

  2. **The Covenant** is the personal pact of friendship between God and His people.

3. **Charity** is the motivating love which inspires the **Covenant**.

4. **Sin** is the offense against God which betrays God's love and breaks the pact of the Covenant.

Section 3. LITURGY, THE PASSOVER AND THE MASS

Against the background of this chapter, we can begin to understand how God prepared the way historically for the sacrifice of the Mass. Instructed by God Himself (Ex. 12:1-32), the Hebrews in their own ancient liturgy were intent upon "keeping alive" the memory of the wonderful historical events which surrounded their triumphal deliverance from Egypt. By God's design this deliverance from bondage is a type of our own deliverance from the bondage of sin as accomplished by the Redemption.

The next step becomes evident: God likewise intends that Christians redeemed by Christ should "keep alive" the historical events which accomplished their redemption. That is why at the Last Supper **Jesus Christ introduced the apostles to the liturgy of the Mass.** The ritual of the Hebrew Passover served as a framework. He added the important words: "Do this in commemoration of me." In other words, He said, "What I have done for you, you should also do in my Church."

We shall discuss at length in another place how incomparably superior the Mass liturgy is to the merely commemorative liturgy of the Passover.

A memory aid

Historical Events	*Liturgical Reliving*
Deliverance from Egypt	Passover celebration
is a	is a
TYPE	TYPE
of the	of the
Redemption	Mass

- LOOK UP in your Missals the famous song of the "Exultet" from the Easter Vigil. Copy out in your notes:

  1. The part recalling the historical events in Egypt over three thousand years ago.

  2. The references to redemption in the life of Christians.

SUMMARY

God called Moses to a great mission: to free the Chosen People from the domination of Pharaoh and to form them into a great nation. God Himself instructed the Hebrews never to forget their liberation from Egypt. Faithfully, therefore, each year they relived it through the liturgy of the Passover. Under Moses, God formed His people into a nation or political unity and also led them to a spiritual maturity which enabled them to proclaim His revelation to the pagan world. On Mount Sinai God made a covenant with His Chosen People.

QUESTIONS

1. How did God call Moses to be a leader of His people?

2. What did God intend Moses to do?

3. How did God answer Moses when pressed for His name?

4. What was the final plague which forced Pharoah to free the Hebrews?

5. Were the Hebrews spared from this final plague? Explain.

6. Who instructed the Hebrews never to forget the Passover? What is meant by the "liturgy of Passover"?

7. Is the Passover a type of the Mass? Explain your answer.

8. What two great problems faced Moses in forming the Hebrews into a nation? Which was the more difficult problem? Why was it more difficult?

9. What was the Hebrew notion of God in the time of Moses? How did it differ from the present day Christian concept?

10. What is the Covenant of Sinai? How did God prepare His Chosen People for this Covenant? How was the Covenant sealed and ratified?

11. What is the Christian parallel to the ratification of the Covenant with God?

12. What is the connection between the Old and New Testament?

13. Why is Moses a type of Christ? Explain this typology.

14. What is a Christian's share in his pact or covenant with God? What is the measure of his fidelity?

15. Explain how God prepared the way historically for the sacrifice of the Mass. Compare the Mass liturgy with the liturgy of the Passover.

CHAPTER VI

LIVING THE COVENANT: JUDGES AND KINGS

Stand with Josue on a high plateau in Moab and scan the horizons to the west. The perspective of the Promised Land thrilled the Hebrews much as the lush California valleys dazzled the eyes of our early settlers in the nineteenth century.

The only trouble was that a downward glance across the Jordan, which lay at the foot of the plateau, was like looking down into the mouth of death. The Hebrews could make out military units moving about like ants on a hill. The inhabitants of Jericho were preparing to resist the invaders. Josue's scouts told him they would be a rugged foe, well trained and heavily armed. But Josue was confident; this was an hour of destiny for God's People.

Section 1. JUDGES AND KINGS
(circa 1200 B.C.-935 B.C.)

I.   THE COVENANT CONTINUES

A. God Is True to His Promises

In this critical hour God had raised up the right man to take Moses' place and rally the Hebrew warriors. Josue inspired confidence in his men, but he knew better than all the rest that their real hope lay in God's protecting hand. God said that this land of rolling hills and fertile valleys would pasture their herds and raise their crops in a glorious future for Israel, and so it would be. To eyes long tired of the rocky and sandy wastes of Sinai, this was indeed "the land flowing with milk and honey," a land worth fighting for.

An aerial view of ancient Jericho, north of the modern town. The Dead Sea and the Mounts of Moab are seen in the distance. THE MATSON PHOTO SERVICE

As Josue mapped out his plans, God reassured him:

"No one can withstand you while you live . . . I will not leave you nor forsake you. Be firm and steadfast, so that you may give this people possession of the land which I swore to their fathers I would give them." (Jos. 1:5-6)

With God at his side, Josue moved to the attack. At the first assault the walls of Jericho stood firm and a siege was set. At God's command Josue marched his men around the city for seven days, with priests carrying the precious Ark of the Covenant, the symbol of God's presence. On the seventh day the wall defenses collapsed. The Hebrews streamed into the town and took it by storm.

- READ the fuller battle account in the Book of Josue, chapters 3-6. Note the literary form of this kind of writing. This is not straight, scientific reporting, but an enthusiastic account of a true historical event. Such accounts glorifying traditional heroes are called "epic" history.

The fall of Jericho in about the year 1200 B.C. marked a break-through. In the wake of this initial success, Josue struck out on a three-pronged attack against the tiny kingdoms of central, southern, and northern Chanaan. But it would be many years before these pockets of stubborn resistance would be overrun.

B. Josue Renews the Covenant Pledges

Josue knew his death was near. He urged his people to stay loyal to the Covenant of their fathers:

"Take great care, however, to love the Lord, your God . . . If you transgress the covenant of the Lord, your God, . . . the anger of the Lord will flare up against you and you will quickly perish from the good land which he has given you." (Jos. 23:11, 16)

The people exclaimed in reply:

"Far be it from us to forsake the Lord for the service of other gods . . . Therefore we also will serve the Lord, for he is our God." (Jos. 24:16, 18)

So Josue renewed the Covenant with the people that day. God had been true to them; they promised to be true to God.

II. THE COVENANT IN TROUBLE

A. The Period of the Judges

1. AFTER JOSUE'S DEATH the battle for total possession of the Promised Land raged on. One petty king after another surrendered, but military victories turned into moral defeats. Gradually pagan ways infiltrated the lives of the Hebrew conquerors. Hebrew warriors married Chanaanite wives, thus striking at the very heart of their national welfare and religious faith.

Men who up to now had known nothing but herds and flocks now settled down on farmlands in Chanaan. They stayed in the fertile valleys among the Chanaanite communities and soon were absorbed into the pagan ways of life, even to the point of idolatry. They worshiped Baal, god of the fields, and his queen-goddess, Astarte. They forgot the Covenant of their fathers with Yahweh.

The next hundred years saw a drama in four acts repeated over and over again in a continuous cycle:

Act I: Unfaithfulness to Yahweh.

Act II: Punishment for their sinful ways.

Act III: Repentance and return to Yahweh.

Act IV: God's forgiveness and deliverance from Israel's enemies, thus ushering in a new era of salvation.

- READ the Book of Judges 2:6 to 3:6 for an account of this slow debasement of religious ideals. Does this cycle of sin and repentance sound familiar from the ordinary experience of men? Explain.

2. DURING THIS PERIOD OF UPS AND DOWNS, punishment for sin swept down upon the Hebrews in the form of armies from the south. These ironclad warriors, brandishing deadly iron weapons unknown to the Hebrews in this early Iron Age (see 1 Kings 13:19) slipped behind the Hebrew borders and ravaged the countryside. Having been repulsed by the Egyptians after their raids upon Egypt from the island of Crete, they pressed farther and farther north looking for soft spots along the Judean boundaries. They were called Philistines and they became the scourge of Juda.

In this epoch the Hebrew authority fell to leaders who were called "Judges," **because they administered the justice of God.** They were, for the most part, faithful to Yahweh. Their efforts to beat back the Philistines and at the same time keep their people loyal to the Covenant met with only limited success. The last of the Judges, a young man named Samuel, received a special call from God.

- READ the extraordinary account of Samuel's vocation in 1 Kings 3:1-21.

3. THINGS WENT FROM BAD TO WORSE IN SAMUEL'S TIME. The Jews needed a shock, something to jolt them hard and bring them to their senses. That shock came and its tremors shook all of the twelve tribes. The Philistines captured and carried off the Ark of the Covenant! The symbol of God's presence and protection had gone out of Israel and over to the hated Philistines. For the first time since Moses' day, faithful Hebrews felt completely alone, abandoned, lost. Their precious Ark lay dishonored by sacrilege in the pagan temple of the Philistine god Dagon.

"The glory is departed from Israel, because the ark of God was taken." (1 Kgs. 4:22)

- READ the story of the ill-fated battle with the Philistines in 1 Kings 4:1-22. Can you detect a sin of presumption on the part of the Israelites?

4. BUT GOD HAD NOT ABANDONED HIS PEOPLE. He had just taught them a good lesson. After seven months of bad luck caused, they believed, by the presence of the Ark, the Philistines were happy to get rid of this useless thing which the Hebrews venerated for some odd reason. Upon the Ark's return, Samuel drove home the lesson to all of Israel:

"If you turn to the Lord with all your heart, put away the strange gods from among you, . . . And prepare your hearts unto the Lord, and serve him only . . ." (1 Kgs. 7:3)

The people answered with contrition:

"We have sinned against the Lord." (1 Kgs. 7:6)

Samuel offered a sacrifice of atonement and the Hebrews shortly afterwards went out to face the Philistines again. Great was their victory that day.

B. The Period of King Saul

As Samuel grew older and less and less capable of ruling with vigor, the Jews pressed for a stronger kind of leadership. Why shouldn't they have a king like their neighbors in the petty kingdoms which dotted the Middle East? Samuel, of course, was deeply hurt and opposed the idea. He prayed to the Lord, Who told him to give them their king. Samuel proved his greatness by bowing to God's will and anointing the new king personally. This first king of Israel was a respected warrior named Saul.

Despite all his early promise, King Saul became one of the most tragic figures in biblical history.

Success against the Philistines swelled Saul with pride. He dared to disregard the commands of Yahweh Himself. Again and again he clashed with Samuel, who tried to bring him back to God's will. Soon "the spirit of Yahweh departed from Saul." He slipped into dark moods of depression and deeper and deeper into sin. Degrading superstition put him at the mercy of a pagan witch and only one final step remained in his complete moral collapse: he took his own life when his army fell before the Philistines.

- READ the account of Saul's defeat and death in chapter 31 of 1 Kings. Can you think of other figures in history who met tragic deaths after evidently turning their backs on God? Consult, for example, the history of the second World War.

III. THE COVENANT SAFEGUARDED: David

A. The Shepherd

1. In his fits of depression Saul used to summon a young shepherd musician to calm his troubled soul with music. The boy's name was David and he came from the tribe of Juda.

Later, the lad proved his worth in battle, too, when he slew in single combat the mighty Philistine hero, Goliath.

- READ the account of David's victory over Goliath in 1 Kings 17:1-54.

2. Before long David's reputation as a warrior eclipsed Saul's. Jealousy blazed into hatred when Saul heard the victory song of his happy citizens:

"Saul slew his thousands, and David his ten thousands." (1 Kgs. 18:7)

- NOTICE again the enthusiastic exaggeration in the literary form we saw before as "epic history." What is the kernel of historical truth contained here?

Once Saul turned against him, David had to flee for his life. He remained in constant danger from the king's evil moods. In fact, had it not been for the loyalty of his friends, David never would have stayed alive. When you consider how important a role David played in God's Plan for man's salvation, all mankind should be grateful to David's friends.

- READ about the devoted friendship between David and Saul's young son, Jonathan. See 1 Kings 18:1-10 and 19:1-7 and 20:1-43. How did Jonathan save David's life?

At a later date Jonathan fell courageously in battle while fighting at his father's side. David mourned his death deeply.

B. The King

1. DAVID, GOD'S CHOICE FOR KING

Once "the spirit of the Lord" had departed from Saul, God wasted no time. He immediately instructed Samuel to anoint secretly the young shepherd David as king.

> *And the spirit of the Lord came upon David from that day forward . . . (1 Kgs. 16:13)*

After Saul's death, David was anointed again, but this time with all the public acclaim due to a newly crowned king of Israel. The elders of the twelve tribes had high hopes for David. He would unite their people into a strong nation and save them from their enemies.

2. DAVID, TYPE OF CHRIST THE KING

As king and savior of his people, David is a type of Jesus Christ.

David	foreshadows	Christ
a. As the king		as the Lord
b. who unified his kingdom		who founded His Church
c. and saved his people		and saved God's People.

NOTE: Read the diagram both across and up-down.

3. CHRIST THE UNIVERSAL KING

Catholics proudly pay allegiance to Christ, their triumphant King. Mary was the first to give homage to Christ the King on earth. Recall again how the Angel Gabriel told her the good news at the Annunciation:

> *"Behold, thou shalt . . . bring forth a son . . . and the Lord God will give him the throne of David his father, and **he shall be king** over the house of Jacob forever . . ." (Luke 1:30-33)*

And, indeed, Mary's son would be a king. Christ strongly affirmed His kingship before Pontius Pilate, much like David's, but with a difference too:

> *"My kingdom is not of this world . . . (but) Thou sayest it; **I am a king.** This is why I was born, and why I have come into the world . . . ." (John 18:36-37)*

After the Ascension, Peter and the apostles will proclaim Christ as King to all the world. He is the long awaited one who

"'. . . should sit upon his (David's) throne,' . . ." (Acts 2:30)

St. John in a vision saw the Kingdom of Christ transported to where it belongs, a Kingdom of heaven and not of earth, where Jesus Christ reigns forever triumphantly as

"King of kings and Lord of lords." (Apoc. 19:16)

The Church today invites all Christians to pledge their loyalty anew. The Feast of Christ the King is the last Sunday of October. Catholics and Protestants alike can pay homage to their Lord:

"Hallowed be Thy name,
Thy Kingdom come!"

- READ, if available, the story of Father Miguel Pro, S.J., who in the Mexican persecutions of 1927 dropped to his knees before the firing squad and sang out, "Long live Christ the King!"

C. **The King's City:** Jerusalem

1. David chose a Chanaanite stronghold for his capital city. He conquered the inhabitants by the clever stratagem of slipping his finest soldiers into the city through a secret water tunnel.

From this time on, Jerusalem became the focal point of all Jewish hopes and ambitions. Since the city contained both the throne of David and the Temple of Yahweh, it always remained the beloved "City of David."

2. Jesus loved Jerusalem, too. That is why we can understand the depths of feeling in our Lord's heart at His triumphal entry into Jerusalem. Yet amid all the rejoicing, **Jesus wept.** He knew His beloved city would never accept Him:

"Jerusalem, Jerusalem! . . . How often would I have gathered thy children together, as a hen gathers her young under her wings, but thou wouldst not!" (Mt. 23:37)

With a heavy heart Christ prophesied the holy city's total destruction:

"Amen I say to you, there will not be left here one stone upon another that will not be thrown down." (Mt. 24:2)

In the year 70 A.D., about forty years after Christ's death, the Roman general Titus punished Jewish resistance to Roman rule by leveling the city to the ground.

God never intended the Jerusalem of David to fulfill men's hopes. This city of stone was only a pale symbol of "the New Jerusalem" in heaven which would be man's final destiny according to God's Plan. St. John records a vision of the eternal Jerusalem in this symbolic passage from the Apocalypse:

> *"And he (an angel) took me up in spirit to a mountain, great and high, and showed me the holy city Jerusalem, coming down out of heaven from God, having the glory of God." (Apoc. 21:10)*

- READ St. John's fuller description in Apoc. 21:9-27. Look for the meaning behind the symbols, not for realistic details which were never intended.

D. A Friend of God Turned Sinner

1. THE SIN

David never doubted that all his success came from God. He loved God in return and enjoyed God's friendship. He was overawed by the magnificence of God's promises for his future and the future of his family line:

> *"Who am I, O Lord God, and what is my house, that thou hast brought me thus far? . . . And what can David say more unto thee? For thou knowest thy servant, O Lord God." (2 Kgs. 7:18-20)*

Nevertheless, in yielding to the temptation of desire for a married woman named Bethsabee, David sinned against his Lord, and sinned grievously. He arranged a hopeless battle mission for her warrior husband so that after his almost certain death on the battle line David might take the widow to be his wife.

2. REPENTANCE

The prophet Nathan stood up to the sinful king and accused him of his crime. His sharp rebuke cut deeply into David's soul. A man has to know what it is to be close to God before he can realize the evil of sin. David now knew both. Few men have ever been closer to God; few men ever understood evil the way David understood it now. Nathan's words stung David into a humble admission of guilt:

"I have sinned against the Lord." (2 Kgs. 12:13)

- LOOK UP the Proper of the Mass for Ash Wednesday and pick out what you think is the most sincere expression of sorrow.

- WRITTEN ASSIGNMENT: Now that you have come to know the many-sided personality of David, try to collect your impressions in a personality profile.

IV. THE COVENANT CHERISHED, THEN ABANDONED: Solomon

A. Builder of the Temple

After David's death his son by Bethsabee ascended the throne of Juda. His name was Solomon and he was a bright, energetic young man. Solomon pleased God from the beginning because "he loved the Lord" (3 Kings 3:3), and when God offered to bless him with any gift he wished, Solomon won new glory with his prayer for wisdom:

"Give therefore to thy servant an understanding heart, to judge thy people, and discern between good and evil." (3 Kgs. 3:9)

Prosperous years passed. If David deserves credit for consolidating the kingdom of Israel against its enemies and bringing the people back to Yahweh, his son Solomon deserves like acknowledgment for guiding the nation shrewdly into an era of unparalleled prosperity. He made all of the Near East look up and take notice of this thriving nation within their midst.

This national prosperity enabled Solomon to realize a dream long cherished by his father David, but reserved by God for his reign: Solomon would build a magnificent temple in honor of Yahweh.

1. THE TEMPLE BLUEPRINT

Solomon chose to build on the very site of David's simple sanctuary, Mount Moriah, which looked out protectingly over the Judean countryside. The blueprint called for the same basic plan as the first tabernacle (i.e., tent) set up long ago by Moses in the desert. Of course, the new temple was much larger than the taber-

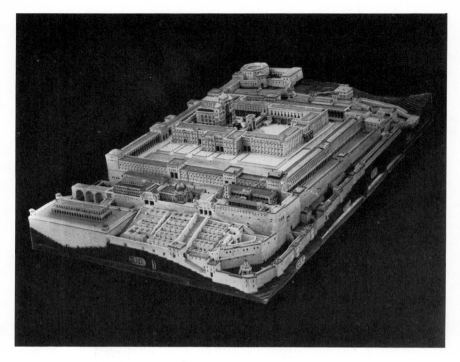

*A Model of Solomon's Temple and the surrounding
environs.* THE MATSON PHOTO SERVICE

nacle of Moses and the sanctuary of David, but the three main
divisions of the plan remained:

    a. a courtyard;

    b. the Holy Place or Sanctuary;

    c. the Holy of Holies.

    a. THE COURTYARD surrounded the main building much as the
fenced-in area had surrounded the tabernacle in the desert. In a
similar arrangement, the altar of the holocausts for sacrificing animals stood within this open courtyard directly in front of the temple
proper.

    b. THE SANCTUARY occupied the larger part of the interior
beyond the vestibule. The stone walls within were lined with boards
of Phoenician cedar and fir all overlaid with gold and precious stones.
The central furnishing was a special altar for offering incense, with
candelabra flanked on either side. A table nearby displayed the

sacred utensils used for sacrifice of animals out in the courtyard. A thick curtain separated this outer sanctuary chamber from the secluded room beyond.

c. THE HOLY OF HOLIES was the name given to this inner chamber beyond the curtain. Here rested the Ark of the Covenant, the symbol of God's presence among men. Within its precious wood were kept the tablets of the Mosaic Law. Two wooden cherubim hovered over the Ark and a small lamp burned in front.

2. THE TEMPLE AS SYMBOL

Since the Ark symbolized God's presence among men, the temple, just as Moses' tabernacle and David's modest sanctuary in earlier times, was **the meeting-place of God and man.** For generations to come, the Jews always felt that they could find God here and converse with Him.

3. THE TEMPLE AS FORESHADOWING

Centuries later, our Lord would show the true role this temple of stone was meant to play in God's Plan of Salvation. The temple of stone was only a foreshadowing of the true meeting-place of God and man which took shape in the person of the incarnate Son of God, Jesus Christ. Man reaches God not by seeking Him in buildings of stone, but by the spiritual contacts possible within the mystical body of Christ. **When the mystical body prays and sacrifices in union with Christ we have what we call the "liturgy."**

- CAN anyone suggest the providential ways given to us for thus making contact with Jesus Christ, God and man? How do we make contact with Christ most closely of all?

NOTE: Should the objection be raised that we Catholics no less than the Jews take great care to build beautiful churches of stone, remember that we do so only because in our human way churches can strikingly symbolize for all visibly to see that we are one with Christ in His mystical body.

- WHAT kind of church architecture do you think best carries the religious ideal of unity with Christ as we are gathered around His altar for the Mass sacrifice? Gothic? Baroque? Some modern design? Discuss the advantages and disadvantages of each for fully participating in the Church's liturgy.

B. Solomon's Downfall

Solomon led the Jewish people farther and farther down the road of worldly success. God was pleased with their success, but not with the attitudes which went with it. Solomon and his countrymen grew soft with luxury and proud with political prominence. Before long many traded their Covenant with Yahweh for the tempting pleasures of the moment. Toward the end of his reign Solomon himself yielded to the coaxing of his pagan wives and built shrines to their pagan gods. From the heights of friendship with God Solomon fell to depths of idol worship. God was angered with Solomon's infidelity, and the dark night of tragedy began to close in.

"Because thou hast done this, and hast not kept my covenant, and my precepts, which I have commanded thee, I will divide and rend thy kingdom . . ." (3 Kgs. 11:11)

C. The Kingdom Divided

Solomon died about the year 935 B.C. Few mourned his passing because he had burdened the people with intolerable taxation in order to finance his own high living. When his son and successor Roboam cracked down still harder upon the complaining citizenry, ten tribes rebelled and formed their own kingdom of the north under another king, Jeroboam. Only the tribes of Benjamin and Juda stayed loyal to Solomon's son. The ax of chastisement had fallen.

The two kingdoms survived the initial blow, but the years clicked away in tragedy. As a political power the Jewish nation tossed in its death throes. And yet no one could even guess the horrible details of its final doom. The next chapter will tell of this tragic decline and of the valiant men who tried to stem the tide. In this era faithful Jews were purified in suffering, and history moved toward its spiritual fulfillments as promised to Abraham, Isaac, and Jacob two thousand years before.

Section 2. SINNERS BEFORE GOD

The monarchy was an interesting epoch of biblical history not only for its fast flow of events, but for its history-making personalities as well. These were real people of flesh and blood facing mature spiritual decisions, and responding in different ways. Contrast David, for example, with the other sinners of his time. The big difference came down to this:

1. David's sense of God, knowing God as He really is.

2. David's sense of sin, recognizing sin for what it really is.

While others continued to offend God again and again, David repented his sin.

Why was this so?

BECAUSE David knew God, loved God. David had a deep sense of God.

THEREFORE, David saw sin for what it was, the rejection of a good and generous Father.

David came out of his sin a holier man with a **strong sense of sin** to protect him for the rest of his life.

A PRACTICAL CONCLUSION: A Christian must first know and love God before he can realize the evil of sin. His reaction to his own sin is called CONTRITION.

Contrition is of two kinds:

1. PERFECT CONTRITION

David's sorrow which dug deep into his heart because he offended the Lord he loved.

> Have mercy on me, O God, in your goodness; in the greatness of your compassion wipe out my offense . . . "Against you only have I sinned, . . ." (but) a heart contrite and humbled, O God, you will not spurn. (Ps. 50:3, 6, 19)

Definition Perfect contrition is the sorrow for sin which comes from love of God.

NOTE: An **act of perfect contrition** takes away all sin instantly (although sins must still be confessed later to a priest).

BUT an **act of perfect contrition** need not be a **perfect act of contrition,** that is, contrition based solely on the love of God, without any lesser motives of fear or reward mixed in. It is rather a question of which is the **dominating motive.**

Perfect contrition is easy for any sincere Christian who loves God.

2. IMPERFECT CONTRITION

The sorrow of so many Jews in David's time, which probably included Solomon.

> . . . and his (Solomon's) heart was not perfect with the Lord his God, as was the heart of David his father. (3 Kgs. 11:4)

Definition Imperfect contrition is the sorrow for sin which comes primarily from fear of God's punishment or from the hope of reward.

NOTE: An act of imperfect contrition **with confession** is enough to take away even mortal sins.

BUT the more imperfect the contrition becomes, the weaker becomes the sense of sin, and it becomes more and more difficult to resist sin's temptation. Such is human experience, as shown in the cases of Solomon, Saul, and so many other people.

Section 3.   DAVID AND THE LITURGY

It is human during some of life's most deeply felt moments to be at a loss for words. Picture an adult convert making his First Communion, a new priest on the day of his Ordination, a really contrite sinner before his Lord. At moments like these we search, but somehow the words seem to fail us.

Our mother, the Church, teaches us things to say before God. Prominent among her prayers are the psalms, particularly when blended into the Liturgy at Mass. For many of the psalms we can be grateful to David.

When lost in wonder beneath a clear and starry sky, we can think of the psalmist's hymn of praise to God:

> Praise the Lord from the heavens . . . praise him, all you his angels . . . praise him all you shining stars . . . Let the kings of the earth and all peoples, the princes and all the judges of the earth, young men too, and maidens, old men and boys, praise the name of the Lord . . . . (Ps. 148:1-3, 11-13)

Or a soldier about to hit beaches teeming with the enemy could pray with thoughts like these:

> The Lord is my light and my salvation; whom should I fear? The Lord is my life's refuge; of whom should I be afraid? (Ps. 26:1)

The sinner comes back to God deeply filled with shame and not knowing what to say. Here is how David expressed his sorrow:

Have mercy on me, O God, in your goodness; in the greatness of your compassion wipe out my offense . . . "Against you only have I sinned, and done what is evil in your sight" . . . A clean heart create for me, O God, and a steadfast spirit renew within me. (Ps. 50:3, 6, 12)

Name the occasion; the psalms provide a ready prayer. Even on the cross our Lord Himself prayed the psalms:

My God, my God, why have you forsaken me . . . I am like water poured out; all my bones are racked. My heart has become like wax melting away within my bosom. My throat is dried up like baked clay, my tongue cleaves to my jaws; to the dust of death you have brought me down . . . they have pierced my hands and my feet; I can count all my bones. (Ps. 21:2, 15-18)

Priests pray the psalms every day in the Divine Office. Thus they give praise and thanks to God, at the same time sanctifying every hour of their day in His service.

More and more lay people are rediscovering the psalms. No one, priest or laymen, should ever be at a loss for words before God because God Himself has taught us what to say in the inspired prayers of the book of one hundred and fifty psalms called the **Psalter**.

- EXAMINE a layman's Breviary and see how many Catholics sanctify their day in God's service by this traditional prayer of the Church.

SUMMARY

Under Josue the Jews enter the Promised Land. But very soon they were absorbed into the pagan ways of life. Punishment for their sins swept down upon them in the person of the Philistine warriors who captured the Ark of the Covenant, the symbol of God's presence among the Jews.

Saul, a great warrior, was the first king in Israel. He later became unfaithful and was replaced by David. David consolidated the kingdom of Israel, and his son, Solomon, brought the nation to unparalleled prosperity. The great temple at Jerusalem was built by Solomon, "the meeting-place of God and man." Solomon sinned and in punishment the kingdom of Israel was divided.

QUESTIONS

1. Who was the successor to Moses? How did he attack and conquer the city of Jericho? Is this account in the Old Testament straight, factual reporting?

2. What drama in four acts do we see repeated again and again by the Israelites after they settled down on farmlands in Chanaan?

3. Who were the Philistines? What connection did they have with the Israelites at this time?

4. Who were the Judges? What was their function? Who was the last of the Judges?

5. Who captured the Ark of the Covenant? Why was its capture such a shock to the Jews? Where was the Ark of the Covenant put by the conquerors?

6. Why was the Ark of the Covenant returned to the Israelites? What lesson did Samuel try to teach the Hebrews at this time?

7. Who was the first king of Israel? Why did the Jews want a king? Who selected the first king?

8. Did Saul remain faithful to Yahweh? What caused his decline? How did he lose his life?

9. Who was David? Why did he incur the hatred of Saul? What happened to David after Saul's death?

10. Why is David a type of Christ? Explain the typology.

11. Why was Jerusalem, the "City of David," the focal point of all Jewish hopes and ambitions? How was it finally destroyed? Was Jerusalem a type? Explain.

12. Was David faithful to God? How did he sin? Who rebuked him? Explain the words, "A man has to know what it is to be close to God before he can realize the evil of sin." Are these words true of David?

13. Did Solomon bring further glory to the kingdom of Israel? Explain. Why did Solomon please God so much?

14. Briefly describe the temple built by Solomon. Of what was it a symbol? What did the temple foreshadow?

15. How did God punish Solomon's unfaithfulness?

16. What is perfect contrition? Can I make an act of perfect contrition and still have the fear of hell? How does perfect contrition differ from imperfect contrition? Explain the condition by which imperfect contrition can take away even mortal sins.

17. What is meant by a "sense of sin"?

18. What are the psalms? Why does the Church make use of the psalms in her liturgy and in the Divine Office?

Beginning of the Liturgical Year

ADVENT

Before moving on to the next chapter, look back a few moments over the general introduction to our entire course located at the very beginning of the book. Note again **the Christocentric focus** of God's Plan. With so much of biblical history now behind us we should begin to see a little more clearly just what this Christocentric focus means. The expectation of the Messianic Age dominates all of the Old Testament even before Christ was born. From Genesis right through the era of the prophets our eyes in looking back have been fixed upon a Savior to be sent by God. Now His coming into this world draws nearer and nearer. With Christ's actual birth we shall mark the end of the first big division of our course, the section entitled "Christ Promised."

Our spiritual mother, the Church, is a good teacher; she does not want us to forget all we have learned thus far. That is why she has organized over the centuries of our Christian era what she calls her "liturgical year."

The Liturgical Year is the commemoration and reliving of God's Plan in our own lives.

Take a look now at the beginning of the liturgical year. New Year's Day in the Church liturgy is the first Sunday of Advent.

I. THE SEASON OF ADVENT

The Latin word "adventus" means a coming. All of the faithful Hebrews looked to the glorious future of a great coming promised by Yahweh. The prophets inspired their people with hope in "the anointed one," the Christ, "he who was to come" in keeping with God's Covenant. Their expectation was certainly beautifully fulfilled

"But when the Son of Man shall come in his majesty . . ." MT. 25:31

in Christ's birth at Bethlehem, but it was not yet completely fulfilled. In the unfolding of God's Plan "the coming" meant much more. Advent, therefore, means much more than waiting for the physical birth of our Savior in the cave at Bethlehem.

Advent awaits not a single, but a triple event in God's Plan for man's Salvation:

A. Christ's Historical Coming

As the central event of all history, the historical birth of Christ gives solid foundation to our Christian faith. But the physical birth alone does not fill out God's wonderful Plan; **it is only the beginning.**

- SEE THE INTROIT for the second Mass of Christmas Day. Is there something more here than Christ's physical birth?

B. Christ's Glorious Coming

The Church looks forward with Advent hope to the day of Christ's **second coming,** the triumph of her Lord on Judgment Day. Without slighting the tremendous fact of God-become-man, we must look beyond the crib to Jesus Christ in His Glory as King and Judge.

- SEE THE GOSPEL for the First Sunday of Advent. Could our Lord have made Himself clearer?

C. Christ's Sacramental Coming

Between His first and second comings our Lord did not abandon us. It is through the Mass and the sacraments that He chose to stay with us during the era of His Church. That is why our era of history is called the era of "Christ living on." Christians do not live in the past cherishing memories of faded greatness; neither do they find strength only in the hopes for a glorious future as did the Hebrews. Christians also share the joy of Christ's coming **now.**

- SEE THE COLLECT for each of the Sunday Masses in Advent:
  "Stir up Thy power, we beseech Thee, O Lord, and come . . . ."

The prayers of the Advent liturgy rise to heaven; we pray for Christ's triple coming. God's answer rings joyously through the three Christmas Masses: "Thou art My Son, this day have I begotten Thee." (See Introit of Midnight Mass.)

- ON THE FRIDAY before each Sunday of Advent search through the coming Sunday's Mass.

In the Mass propers discuss which of the three comings seems to predominate. Do you think some of the passages in the Masses could be interpreted to fit two or even the three of these comings of Christ?

Can you agree upon any theme predominating in each of these Sunday Masses? Hope? Repentance? Joy?

SUMMARY

A Triple Coming in the Advent Liturgy — Fulfillment

Past: Christ's historical coming — Christ's birth, 6 B.C.

THEREFORE. A memorial of an event.

Future: Christ's triumphant coming — Judgment Day, ? A.D.

THEREFORE. An expectation of an event.

Present: Christ's sacramental coming — Today, or any day A.D.

THEREFORE. A spiritual reality now.

NOTE: Be on the alert from now on in our course to synchronize the historical unfolding of God's Plan with the liturgical reliving of it in the Church's liturgical year.

With the first Sunday of Advent, the season of Christ Promised, we begin the historical period in Jewish history which was dominated by those great men of God, the prophets. In history they rallied their people with hope in the Messiah's coming; in the liturgy of Advent we once again share their expectations.

In the same way our historical study of Jesus Christ and His mission on earth will stay geared to the progress of the liturgical year. In Gospel accounts and Missal we shall follow our Savior as step by step He approaches the high point of His life, the day of His glorious Resurrection, our liturgical Easter Sunday.

CHAPTER VII

THE NEW COVENANT IN PROPHECY: THE PROPHETS

We should not be surprised that in this era following Solomon's death devout Jews kept looking back to the bright past of David's kingship, and then forward to the still brighter future of a promised New Israel. The present for them stayed dark and menacing, much like a mountain tunnel between two sunny valleys. From roughly the year 900 B.C. to 500 B.C. the religious-minded people of the nation would be tried in suffering, and the Covenant would be purified of its earthly ambitions. The process was painful, but God sent ambassadors to help and guide His children. Not for a moment would He abandon them or His Master Plan for their salvation. The men who thus spoke in God's name were called **prophets,** a name derived from the Greek word "to speak in behalf of someone."

Section 1. THE PROPHETS IN BIBLICAL HISTORY

I. ISRAEL: the Kingdom of the North (935 B.C. - 721 B.C.)

The ten northern tribes sliced off the richest part of the nation by their secession. The land was rich and fertile; water was plentiful. And so the farmers and herdsmen prospered. The merchants and tax-collectors were happy too, because as a bonus for their efforts, they cashed in on the wealth of trade brought by caravans. These caravans tracked up and down their land north to Damascus and south to Egypt, or around the Fertile Crescent to the sea on the west and Mesopotamia on the east.

With their prosperity, however, they drifted farther and farther away from the true worship of Yahweh. Their first king, Jeroboam, built two shrines, at Dan and Bethel, in order to keep his people from visiting to Jerusalem for yearly worship in Solomon's Temple. As shrine attractions, two metal bulls were set up representing Yahweh, thus imitating the pagan bull-worship common in the Middle East of this era. A few generations of mixing religions in this way and for all practical purposes the young kingdom was lost to Yahweh.

A. Achab and Jezabel

If Jeroboam had led the northerners down the road of idolatry, a later monarch named Achab led them over the cliff. As a political move he married a Phoenician princess named Jezabel who from that day on dedicated her life to stamping out all worship of Yahweh. She drove out the religious leaders of Israel and brought in hundreds of pagan priests from Phoenicia, hoping to plant the worship of Baal deep into Israel's soil. The irreligious Achab stood by with indifference; only power politics interested him.

B. Elia

A fearless spokesman for God challenged the king and queen to their faces. His name was Elia. He predicted a famine in this land of usual plenty, and told Achab it would be a sign of God's displeasure. The famine struck, and of course Achab blamed Elia. With his life now in danger, Elia hit upon a stratagem. He threw out a challenge to the king and staked his own life on the outcome: Let him, Elia, the prophet of Yahweh, pit his Lord against Baal with his hundreds of pagan priests. Let both sides pray for rain to end the drought and famine. By answering His prophet's prayer, Yahweh would prove Himself the one, all-powerful Lord of Creation.

- READ the account of this match between the priests of Baal and the prophet of Yahweh in 3 Kings 18:20-40.

Jezabel was furious at the outcome. She was more determined than ever to kill Elia. He fled for his life to the mountains of Sinai. But by a sudden turn of providence, the day of retribution caught up with Achab and Jezabel. Achab was slain in a senseless attack upon neighboring Syria, and a year or two later the hated Jezabel was hurled from her room to the pavement below when the success of an army revolt first reached the ears of her servants.

According to Jewish tradition, Elia was taken up to heaven alive (4 Kings 2:11-12) and was expected to return to earth just before the coming of the Messiah. That is why some of the Jews who first met John the Baptist at the Jordan centuries later thought that he must be Elia come back to life.

- READ and compare this incident at the Jordan in John 1:21 with a real appearance of Elia in Matthew 17:3. See what our Lord had to say about Elia in Matthew 18:10-13.

C. Collapse of Israel

Years passed, and still the people and rulers failed to listen to the later prophets of Israel like Eliseus, Osee, and Amos. The tide of sin and paganism rose; it brought the house of Israel crashing down in ruins. Final punishment for sin swept down upon the kingdom of the North through the armies of Sargon, the mighty Assyrian conqueror. Samaria, Israel's capital, fell in 721 B.C., and thousands of Israelites were dragged off to Nineve. To enjoy the rich homes and prosperous farms of the deported Israelites, Sargon moved in thousands of favored subjects from other parts of his empire. The people later known as Samaritans would descend from this mixture of Jewish and foreign stocks. We can see why the Samaritans were hated so. As for the ten scattered tribes, history closed its pages for good upon the once proud kingdom of the north.

II. JUDA: the Kingdom of the South (935 B.C. - 586 B.C.)

The kingdom of the South, Juda, held on much longer, but life was hard among the two tribes of Juda and Benjamin. The soil in that part of the country was rocky, and the water was scarce. Even the trade routes usually bypassed Jerusalem. The people, therefore, were poor, but intensely proud, too. In the ups and downs of national religious fervor many lost their faith in Yahweh, but the solidly religious among them never let their children forget their heritage. Theirs was the promise made to their father David. Theirs was the holy city of Jerusalem, the City of David, and the sacred Temple of Solomon, still symbolizing the meeting-place of God and man. Was not God still with them in the Ark of the Covenant, hard though life might be? Thus they looked to a brighter future in a spirit of hope which was nourished by a succession of holy prophets.

From the year of Solomon's death in 935 B.C. to the fall of

Jerusalem in 586 B.C. no less than twenty-six kings ruled Juda. Only a few were true sons of David who inspired their subjects in the worship of Yahweh. King Achaz and his son, Ezechia, typified the opposite extremes of wickedness and righteousness before Yahweh. A third personality, the prophet Isaia, figured prominently in the lives of both.

A. King Achaz

More to cement good relations with the powerful Assyrians than from any religious conviction, Achaz took to the worship of Assyrian idols. He had long lost faith in Yahweh, trusting only in the size of armies and power in battle. With the Assyrian battalions as allies, he felt that no one would dare raise a hand against Juda. But his policy made Juda a puppet state forced to pay high tribute to the Assyrians. The smoke of pagan sacrifice which defiled the skies above Jerusalem was a fitting symbol of the reign of Achaz.

B. The Prophet Isaia

In those unholy days God raised up another prophet, named Isaia. Isaia was born to a noble family of Jerusalem, was well educated, and showed all the promise of becoming an outstanding statesman. He reproached the king for his infidelity and lack of confidence in Yahweh. He begged Achaz in the interest of his people to stir up a religious renewal, to bring those who had strayed back to the all-holy and all-powerful God of their fathers. Achaz sneered at Isaia's way of saving Juda; he preferred the plans of his own political maneuvering to the Master Plan of God for the welfare of God's Chosen People.

- WHAT would you say are the essential differences between God's Plan for man's salvation and the plans of men like Achaz? Do you know any such rulers who have upset the peace of the world in modern times?

C. King Ezechia

Achaz died in 716 B.C. and his son, Ezechia, ascended the throne of Juda. Because of Achaz's misrule, the country was now a vassal-state, permitted survival only for the heavy taxes which swelled the Assyrian treasury.

Ezechia was a sincerely religious man and made a fine king, but in these dark days little could be done for the economic welfare of the country, short of a hopeless attempt at revolution. He set his sights, therefore, on the revival of religion counseled by Isaia to Achaz years before. He understood well that Juda's safety depended upon the powerful arm of Yahweh. This is the way Ezechia rallied his people:

> *"Our fathers have sinned and done evil in the sight of the Lord God, forsaking him . . . Now therefore I have a mind that we make a covenant with the Lord the God of Israel: and he will turn away the wrath of his indignation from us."* (2 Par. 29:6,10)

The king first put large wrecking crews to work at smashing the pagan altars and shrines. Then they turned to repairing the Temple, so badly neglected during Achaz's reign. Soon the inner sanctuary sparkled again with fresh beauty, and priests and levites were appointed to tend it. Sacrifice to Yahweh once more lifted the smoke of burnt offerings aloft as the symbol of fidelity and worship. To climax the religious rebirth of his people, Ezechia dispatched messengers far and wide to invite his countrymen to join him in the year's Passover celebration. Many had become so hardened and irreligious that they treated the messenger with ridicule, but many others came, flocking to the Holy City as in the days of David. Jerusalem again echoed with the psalms of old as the Temple once more became the meeting-place of God and His People.

The Jews returned to God none too soon. When Ezechia's alliance with Egypt disturbed the new monarch of Assyria, Sennacherib, he invaded Juda in retaliation and laid siege to Jerusalem about 701 B.C. Isaia warned Ezechia not to make the mistake of his father Achaz. This was his message to the king: Prepare to resist, but put your trust in Yahweh. Yahweh will deliver Jerusalem from the Assyrian horde! Ezechia listened to the prophet. Then he inspired new courage in his people:

> *"Behave like men, and take courage: Be not afraid nor dismayed for the king of the Assyrians, nor for all the multitude that is with him . . . For with him is an arm of flesh: with us the Lord our God, who is our helper, and fighteth for us."* (2 Par. 32:7-8)

The night before Sennacherib's intended attack, an angel of the Lord scattered the Assyrian army. Bewildered at the sudden turn in fortune, they fled back across the eastern borders.

- READ the account of the siege. Note Sennacherib's blasphemous boasting, and then the final outcome in 2 Paralipomenon 32:1-23.

D. The Prophet Jeremia

Two unfaithful kings followed Ezechia and undid all his religious reform. The saintly king Josia led the people back to Yahweh during the kingship from 640 B.C. to 609 B.C., but with his death the country slid faster and faster down on its way to destruction. The last of Juda's kings may have been the worst of all, an insolent young king by the name of Sedecia.

To represent Him before the king and to champion the cause of the faithful, God chose a young priest, Jeremia. Jeremia pulled no punches in wording God's message to Sedecia: Return to Yahweh or perish. Like the voice of conscience Jeremia prodded the king and all the faithless in Juda. He promised the New Covenant in a New Israel:

> *"The days are coming," said the Lord, "when I will make a new covenant with the house of Israel and the house of Juda . . . I will place my law within them, and write it upon their hearts; I will be their God, and they shall be my people." (Jer. 31:31-33)*

Could God have been more gracious and kind in the generosity of His promises? But God's spokesman, Jeremia, was ridiculed and spurned. Disappointment scarred his sensitive soul, but he pressed on bravely in the service of Yahweh. Finally, Sedecia threw the prophet into prison and the doom of Juda was near.

E. The Collapse of Juda

In the year 586 B.C. the ax fell. To counter a senseless revolt by Sedecia, the ruthless king from Babylon, Nabuchodonosor, waged an attack against Juda. The unheeded warnings of Jeremia took on shocking reality when Babylonian battalions rushed the city's walls. Defenses toppled quickly and King Sedecia fled to the hills. Nabuchodonosor pursued, tracked down Juda's last king, forced him to watch the slaughter of his children, and then commanded that Sedecia's eyes be gouged out before dragging the helpless Sedecia to Babylon as a prize of war.

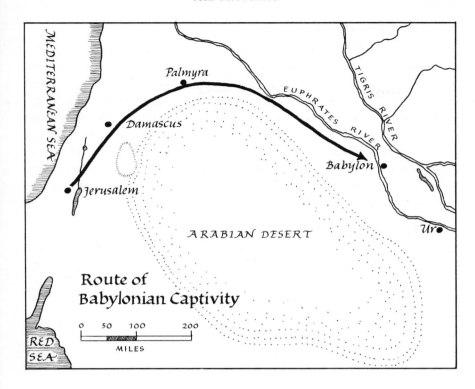

Route of
Babylonian Captivity

With the humiliated king went thousands of Juda's craftsmen and laborers — brains and muscle for building up the capital city of Babylon. Nabuchodonosor left the weak and helpless Jews behind. The pick of Juda's population faced exile in an ungodly land. Thus began what is known in history as the Babylonian Captivity.

Nabuchodonosor freed Jeremia from Sedecia's prison, and since the prophet had boldly opposed the senseless revolt, offered him a privileged position in Babylon. Jeremia chose to stay behind with the weak and the helpless in Jerusalem; a friend and fellow prophet of God named Ezechiel would accompany the captives into exile. Some time later fanatic revolutionaries took Jeremia to Egypt by force where he died, perhaps murdered in revenge for his opposition to the revolt of Sedecia.

- • READ the account of Jerusalem's fall in 4 Kings 25:1-18. Note the total desecration of the Temple. The Ark of the Covenant is never heard of again. What would its tragic loss symbolize to faithful Hebrews?

F. The Prophet Ezechiel

Ezechiel had also been trained as a priest. That was probably how he came to know Jeremia. God called him now for a demanding assignment. In the black days of exile he must convince the Jewish D.P.'s that God had not abandoned them. He must help them accept their suffering and disgrace in a spirit of penance for their sins. When all seemed lost, he had to preach hope; the hope of the Covenant promises, the hope of a glorious future which at a time like this must have sounded like a cruel, cynical joke. Picture the downhearted Jews Ezechiel had to work upon as they spoke in the words of a psalmist:

> *By the streams of Babylon we sat and wept when we remembered Sion . . . If I forget you, Jerusalem, may . . . my tongue cleave to my palate . . . O daughter of Babylon you destroyer, happy the man who shall repay you the evil you have done us! Happy the man who shall seize and smash your little ones against the rock! (Ps. 136:1, 5-9)*

These were the kind of men whom Ezechiel knew and worked with, weak men softened by self-pity or feverish for revenge. A special vision God gave him proved an apt description of his task. Truly these exiled Jews were much like dried-out bones; he, their prophet, must give them flesh and new muscle, and above all, the spirit to live by.

- • READ the full "vision of the dry bones" in Ezechiel 37:1-14, and marvel at the mercy of God and the generosity of His promise to these broken men beside the streams of Babylon:

  "O my people, I will open your graves and have you rise from them, and bring you back to the land of Israel. Then you shall know that I am the Lord, when I . . . put my spirit in you that you may live . . ." (Ezech. 37:12-14)

  The "vision of the dry bones" takes on special meaning for the Church of Christ in the liturgy of Holy Week, especially of Easter. Does anyone see why it is appropriate then? What sacraments are strikingly symbolized in these pictures of coming to life and receiving a new spirit?

As time passed the years became kinder to the exiled Jews. Many as skilled, valuable workmen achieved a decent standard of living. Many Jews married Babylonian wives and mixed more and more into the stream of prosperous city life. Soon they took on the ways and beliefs of their pagan neighbors. As material conditions thus improved, Ezechiel's task became increasingly difficult. As so often in Jewish Old Testament history, some felt no need for Yahweh when fortune smiled upon them. They looked up to God again for help only when flattened by catastrophe.

- WHAT resemblance do you see between this behavior on the part of some Jews in Babylon and some Christians you may meet with today? Do men more usually turn to God in prosperity or in adversity? What is the truly Christian point of view?

NOTE: At about Ezechiel's time in history another holy man whose identity is not known wrote about suffering and its place in God's Plan of salvation. Since scholars for many centuries thought that this beautiful book was authored by Isaia, it is usually referred to as "the book of Second-Isaia." You will find these writings in chapters 40-55 under the name of the prophet Isaia. Later in the course we shall return to these precious documents when studying Christ's passion and death.

G. Deliverance from Captivity

History marched forward, and even mighty Babylon toppled from power. Its magnificent temples, its hanging gardens — one of the seven wonders of the world — its palaces and beautiful avenues, all fell as prizes of war into the hands of the Near East's latest conqueror, the Persian Cyrus. He believed in keeping peoples in subjection by making them contented, so he signed an edict permitting those who wished to do so to return to their native land. The Judea to which they returned became a segment of the vast Persian empire. The year was 538 B.C., about forty years after the Captivity had begun. The edict of Cyrus which encouraged the Jews to practice their religion was a landmark in the history of religious toleration.

Some Jews who had come to prosper while in captivity stayed on in Babylon under Cyrus' rule. Why should they give up the comforts they had worked so hard to achieve? The City of David and the Temple of Solomon held little attraction for any who had long forgotten Yahweh and the faith of their fathers. They sold their Covenant birthright for a few years of comfortable living.

• ARE YOU REMINDED of any other biblical personality who did
something similar? What common human experience should
you note here? Why is the temptation of the moment so strong?
Use some examples of temptation and show how a man must
think clearly to protect himself.

But among those who turned their steps toward holy Jerusalem
were to be found the spiritual elite, the faithful of Yahweh, formed
by the prophet Ezechiel and the unknown scribe who told them of
suffering's true role within God's Plan. Purified in suffering and
more confident than ever of Yahweh's promises for a glorious future,
they radiated hope as they strained their eyes for the first glimpse of
Mount Moriah where the Temple of God once stood. This little
community of the faithful, called in Isaia's prophecy "the remnant
of Israel," from this time onward continued to cherish the Covenant
with Yahweh and kept their eyes fixed forward. They looked with
mounting hope and expectation for the dawn of a new day, "the
Day of Yahweh," when a New Israel would arise under the banner
of God's "anointed one," the Messiah, the Christ.

Section 2. THE PROPHETS AS THE VOICE OF GOD

I. FOR THEIR OWN TIMES: Men of Action

After watching the prophets in action, we get a good idea of
how God used them in their own times. They spoke for God; they
represented God before the Chosen People. But just as God Himself
spoke in action throughout biblical history and not just in words,
so the prophets also were men of action. They were men of influence
deeply involved in the big doings of their period in history.

The prophets were sure that nothing could ever derail the plan
God worked out for man's salvation. But they also understood well
that men could forfeit their privileged position in God's Plan. Such
was the frightening power of man's free will; he could throw away
his destiny. The prospect horrified the prophets. Out of love for
their fellow men as well as love for Yahweh, they served as voice
of conscience for their Jewish brethren to try to keep them loyal
sons of Yahweh, true to the Covenant made with their fathers.

As middlemen between God and man, the prophets had to help their brethren meet and conquer **five big temptations.** They met each head-on by countering it with a corresponding message from Yahweh.

A. Idolatry

Always a threat as in the past, from Egyptian masters, Chanaanite neighbors, Assyrian and Babylonian conquerors.

MESSAGE Adore the one, true God of your fathers, and Him alone, the all-holy, the all-powerful Lord.

B. Lack of Confidence in Yahweh

Trusting instead in military might and political alliances.

MESSAGE Trust wholeheartedly in Yahweh; He alone has the power to protect Israel from its enemies.

C. Formalism in Religious Worship

A "going through the motions" kind of religious worship, an empty formality of exact, but meaningless ritual.

MESSAGE God does not need nor does He want fancy sacrificial rites for themselves. He wants men's hearts freely and generously given with the sacrifice.

D. Religious Nationalism

An effort to fence God within Juda's or Israel's boundaries; putting God at the service of national ambitions for this world.

MESSAGE Yahweh is the God of all men. His rule extends "to the ends of the earth."

E. Social Injustice

Permitting a wide gap between the "haves" and the "have nots," an unjust distribution of the nation's wealth; a holdover from the quick developments in business and trade from the time of Solomon.

MESSAGE There will come a day of retribution for the luxury-loving and the greedy who make victims of the poor.

- READ the prophecies of Amos in Amos 4:1-3, 5:21-24 and 6:1-7. To which of the above temptations had the people of the Northern Kingdom of the eighth century B.C. succumbed?

- WOULD the prophets find any similar attitudes and situations to condemn today? Discuss each of the above temptations as possibly met in the world today, as for example: worship of power or money, religious or racial bigotry, indifference to poverty-stricken people at home and victims of famine abroad, the "Sunday only" kind of Christianity.

II.   FOR THE TIMES TO COME: Seers of the Future

By flashes of inspiration God gave the prophets glimpses into the future. Sometimes God made the light ahead bright and clear, but often He left the prophecies shrouded in shadows, too. Even these dim and shadowy prophecies took clearer shape as time went by, but their focus was clearest at the crossroads of time, the meeting of the Old and New Testaments in Jesus Christ.

The coming of God's Kingdom spoken of by these men of God was this kind of dim and shadowy prophecy. God would keep His part of the Covenant; that was sure. But how would God do it? His Plan gradually unfolded as the figure of a remarkable person became more and more distinct in the distance, the figure of the Messiah.

Picture this remarkable person as if he were walking toward you on a foggy night. As he crosses the street a block away from you, you can make out nothing but a misty silhouette. The steady tap of footsteps echoes louder and louder until now you can distinguish his height and physical form, even the cut and style of his clothing. In a matter of seconds he stands before you at the same street corner where you have been waiting anxiously. You see him face to face, eye to eye, and you recognize him as your friend.

The experience of the prophets and the "faithful remnant" who waited anxiously for the Messiah was something similar. But each caught glimpses of the Messiah from different distances. The earlier prophets saw little except his silhouette while the later ones distinguished his features vaguely, but without the clarity of a face-to-face encounter. It was only with the actual coming of Christ that the faithful "remnant" recognized their Savior just as He was supposed to be. The first actually to meet the Messiah was a young maiden named Mary who lived in a tiny mountain town called Nazareth. The Angel Gabriel told her that the Messiah was coming, coming right now, and He would be her son:

"Do not be afraid, Mary . . ." LUKE 1:30

*"Behold, thou shalt . . . bring forth a son . . . and the Lord
God will give him the throne of David his father, and he shall
be king over the house of Jacob forever; and of his kingdom
there shall be no end." (Luke 1:30-33)*

The angel's message stirred up echoes of other words she had
often heard and studied before. Go back with her now, and read
aloud the inspired prophecies which prepared the coming of the
Messiah. She knew them well; soon they would be fulfilled in her
son. Mary remembered Isaia:

*. . . **the virgin shall be with child,** and bear a son, and shall
name him Emmanuel. (Isa. 7:14)*

*For **a child is born to us,** a son is given us . . . They name him
. . . Prince of Peace. (Isa. 9:5)*

And from whose family would this "Emmanuel" arise, this "God
with us"? Mary knew, as did all the faithful of Juda:

*But a shoot shall sprout **from the stump of Jesse** . . . . (Isa. 11:1)*

That was why Mary and other members of David's family, the
tribe of Juda, saw in the Messiah's coming the fulfillment of God's
promises to David a thousand years before:

*"I (God) will raise up thy seed after thee, which shall proceed
out of thy bowels: and I will establish his kingdom. He shall
build a house to my name: **and I will establish the throne of
his kingdom for ever."** (2 Kgs. 7:12-13)*

And the world in which this Emmanuel was to reign would be a
new creation, a glorious world of peace and happiness for all the
faithful of Yahweh. It would be the Kingdom of God as pictured
in symbol:

*Then the wolf shall be a guest of the lamb, and the leopard shall
lie down with the kid; the calf and the young lion shall browse
together, **with a child to guide them** . . . .*

*On that day, **the root of Jesse** . . . the Gentiles shall seek out
. . . . (Isa. 11:6, 10)*

- READ and compare the prophecies that follow concerning the
  Messiah. They are to be viewed in retrospect from the New
  Testament fulfillment.

1. BETHLEHEM, the town of the Messiah's birth
- SEE Michea 5:2.
- COMPARE Matthew 2:1-6.

2. KINGDOM OF GOD SPIRITUAL, not of this world
- SEE Ezechiel 21:26-27 (Sedecia, the last of Juda's temporal kings).
- COMPARE John 18:36.

3. JOHN THE BAPTIST announces the Kingdom
- SEE Malachia 3:1.
- COMPARE Matthew 11:10.

NOTE: Other prophecies about different aspects of the Christ-Messianic mission will come up later.

III. FOR OUR OWN TIMES: Friends from the Past

In the famous medieval cathedral at Chartres, France, there is a stained-glass window which brings a smile to American tourists. The artist pictures the four evangelists standing on the shoulders of the four great Messianic prophets: Isaia, Jeremia, Ezechiel, and Daniel. A twentieth-century tourist may see here an exhibition in gymnastics, but the striking picture carried a profound truth to the simple people of medieval times who studied their Catholic faith in Chartres' stained-glass windows:

The New Testament is built upon the Old.

The Evangelists rest upon the Prophets.

It might be said as a figure of speech that we of the later Christian era stand astride the evangelists' shoulders in that we are the heirs by God's special favor of the revelation spanning both Testaments. In preaching Christ's redemptive triumph the evangelists searched back through the Old Testament and found there the many types and prophecies that prepared the way for the saving events they were privileged to witness. How grateful we should be to both evangelists and prophets, our spiritual ancestors and friends.

Section 3. THE PROPHETS IN THE ADVENT LITURGY

The Propers in the Masses of Advent cluster around three great personalities, two prophets and the Virgin Mary. Each in his or her own way is a symbol of the Christian hope which runs through the Advent liturgy.

Hope is the theological virtue by which we trust that God will fulfill in us the wonderful designs of His Covenant.

I. ISAIA

The prophet Isaia's voice echoes throughout Advent. His is the message of Messianic promise:

> *"People of Sion, behold the Lord shall come to save the nations. . . ." (Introit of second Sunday of Advent)*

- SEE IN YOUR MISSALS the epistles of Ember Week, i.e., the Wednesday, Friday, and Saturday after the third Sunday of Advent. Do you note any expressions referring to the three comings of Christ?

II. JOHN THE BAPTIST

The last of the Old Testament prophets, John the Baptist, is a towering figure in the Advent liturgy. But the Church wants us to remember him not just as the precursor of the Messiah two thousand years ago, a prophet who came, spoke, and then passed for good from the stage of biblical history. John the Baptist is a prophet for all time, always proclaiming "the good news" of the Gospel: "The Kingdom of God is at hand" (Matthew 3:2). His message for men of all time is threefold:

> *"I am not the Christ. I am the voice of one crying in the desert, 'Make straight the way of the Lord.' . . ." (John 1:20-23)*

"He it is who is to come after me, who has been set above me, the strap of whose sandal I am not worthy to loose." (Gospel of the third Sunday of Advent.)

THEREFORE **Christ's historical coming.**

And he went into the region about the Jordan, preaching a baptism of repentance for the forgiveness of sins . . . . (Gospel of the fourth Sunday of Advent.)

THEREFORE **Christ's sacramental coming is prepared.**

For even now the axe is laid at the root of the trees; every tree therefore that is not bringing forth good fruit is to be cut down and thrown into the fire. (A prophecy from Matthew 3:10, backed up by Christ Himself in the Gospel of the first Sunday of Advent:*"And then they shall see the **Son of Man coming** in a cloud with great power and majesty."*)

THEREFORE **Christ's triumphant coming on the last day.**

III. THE VIRGIN MARY

Not a prophetess, but greater than all the prophets, Mary shines brightest of all in the Advent liturgy. More than anyone else this young girl from Nazareth lived the ideal of Christian hope; her confidence in her God was supreme. Free from any touch of sin by her Immaculate Conception, Mary's vision of God's Plan was extraordinarily clear. She never doubted that God would stay true to His Covenant promises, that the Messiah would come, but even she did not know how or when. It never dawned upon her that she would be the one chosen for such an essential role in God's Plan.

The Angel Gabriel brought word of the favor she had found with God:

*"Hail, **full of grace,** the Lord is with thee, Blessed art thou among women.*

*Behold, thou shalt conceive in thy womb and **shall bring forth a son; and thou shalt call his name Jesus.** He shall be great, and shall be called the Son of the Most High; and the Lord God will give him **the throne of David his father,** and he shall be king over the house of Jacob forever; and **of his kingdom there shall be no end."** (Gospel of Wednesday in Ember Week of Advent)*

Thus in the Advent liturgy the Church stirs up the same prophetic echoes in our minds that must have rung through Mary's during this historical event of the Annunciation. We unite ourselves with her as we relive the months of her pregnancy counting off the days to the birth of our Savior.

- TRY to translate what is probably the most famous of all Advent hymns:

    "Rorate, caeli, desuper et nubes pluant justum."

SUMMARY

The two kingdoms of Israel and Juda drifted further and further away from God.

In Israel, the kingdom of the North, Jezabel, the Phoenician wife of King Achab, dedicated her life to stamping out all worship of Yahweh. Achab stood by with indifference. In a religious encounter, Elia, a prophet, defeated Jezabel and her priests and had to flee for his life. Years passed and finally Sargon, the Assyrian conqueror, defeated Israel, forcing its ten tribes into captivity and oblivion.

Juda, the kingdom of the South, was ruled by Achaz. He believed in power politics and allied himself with the Assyrians to the extent that Juda became a vassal state. He paid no attention to the prophet Isaia when reproached for his infidelity and lack of confidence in God. His son, Ezechia, was a religious man who brought the people back to God and conquered their enemies, the Assyrians. But after his death, successive rulers and people once more turned to paganism and were eventually crushed by the Babylonians under Nabuchodonosor.

God did not desert His captive people. He sent a prophet, Ezechiel, to remind them of the Covenant and of the need to accept their suffering in punishment for their sins. Through the years that followed, the Jews bettered their lot and to such an extent that when the Persian Cyrus offered them permission to return to Jerusalem only a part remained faithful and returned to Jerusalem.

The liturgy of Advent is dominated by three personalities. Each is a symbol of hope.

QUESTIONS

1. Who were the prophets?

2. In parallel columns, name: (a) the kingdom of the North and the kingdom of the South; (b) the number of tribes in each; (c) a great prophet whom God sent to each; (d) the pagan people and leader who finally conquered each kingdom; (e) the date when each kingdom fell.

3. Identify by a sentence or two: (a) Achab, (b) Jezabel, (c) Elia, (d) King Achaz, (e) Isaia, (f) King Ezechia, (g) Sargon, (h) Sennacherib, (i) Jeremia.

4. What was common to both the kingdom of Juda and Israel which eventually caused their downfall?

5. What is the "Babylonian Captivity"?

6. Why was the prophet Ezechiel sent to the captive Jews? What did he try to teach them?

7. Describe the conditions of the Jews in the later years of exile. Did they remain faithful to God and the Covenant? Why?

8. Who was Cyrus? Why did he, a conqueror and pagan, treat the Jews in a different way than other conquerors?

9. Explain why all the exiled Jews did not return to Jerusalem when permitted by Cyrus.

10. What is "the remnant of Israel"?

11. The prophets had to meet five great temptations or obstacles among the Hebrew people. Name these five temptations and in a WORD or PHRASE show how the prophets met these temptations.

12. The prophets are called "seers of the future." What does this expression mean? What does it mean with reference to the coming Messiah?

13. Explain: THE NEW TESTAMENT IS BUILT ON THE OLD.

14. Besides the expected Messiah, what three personalities dominate the Advent liturgy? Give examples of each.

15. Show from the Sunday Gospels of Advent how St. John the Baptist makes some reference to each of Christ's three comings.

CHAPTER VIII

DAWN OF THE NEW COVENANT: CHRIST COMES

If it took a strong sense of religious faith and national patriotism for Jews to pull up roots from prosperous Babylon, only a rugged courage could make the repatriated stay on in the battered Jerusalem of 538 B.C. The biblical account tells us that the first wave of returnees numbered about forty thousand; their leader was Zorobabel, born of the kingly line of David. The squinting eyes of older men and women who had known the Holy City in its splendor must have welled up with tears at the sight of the toppled walls, the rubble-littered streets, and most crushing of all, the once magnificent Temple of Solomon, now one big shamble of rock and burnt-out timber.

Section 1. RETURN FROM CAPTIVITY

I. REBUILDING THE HOLY CITY

With heavy but willing hearts the priests of the returning populace set up an altar amid the Temple ruins and offered a holocaust to the Lord. As of old, the people observed the Feast of Tabernacles, and in response to Zorobabel's leadership they were determined to put their backs at once to the gigantic task of rebuilding God's Temple.

An unexpected offer of assistance came from the North, from the Israelites who had intermarried with the Assyrian colonists after the fall of the Northern Kingdom. Along with Assyrian gods, they still worshiped Yahweh.

"Let us build with you, for we seek your God as ye do."
(1 Esd. 4:2)

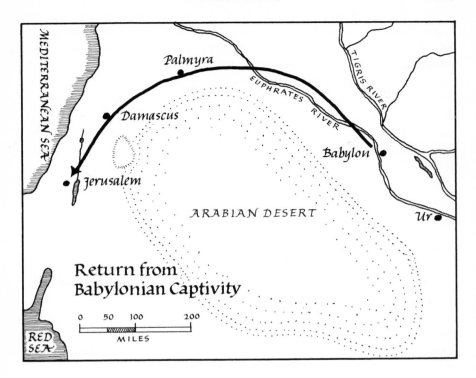

Return from Babylonian Captivity

But Zorobabel snubbed their offer rudely, branding these north-erners "unclean" apostates and traitors to their nation and their Jewish faith:

> "You have nothing to do with us to build a house to our God; but we ourselves alone will build to the Lord our God . . ." (1 Esd. 4:3)

From that day forward, a fierce feud split the faithful Jews and the mixed stock in the North who came to be called "Samaritans."

- DO YOU REMEMBER any signs of such a feud in the life of our Lord? As as example, look up John 4:4-42.

The work on the Temple dragged on for over twenty years, hampered by poor materials, shortage of funds, some bickering among the Jews themselves, and even sneak attacks from hostile neighbors. After Zorobabel's recall to Babylon, only the unbending determination of two of God's spokesmen, the prophets Aggai and Zacharia, drove the weary Hebrews to complete the job. The year of the Temple's dedication was 515 B.C.

The building could hardly compare with Solomon's masterpiece, but the people were proud of it nonetheless. This symbol of God's presence among His people gave them new life, a fresh sense of dignity with pride in themselves and the destiny of their tiny nation. For the "faithful remnant," this day of Temple dedication marked another turning point in the spiritual mission of Juda. **God was with them again.** Hope flourished anew that Yahweh would lead His chosen ones to the day of triumph promised through Isaia, Jeremia, and Ezechiel. Juda again looked to the coming of its glorious Messiah.

● COMPARE Zacharia 9:9 with Matthew 21:1-11.

Years later the Jews turned to the other big construction job of some urgency, the city's walls. The Holy City of David, the symbol of God's Kingdom, had to be defended from its enemies; without outer fortifications the city invited attack. That this second vast project was ever completed was due to the dedication of another great man who rose to the challenge, an influential friend of the Persian monarch, Artaxerxes. His name was Nehemia. As governor, with full powers and even a financial contribution from Artaxerxes, Nehemia never wavered from his objective to protect the City of David. At times his workmen labored with swords at their sides, but the sneak attacks only succeeded in delaying the work Nehemia was determined to finish.

● READ the inspiring story of this dedicated layman in 2 Esdras 4:1-23. In "a war of nerves" he put his total faith in God. As a man of action, Nehemia set a fine pattern for lay apostles in our Church today. What careers that you know of would particularly demand the determination and courage of a man like Nehemia? Discuss.

II. REBUILDING A NATION'S SPIRIT

City walls and even a Temple's towers are still only stone and mortar. The true test of Juda's greatness came in forging the spirit of its people. Moses had formed the spirit of God's People in the desert proving grounds; now God would raise up another holy man to direct the religious mission of the Jewish people in the post-exile period. He was a priest named Esdras who had won favor with

Artaxerxes. The king sent him to assist the governor, Nehemia, in the latter part of the sixth century B.C.

A. Renewing the Covenant

Working as an efficient team, the governor and the priest, Nehemia and Esdras, labored to re-enkindle in the Jewish people the Covenant spirit which had been their heritage from their fathers. Purified in suffering and humiliation, many of the faithful now saw in a clear light what generations before them had never clearly understood or had never wanted to accept: Juda's greatness did not lie in worldly power or material riches. Now that they were stripped of both upon their return from captivity, "the remnant" could catch a glimpse of God's Plan and the spiritual role to be played in it by God's Chosen People. The spiritually alert among them would keep their eyes forward to "the Day of the Lord" foretold by the prophets, the glorious fulfillment of God's Kingdom through the triumph of Him "who was to come," the Messiah.

On a momentous day Esdras summoned the faithful together for a solemn renewal of the Covenant with Yahweh. The Bible reported the occasion in the second book of Esdras:

> *Then Esdras the priest brought the law before the multitude of men and women, and all those that could understand . . . And he read it plainly in the street . . . and the ears of all the people were attentive to the book . . . And Esdras blessed the Lord the great God. And all the people answered: "Amen, Amen." . . . And they bowed down, and adored God with their faces to the ground. (2 Esd. 8:2, 3, 6)*

The report went on to recount the high point of the ceremony when Nehemia and all the influential people of the city pledged themselves to the Covenant together:

> *"And because of all this we ourselves make a covenant, and write it; and our princes, our levites, and our priests sign it." (2 Esd. 9:38)*

- THE Hebrew "Amen" is a solemn ratification by the people of all that was said and done. It was like putting their own personal signatures to a legal document; they pledged themselves "to live" the Covenant. Do you remember any similar approval and ratification given by the people in our Mass as we have it today?

B. **The Soul of the Old Covenant:** the Law

Once the Covenant with Yahweh was joined again, Esdras was most concerned with bringing his people back to loyal observance of the Mosaic Law which spelled out man's side of the pact with God. While still at Babylon Esdras had worked with other Scriptural scholars called "scribes" in preparing a written text of the sacred traditions, both written and oral, which had come down the centuries. This was the book of the Law, the **Torah,** which he and his fellow priests had interpreted for their people. It corresponds to the first five books of our Bible. The use of the written Torah marks a turning point in Jewish history. From this time onward, the Torah replaced the oral message of prophecy, and the scribes, interpreters of the Law, replaced the prophets as the most influential spiritual leaders in Juda. The Bible as we know it had begun to take shape.

C. **Other Voices of Israel:** the Wisdom Literature

The next few hundred years of "the remnant's" religious fervor produced other sacred writings, each of which was divinely inspired. Even though we do not always know the human authors by name, Jews and Christians alike can look to these books for the Word of God addressed to His children.

For us who live so many centuries removed from these pre-Christian times it is understandably difficult always to catch the message of the Wisdom literature. We can experience the difficulty each day at Mass when we discover that so many of the readings, hymns, and prayers of our liturgy are taken from these ancient works. The fact is that no matter how old these psalms, proverbs and the rest may be, **God continues to speak through them. We must learn to listen.** And to listen intelligently we must know something about each of the books of Wisdom literature. The brief introductions that follow are only a small beginning to a long-term effort.

1. THE PSALMS

It may be a surprise to learn that many of these liturgical songs were composed long after David had composed his share of the psalms. Pilgrims sang psalms while winding their way up the roads to the hill of Jerusalem for religious celebrations. The Jews prayed the psalms in the Temple or at home, considering them as a God-inspired way to reach their Lord. In her liturgy today the Church makes much of these psalms, and for the same reason.

- READ the Gradual-hymns which are sung or recited in the Sunday Masses of Advent. Notice they are all *snatches of psalms;* so you see how much the psalms figure in our liturgy. What is the dominating theme you detect in each of these Graduals?

2. PROVERBS

These were bits of practical advice handed down from older men to the nation's youth. Many of them ring true with human experience. It is noteworthy that the Jewish sages borrowed from the treasures of wisdom of the peoples they knew, like the Egyptians, and they adapted the foreign sayings to their own religious beliefs.

- READ the Epistle for the Mass of the Immaculate Conception, Dec. 8. Don't try to understand every word, but see how its beautiful poetic thoughts can be applied to our Lady:

  ". . . he who finds me finds life, and wins favor from the Lord. . . ." Prov. 8:35.

- READ the Epistle for the Mass of St. Elizabeth, Nov. 19, and elect someone to study her life and report whether this selection from Proverbs was well chosen.

- READ a few of the proverbs traditionally traced back to the wisest of all men, Solomon; e.g. Proverbs 22:14
  Proverbs 27:1-2
  Proverbs 29:15-17

3. ECCLESIASTICUS OR BOOK OF SIRACH

This is a book of moral training and religious education, written by a scribe named Sirach around 180 B.C. It was very popular in the early Church, so that we find it much quoted in the liturgy of the Mass.

- READ the Epistle for the Mass of St. Aloysius Gonzaga on June 21. Elect someone in the class to study the life of St. Aloysius and report whether this selection from Ecclesiasticus was well chosen.

- READ the Epistle for the Mass of St. Cecilia, Nov. 22, or Saints Perpetua and Felicitas, Mar. 6, with the same type of assignment.

- SEE ALSO Ben Sirach's counsel to young men in the famous passage of Ecclesiasticus 2:1-6.

4. BOOK OF WISDOM

Written by a cultured Jew from Alexandria, this book encouraged fellow countrymen living in exile to stay true to their Jewish traditions. Scholars date its writing during the last hundred years before Christ's birth. It contains many spiritual insights which are valid for Christianity as well.

- READ the Epistle for the Mass (Nov. 13) of St. Stanislaus Kostka, the young Jesuit who is a patron of youth. Have someone in the class read up a bit on his life and discuss whether the selection from Wisdom is appropriate.

5. ECCLESIASTES

A Jewish teacher wrote this book in the third century B.C. The book is noted for its pessimistic outlook on life, but some of the counsel which it offers young men is very wise.

- READ as an example Ecclesiastes 11:9 and 12:1-7 with its punch line in v. 8. In a poetic passage like this, just look for the dominating idea, not the many details.

6. CANTICLE OF CANTICLES

Often called the "Song of Songs," this short book of poetry portrays God's love for His people. The author is unknown, but he probably lived about the fourth century B.C. In one of his letters (see Eph. 5:25-33) St. Paul uses the same image of love of husband and wife to portray the love of Christ for His bride, the Church.

- READ the Epistle for the Feast of the Visitation of our Lady on July 2. The poetry of the Canticle is applied here to the Virgin Mary and her great love for her Son.

- ALSO in the Epistle for the Mass of St. Mary Magdalene on July 22 you will find some lines from the Canticle which express Magdalene's love for her Lord. Remember how our Lord showed special concern for Mary by appearing to her after His Resurrection.

7. THE BOOK OF JOB

Written around 450 B.C., this story of a good man tried by God in suffering seeks to explore the meaning of suffering in this life.

- COMPARE John 9:1 and Luke 13:1.

- READ the Offertory prayer for the Mass of the 21st Sunday after Pentecost; it sums up the story of Job. Do you see any connection with the Epistle?

Section 2. GREEK CONQUEST

Just when it seemed that Juda had finally come to recognize and properly value her spiritual mission, once more the topsy-turvy events of history shattered her peace and threatened to rock the very foundations of her Jewish faith. A new conqueror swept in from the west, riding a tide of military victories which set him off as the military genius of his time. This young and vigorous warrior was Alexander the Great. In the year 336 B.C. he took command of his father's Grecian armies at the age of twenty, and for thirteen years ranged far and wide, to Egypt on the south and to the very borders of far-off India on the east. One foe after another collapsed before his onslaught. Mighty Persia was brought to its knees, and of course with the Persian Empire the tiny province of Juda fell as a prize of war to the conquering hero from Greece.

I. THE HELLENIZATION OF JUDA

Trading one master for another would hardly seem too much of a catastrophe for the Jewish people. The trouble was that, unlike the tolerant rulers of the Persians, Alexander pressed his ambition to spread the highly advanced Grecian culture throughout the known world. Hellas is another name for Greece, and this movement to impose Greek ways upon conquered peoples is called "Hellenizing." It is important because from that time on in Jewish history Greek customs colored Jewish life; early Christianity reflected those Greek influences.

You can imagine the horrified reaction of the proud Jews, God's Chosen People, bearers of religious truth, now at the mercy of those insolent pagans who worshipped strange gods. Instead of the triumph the Jews expected with their all-conquering Messiah, the bitter humiliation of bowing down to a foreign upstart was a shattering experience for their faith. The clash in ideals could not be sharper for the Jewish mind:

Greek Ideals	vs.	*Jewish Ideals*
1. Man's full purpose in life is his own and his country's contentment.		Man's full purpose in life is serving Yahweh, with hope in Yahweh's promises.
2. Man must depend upon himself to train his powers of soul and body to achieve that contentment.		Man must depend upon God and not himself to achieve the purpose of life.

- OUR CIVILIZATION today is heir to both the Greek and the Jewish ideals. Discuss what is true and good in both sets of ideals. How has Christianity tried to combine them in a proper balance according to God's Plan for men? What different kinds of education are essential to achieve this balance? Discuss.

II. THE AFTER-YEARS OF HELLENIZATION

Greek influence made deepest inroads among the upper classes of Juda. The educated learned the Greek language; children wrestled in Greek gymnasia and threw the discus in Greek track and field games. Adults read Greek books and attended Greek plays. Greek weights and measures became the standard in business and trade. Where was it all to stop?

What even Alexander never dared to try, later monarchs after his death imposed by law: **The Jews must worship Grecian gods.** The choice became clear: heroic loyalty to the faith of their fathers or an easy surrender to Greek paganism.

A. **New Masters:** Alexander's Death

By a sudden twist of fortune, Alexander died almost as suddenly as he had burst upon the lands of the Near East. A deadly fever wracked his once powerful body and snuffed out his brilliant mind at the age of thirty-three, in the year 323 B.C. The unwelcome intruder's sickness and death made a mockery of Greek ideals.

The fight for the spoils split Alexander's vast empire. Palestine became the battle area between two opposing forces, the one centered in the North with a capital at Antioch and the other in the South with a capital at Alexandria. Little Juda lay helpless, a frightened lamb trapped between two hungry lions. In 168 B.C. Antiochus IV, ruthless monarch of the North, gobbled up the province of Juda and vowed so to Hellenize the Jewish people making Jerusalem itself the Antioch of the south.

The stumbling block to Antiochus' ambition to Hellenize Juda was the strong Jewish faith. He met the problem head on by forbidding all worship at the Temple. When word got back that the Jews were unshaken in their religious observance, he dispatched his Syrian troops to enter Jerusalem and massacre whatever participants they discovered at worship. Many martyrs fell that day under the Syrian sword, but most sacrilegious of all, pagan priests set up a statue of the Greek god Zeus in the Holy of Holies. The horror of that day went down in Jewish history as the "abomination of desolation," with the Temple, the symbol of God's presence among His People, defiled by pagans, and the Holy of Holies, the pulsing heart of the Jewish religious community, desecrated by idols. From that day on, a reign of terror set in for all the faithful of Yahweh. The mettle of Jewish faith was severely tested.

B. **A Voice of Courage:** the Book of Daniel

1. FOR THEIR PRESENT PLIGHT

In those dark days of persecution less than two hundred years before Christ's coming, an unknown scribe composed a work which retold some popular traditions from Exile days about a national hero named Daniel. The story of Daniel gave new heart to the faithful.

- READ the account of Daniel's courage before a similar threat of death in the Book of Daniel 6:1-28.

The message of Daniel hit the mark for the persecuted Jews of 168 B.C.:

1. Keep the faith with all courage.
God will not abandon His children.

2. Final deliverance is at hand.
God is more powerful that earthly kings.

- FOR WHOM would the message of Daniel have special significance in the world of today? Would "deliverance" always mean liberation from physical suffering? Discuss the meaning of suffering and persecution in the full perspective of God's Plan.

- READ an inspiring story related in 2 Machabees 7.

2. FOR THE FUTURE

The book of Daniel carried another though mysterious message for the future. The inspired author tells of a vision:

> *"As the visions during the night continued, I saw* **one like a son of man coming on the clouds of heaven;** *. . . he received dominion, glory, and kingship; nations and peoples of every language serve him . . .*
>
> *His dominion is an everlasting dominion that shall not be taken away, his kingship shall not be destroyed." (Dan. 7:13-14)*

Whether the human author in this passage is also making a reference to the Messiah who is to come, or whether the expression "Son of Man" is only a symbol in the author's mind of the entire people of Israel, is not definitely determined. Nevertheless, Christ is recorded as having often referred to Himself as the "Son of Man," so that we can see in this text another example of the "fuller sense" which we explained earlier.

- READ Mt. 8:20 and 26:64 for examples of our Lord's use of the title, "Son of Man."

III. THE REVOLT AGAINST GREEK DOMINATION

A. The Machabees

Even against impossible odds the time was ripe for revolution. Better to die for their faith than give up their heritage. In little bands Jewish men, young and old, slipped away to the hills where they formed a small army of liberation. They rallied around a village priest and his five sons, later called "the Machabees" from the Hebrew word for "hammer." And hammer away they did, with one attack after another, boldly matching their ill-equipped revolutionists against the Syrian army units. The oldest son, Judas Machabee, took command after his father's death and inspired his men with words like these:

> *"Fear ye not their (the Syrians') multitude, neither be ye afraid of their assault.*
>
> *"Remember in what manner our fathers were saved in the Red Sea, when Pharao pursued them with a great army.*

"And now let us cry to heaven: and the Lord will have mercy on us and will remember the covenant of our fathers and will destroy this army before our face this day.

"And all nations shall know that there is one that redeemeth and delivereth Israel." (1 Mach. 4:8-11)

- READ the account of one of Judas' greatest victories in 1 Mach. 4:1-25.

The combination of faith in the Lord and courage in battle turned the tide in favor of Jewish independence. The Machabees became national heroes.

B. A Liberated Juda

On their day of victory Judas Machabee led his men into Jerusalem in triumph. An edict of tolerance was granted to the Jewish people in 162 B.C. Down came the pagan altars; in a special religious ceremony lasting eight days the Temple, after years of desecration, was purified and rededicated.

- TILL this day faithful Jews celebrate the victory of Judas Machabee around Christmas time. It is called the Festival of Lights (Hannukkah) . Did our Lord celebrate this feast? Look up John 10:22.

But the total political victory was not yet won. The war raged on even after the death of Judas Machabee in 160 B.C. His brothers carried on until the Syrian king wearied of tracking down the revolutionists. When political independence became a reality in 143 B.C., a new dynasty ascended the throne of Juda, that of the Hasmonean kings who were so named after the family name of the Machabees. Greek rule came to an end, but Greek culture, however, had left an indelible mark. Greek language and customs seeped down into the very roots of Palestinian life.

IV. GOD'S PROVIDENCE AT WORK

As so often in the unfolding of God's Plan for men, even in allowing free play to men of evil purpose God directed the course of history. The great design for man's salvation moved ever forward. From the humiliation and suffering of the Babylonian Captivity and the Hellenizing persecutions God drew out two providential developments:

A. The Spread of Judaism

By the time of Christ's birth, Jewish colonies dotted the outer rim of the Mediterranean world. The Captivity was responsible for the large colony which chose to remain in Babylon after the Edict of Cyrus in the sixth century B.C., as well as for important Jewish colonies in Egypt. Other Jews, both before and after the Captivity, followed the trail of business opportunity to other parts of the world. This was particularly true of the many who continually moved south and west into the thriving Greek city of Alexandria to expand the colony there. From this fine port ships fanned out over the Mediterranean, to Carthage in North Africa, to Rome on the Italian peninsula, to Greece, and into the northern reaches of Asia Minor. Frequently Jewish families went along, impelled by the desire for new opportunities.

- CONSULT a map of the Mediterranean world and calculate the distance of the journeys made by Jewish families migrating to the various centers of the ancient world: Rome, Athens, Antioch, Alexandria, etc.

B. The Greek Bible

It was inevitable that in the middle of this period of change ancient Hebrew and even more popular dialects like Aramaic should give way to other tongues as the spoken language of the dispersed Jewish people. Since Greek was the most popular and useful language of all, it is not surprising that the Jewish community in Alexandria launched the project of translating the Hebrew Bible into popular Greek. According to an ancient account, seventy-two Jewish scholars were brought in to do the task. This Greek Bible of the third century B.C. is called the "Septuagint," after the Greek word for seventy. Thus, **for the first time a large number of Gentiles could read the Word of God.**

How did these two developments help God's unfolding Plan?

1. Jews in foreign lands won over many converts to worship of the one, true God.

2. They laid the groundwork for the spread of Christianity by the great missionary, St. Paul.

3. They brought their Greek Bible with them so that all — Jew and foreigner alike — could listen together to the Word of God.

- IN WHAT language would you expect that the Gospels were written? What characteristic or mark of the Church of Christ was prophesied in Isaia 2:1-4?

Section 3. THE ROMAN CONQUEST

At the turn of the first century B.C. the nations of the Near East shot nervous glances westward. A warlike nation bursting with youthful vitality was building up power and looking greedily eastward — Rome. Undoubtedly, it was anxiety about this threat from the west which had pushed Syria to grant Judean independence in 143 B.C. rather than prolong a guerrilla war on its southern flank. Syria tried to stay poised and ready for Roman attack, but the short-sighted politicians in Juda frittered away their political control with endless bickering among themselves.

I. JUDA IN PERIL

The Hasmonean kings who had taken power after independence was won not only failed to bring a stable peace to the tiny nation, but foolishly thought to push out Juda's borders by a campaign of conquest. They succeeded in swallowing up some smaller peoples in the immediate area, but their expansionist policies split the thinking of their own people right down the middle, thus causing family squabbles which distracted attention from the real menace of the times, the Romans. The factions which split the nation at this time set the climate of hostility right down to the day when the Son of God walked down Jerusalem's streets.

A. The Pharisees

The name means "the separated ones." They were religious-minded men who branded mixing with foreign "unclean" peoples as a betrayal of their sacred trust; the Jews and the Jews alone were God's Chosen People. The Pharisees bitterly opposed the conquests of the Hasmonean kings. Since they wielded great influence over the common people, they could organize civil war in later years in defiance of national policy.

Religious Beliefs. Originally an admirable group of sincere patriots and lovers of God's Law, they fell prey to an exaggerated nationalism and a fanatic formalism in religious observance. The "letter of the Law" became more important than the spirit of love taught in Deuteronomy, an attitude that led to pride and hypocrisy. And yet, strangely enough, the Pharisees had a strong sense of Messianic expectation and they believed in the resurrection of the dead.

- READ Chapter 23 of St. Matthew and in our Lord's ringing condemnation you will understand how low the Pharisees fell by the year 30 A.D.

B. The Sadducees

The name means "the just ones." These men claimed to be descendants of Solomon's great high priest Sadoc. They were really an aristocracy of the first families of Juda, who ruled both the nation's government and its religion. Ambitious for worldly power, they favored the expansion of Juda's borders. Later on they took easily to Roman domination, once they discovered how they could profit immensely by aligning themselves with Rome. Annas and Caiphas in our Lord's time were this type of religious opportunist, as were also probably a majority of the members of the Sanhedrin.

Religious Beliefs. They recognized only the five books of the Torah (Law), rejecting the other books of the Old Testament. This partly explains their denial of the resurrection of the dead, a belief which is found in the Old Testament, only in the Book of Daniel. They did not look for the Messiah as did the "faithful remnant." Their leading characteristic was a fanatical observance of the Mosaic Law.

- READ Matthew 3:7-10 for John the Baptist's condemnation.

C. The Essenes

In many ways similar to the Pharisees, these religious men preferred to keep clear of all politics by leading a community life among themselves in what today we would call monasteries. Their physical existence was rugged indeed, but they observed the Law carefully and took great pains to preserve the written text of the Sacred Books.

Religious Beliefs. Besides the ordinary faith shared with the Pharisees, they had a strong sense of charity within their own community, but like the Pharisees they bore no love for anyone else. Much more is known about these Essenes and the era in which they flourished because of an extraordinary discovery within recent times, the discovery of the "Dead Sea Scrolls."

NOTE: The Dead Sea Scrolls

In the spring of 1947, a young Bedouin while searching on a hillside for a wandering lamb discovered by chance an opening through the rock. He managed to wriggle his body through the crevice and found himself in a grotto hollowed out of the hillside. A strange sight met his gaze: the floor was littered with broken pottery, but eight sturdy-looking jars seemed to be standing sentinel over in one corner. Hoping that the big jars might be of some commercial value, he examined them and found on the inside of a few of them some rolls of curling leather. Later investigation showed the rolls to be biblical manuscripts of a fantastic age, just about two thousand years old. They must have been hidden for safekeeping, but who wrote them and who hid them away?

Since that first day, natives scoured the hillsides near the Dead Sea and found ten other grottoes which gave up similar treasures, mostly manuscripts of the Bible written in ancient Hebrew. To top off their discoveries, workmen unearthed the remains of what appears to be an ancient "monastery" nearby. The picture of what happened is beginning to come into focus and the facts it reveals throw a new light on the century before and after Christ so that we can understand with new accuracy many things which were going on around our Lord's own time.

Archaeologists and biblical scholars draw these conclusions:

1. The monastery belonged to a community of Essenes in existence **before, during,** and **after** our Lord's life on earth.

2. The members of the community living in 70 A.D. either fled or were captured when the Romans subdued the famous Jewish revolt of that year.

3. Before the Romans arrived, the Essenes managed to hide away in neighboring grottoes the precious manuscripts of the Bible which they did not want to fall into pagan Roman hands.

- WHY are these documents so precious for correct understanding of the Bible today? Recall what you learned about biblical authorship and inspiration.

II. THE ROMAN LEGIONS MOVE IN

Torn by all the political and religious dissension of the first century B.C., Juda was ripe for easy conquest. Once the Roman legions under their general, Pompey, had conquered Syria, they moved south with little expectation of resistance from tiny Juda. But the Jews would not surrender their liberty so easily. For three futile months the siege lasted, until Pompey's machines of war scaled the city's walls and then battered down the gates of the Temple, where the last die-hards had holed up as a final pocket of resistance. The Jewish historian Josephus paints a horrible picture of the massacre that followed, as the bloodthirsty Romans burst in upon the soldiers in the Temple courts and the priests at worship in the sanctuary of the Holy of Holies. The raging Romans cut down Jewish priest and soldier alike without a scruple. Jewish liberty died a horrible death that day.

III. ROMAN RULE

In the aftermath of battle, the Roman Pompey did not repeat the blunder of the Greeks. He made no effort to Romanize the Jewish people. He permitted them their own cultural ways and even a certain measure of self-rule.

Events, however, moved on and a shuffling of power took place within the Roman Empire itself. Julius Caesar, then Marc Antony, and finally a young soldier named Octavian came to power. The latter, who called himself Caesar Augustus, proved to be a shrewd ruler of men. Beginning with the year 27 B.C., the world knew peace, the peace of the Golden Age of Rome, during which the Emperor Augustus tried to consolidate his far-flung empire.

A. King Herod the Great

Back in the province of Juda, an Idumean named Antipater had won his way into the confidence of the Romans. He and his son, Herod, were permitted to rule in the name of Rome, with the Jews themselves represented by an assembly of priests and leaders called the Sanhedrin. After Antipater's death, Herod so impressed the Romans that they set him over all of Palestine. He ruled with a strong but competent hand. Best of all for the Romans, he kept the taxes flowing back to Rome. You can imagine how the Jews hated him and his tax-collectors.

King Herod's greatest achievement was the beautifying of Jerusalem, especially in building another magnificent Temple for Jewish worship. It was within the courts of Herod's Temple that Jesus Christ walked as a boy of twelve and from its gates later on that He drove out the money-changers who made His Father's house "a den of thieves."

At the death of Herod the Great in 4 B.C. the Romans divided the rule of Palestine among Herod's three sons:

1. **Archelaus** ruled Judea, Samaria, and Idumea.

2. **Philip** ruled the districts north and east of Galilee.

3. **Herod Antipas** (not to be confused with his father) ruled Galilee and Perea.

- CONSULT a map of Palestine at the time of Christ's birth and note the division of Herod's kingdom.

Philip and Herod Antipas had long reigns, beyond Christ's crucifixion, but Archelaus fell out of favor with Caesar Augustus for mismanagement of his authority. At his banishment in 6 A.D. the emperor decided to control the area through Roman procurators answerable directly to himself. This was the post which some years later fell to an ambitious Roman named Pontius Pilate.

B. The Census

Roman efficiency called for a careful census of all its provinces. Such a census was decreed by Caesar Augustus in the year 6 B.C. The people of Palestine were not happy about it because they realized more than ever their humiliating dependency upon Rome, and they also suspected an increase in burdensome taxes. But obey they must; each family prepared to return to the village whence their clan originated in order to be enrolled. Among many thousands of others, a carpenter from the hilltown of Nazareth in Galilee informed his young wife, and together they prepared for the rough journey down to Bethlehem, the city of David, since they were of the house of Juda. It was particularly hard for them because the young wife was expecting a child.

- READ St. Luke's account in Luke 2:1-4.

Section 4. THE MESSIAH IS BORN

I. THE TRIP TO BETHLEHEM

The trip today from Nazareth to Bethlehem runs about ninety-five miles by modern highway. By the caravan routes of the first century B.C. it was probably somewhat less, but the terrain was all the more rugged. The so-called roads were so narrow that in a period of travel as busy as census time simple foot-travelers leading a mule with provisions would time after time be shoved off the road surface by camel caravans or passing detachments of Roman soldiers. The most such folk of moderate means could expect as lodging for the three nights required on the road would be a space in the courtyard of a caravan station where they would encamp, using the outer walls for shelter from the cool night breezes. The animals would be left tied to posts in the middle open space of the courtyard. Well-to-do people might find lodging in a few private rooms in the back of the enclosed court, somewhat removed from the hubbub and all the coming and going of men and animals. All in all, "an inn" in the Orient was not a very comfortable place for a good night's rest.

II. "AND SHE BROUGHT FORTH HER FIRST-BORN SON"

Arriving at last in Bethlehem, Joseph and Mary, the carpenter and his young wife from Nazareth, were faced with a very delicate problem.

And it came to pass while they were there, that the days for her to be delivered were fulfilled. (Luke 2:6)

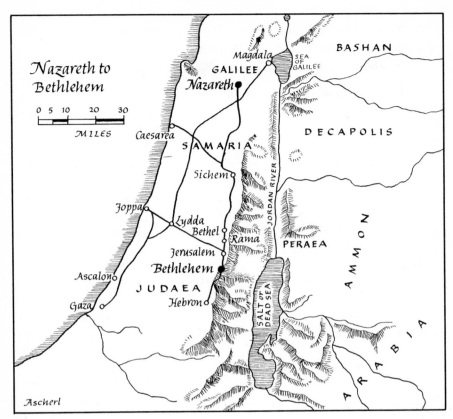

Surely they could not put up with the primitive accommodations
of the last few nights. Better to be off someplace where at least they
could know privacy for this sacred moment in the lives of both of
them, the moment when their child would be born.

There is no evidence to suppose rudeness on the part of inn-
keepers, who surely at this busy time would have already rented
out the few private rooms they had. In fact, the traditions of oriental
hospitality would argue that it was probably a sympathetic innkeeper
who made the suggestion to use a nearby cave cut out of a hill.
At least it was out of the wind, and most of all, Mary would not be
disturbed. In those primitive times, not much more could have
been expected; Mary and Joseph gladly accepted the suggestion.

> *And she brought forth her firstborn son, and wrapped him in*
> *swaddling clothes, and laid him in a manger . . . . (Luke 2:7)*

No description can communicate the sacredness of this moment awaited by so many since the dawn of man:

God's Plan to redeem men reaches its climactic stage.

God's own Son has become man.

SUMMARY

The repatriated Jews found Jerusalem in complete ruin. They set to work rebuilding the Temple and the city walls. More important still, Nehemia and Esdras renewed the Covenant with Yahweh and inspired a spiritual revival. The Mosaic Law appeared as a carefully edited text for the first time and over the next few centuries a series of books called the Wisdom literature sprang from the heart of the Jewish people.

Alexander the Great replaced Persian rule and the menace of Hellenization shook the Jewish nation. Persecution followed, during which the people found courage in the message of Daniel the prophet. A revolt under the leadership of the Machabee family brought temporary freedom, but the nation was soon forced to surrender to the new rulers of the world, the Romans.

Under Roman rule religious factions split Jewish loyalties more than ever. The "faithful remnant" longed for the Messiah to deliver them. From a little Galilean town a carpenter brought his wife to their ancestral town of Bethlehem for a census, and there she gave birth to a son. In fulfillment of prophecies, the Messiah was born. We commemorate the event in the liturgy of Christmas day and the Nativity-Epiphany season.

QUESTIONS

1. Discuss the role played among the repatriated Jews by each of the following: Zorobabel, Aggai, Zacharia, Nehemia.

2. What was the religious message which Nehemia and Esdras tried to impress upon the people?

3. How did Esdras go about rebuilding the nation's religious observance?

4. In what sense was this period a turning point in Jewish religious history?

5. What books of the Old Testament make up what is called "the Wisdom literature"? Briefly sum up the contents of each.

6. What is meant by "Hellenization" in the time of Alexander the Great and his successors? Contrast Greek and Jewish ideals.

7. Why was the Book of Daniel so well timed in appearance and what was its basic message?

8. What two developments show the providential influence of Hellenization upon the spread of Christianity later on?

9. Briefly describe the religious factions which divided the people during the Roman occupation.

10. What are the "Dead Sea Scrolls" and why are they so important?

11. How did Herod the Great come to power and what happened to the rule of Palestine after his death?

12. Describe Joseph and Mary's trip from Nazareth to Bethlehem and discuss how they probably came to the cave where Christ was born.

"And the Word was made flesh . . ." LAST GOSPEL

Liturgy of Christmas and Epiphany

The liturgy of the season centers around the two feasts of Christmas and Epiphany. From the beginning the Catholic Church of the west emphasized the historical event of Christ's nativity while the Catholic Church of the east emphasized the spiritual aspects of the coming of Christ, especially each Christian's rebirth in grace. East and west exchanged feasts and in the exchange enriched immeasurably their liturgical celebration of the season.

I. COMMEMORATING THE NATIVITY: Christmas

The early Church commemorated Christ's coming in the three Masses composed for the feast of the Nativity, December 25:

A. The Midnight Mass

The midnight Mass was a custom begun by the community of Christians at Jerusalem who celebrated Mass in the quiet of the night at the traditional grotto of Christ's birth in Bethlehem.

- FIND the reference to darkness and night in this first Mass of Christmas. What is the symbolism and how is it used effectively, as for example in the Collect?

B. The Mass at Dawn

Upon returning from Bethlehem, the early Christians attended a second Mass at dawn.

- LOOK FOR the references to light in this second Mass of the Christmas liturgy. Why is the reference in the collect to the rising sun such a favorite symbol of Christ?

C. The Mass at Mid-day

For a third time the Christians of Jerusalem gathered for Mass, this time for a solemn Mass at the place of worship reserved for the bishop.

- PICK OUT parts of this third Mass which convey the triple coming of Christ awaited through the Advent liturgy.

- LOOK ALSO for references to the main theme of Christ's sovereignty over the world as the Lord of History.

The three Masses of Christmas day drive home in striking fashion one of the key ideas of our course. The Son of God became man in order to bring new light to a world darkened with sin. His light illumines the Old Testament in the past and throws its beams far into the future of God's Plan for man's salvation.

Jesus Christ is the Light of the World.

Jesus Christ is the Lord of History.

- REFRESH the meaning of these important themes by reviewing the introduction to this book.

II.   MANIFESTING CHRIST TO THE WORLD: Epiphany

On January 6 the Catholic Church of both east and west explores the wondrous implications of Christ's coming among men. The word epiphany derives from the Greek word meaning appearance or manifestation. The Son of God has entered the world and manifested Himself through three particular episodes, each of which provides a major theme for the feast of Epiphany:

A. **The Coming of the Magi**

St. Matthew's Gospel speaks of a visit of wise men from the east in a manner that strongly links Christ's coming to the fulfillment of Old Testament promise, to the dawning of the Messianic Age. In her liturgy the Church has traditionally applied this prophecy of Isaia to the People of God and its Messiah:

> *Rise up in splendor! Your light has come, the glory of the Lord shines upon you. See, the darkness covers the earth, and thick clouds cover the peoples; but upon you the Lord shines, and over you appears his glory. Nations shall walk by your light, and kings by your shining radiance. (Is. 60:13-3)* (Used in the epistle for the feast of Epiphany.)

- EXPLAIN the light and darkness symbolisms in the passage above. Can you find any other uses of these symbolisms in the Mass for Epiphany?

● READ Michea 5:1-4 and Psalm 71:10-11 for two other prophecies connected by St. Matthew with the Epiphany story. Discuss the theme of universality contained there and point up its relevance for many problems of world peace and international relations. Do you see any link with the spirit of the United Nations? Consult and quote the United Nations' Charter to bring out your point.

B. The Baptism at the Jordan

Though not stressed in our western liturgy as much as in the east, the episode of Christ's baptism at the Jordan is also part of the Epiphany tradition. We commemorate the event later in the Epiphany season on January 13. Christ's baptism, as we shall see more fully later, manifests Christ in a special way and marks the solemn dedication of Christ to His redemptive mission and His anointing for the task by the descent of the Spirit. The salvation that Christ will bring will reach us in the sacraments. Baptism and confirmation will dedicate each one of us to a share in the sacred mission of Christ to the world, and the Eucharist will seal our commitment in faith and love.

● READ the introit from the Mass of January 13 and interpret the prophecies contained there in the light of New Testament fulfillment.

C. The Miracle at the Cana Wedding Feast

The Gospel for the second Sunday after the feast of the Epiphany records the changing of water into wine, the first of our Lord's miracles. The Cana theme belongs to the Epiphany tradition, too, in that through the miracle performed at Mary's request Christ manifested His sacred power to the world for the first time. In doing so, He revealed Himself. As the Gospel itself puts it, "And he manifested his glory" (Jo. 2:11).

It is significant that this manifestation of Christ's power took place at a wedding feast. Besides giving our Lord's blessing to festive occasions such as this, the banquet at Cana stirs up many echoes in Scripture of the banquet theme with its rich symbolisms. We shall see more at length later that Christ compared the Kingdom of heaven to a festive banquet, and as a foreshadowing of heaven He planned that the Eucharist which would unite men to Himself should also take the form of a meal. Around the table of the Eucharist Jesus

Christ, the bridegroom, enjoys the nuptial feast with the Church, His spouse. As children of our Mother the Church we are meant to share the delights of the Lord's table.

In a skillful blending of words an unknown poet of the liturgy has woven the three themes of Epiphany together beautifully:

> *This day the Church is joined to her heavenly Spouse,*
> *for Christ has cleansed away her crimes in the Jordan;*
> *with the gifts the Magi hasten to the royal nuptials,*
> *and the guests are gladdened with wine made from water.*
> *Alleluia.* (From the Benedictus antiphon in Office of Epiphany)

- RECALL from Mt. 2:11 that the offering of gifts is part of the Epiphany spirit. What is the finest gift we can offer to God? See the secret in the Mass for the Epiphany for the answer. Do some research on the celebration and significance of Epiphany among our Christian brethren of the Eastern Church.

SUMMARY OF MESSIANIC EXPECTATIONS

With Christmas so close, look back a minute over our course thus far. Many of the things which we saw as shadowy and indistinct in the Old Testament will now become clear in the person of Jesus Christ. The figure of the Messiah stands before us in the New Testament's dawning light.

Here is a summary of what the Old Testament said about the Messiah in its shadowy, indistinct way. Note the corresponding clarification and fulfillment in the column on the right:

The Prophet	*Old Testament* The Prophecy in Shadow	*New Testament* The Prophecy in Fulfillment
1. Moses speaks of	"the prophet" Deuteronomy 18:15-18	Acts 3:22 John 1:21; 6:14; 7:40
2. Nathan speaks of	"the son of David" 2 Kings 9:6-7	John 7:41-42
3. Isaia speaks of	"the King-Messiah" Isaia 9:6-7 "born of a virgin" Isaia 7:14 "a miracle-worker" Isaia 35:4-6	Luke 1:30-33 Luke 1:26-27 Matthew 1:22-25 Luke 7:20-22

4. Ezechiel speaks of   "the shepherd of his people"
Ezechiel 34:5-6, 11-16, 23-24   John 10:11-18; Luke 15:3-7

5. Second Isaia speaks of   "the victim of suffering"
Isaia 53:4-7, 12   Mark 10:32-34; 15:15-20

6. Daniel speaks of   "the Son of Man"
Daniel 7:9-14   Matthew 24:27-30; 26:64

- IT WOULD be a good idea to type or write out these texts in two columns with the corresponding texts opposite one another. Study their connections.

AN IMPORTANT CONCLUSION

The figure of the Messiah from the Old Testament shows many different faces: The Prophet — Son of David — King Messiah — Miracle Worker — Shepherd — Victim of Suffering — Son of Man.

We are not surprised that the full and clear picture of the true Messiah with all these different faces from Old Testament preparation would only come into focus when the faithful could see them blended into the living personality of Jesus Christ.

Jesus Christ is the answer to all that the Jews had hoped for and had heard about from their prophets. In Him the Old Testament finds its meaning and fulfillment.

A CHRONOLOGY OF ISRAEL'S HISTORY

Approximate Dates	*Events of Importance*
THE EARLY ORIGINS B.C.	
1850	Call of Abraham into Chanaan
1710	Joseph in Egypt
1700	Hebrew migrants in Egypt
1560	Oppression of Hebrews
1290	Exodus under Moses
1250	Reconquest of Chanaan
1075	Samuel, last of Judges

Approximate Dates	*Events of Importance*
THE ROYAL PERIOD B.C.	
1045	Saul, the first king
1005	David, king of Israel
972	Solomon succeeds David
935	Split of two kingdoms
874	Achab and Jezabel in Israel – Elia
736	Achaz in Juda – Isaia
721	Fall of Israel to Assyrians
716	Ezechia – Isaia
701	Siege by Sennacherib
640	Reform under Josia – Jeremia
609	Collapse of reform
THE PERIOD OF EXILE B.C.	
586	Fall of Juda to Nabuchodonosor
587	Babylonian captivity, Ezechiel
THE PERSIAN PERIOD B.C.	
545	Cyrus the Persian conquers
	Second – Isaia
538	Cyrus' edict of liberation
	Return to Jerusalem
515	Dedication of second Temple
	Aggai and Zacharia
458	Missions of Esdras and Nehemia
	Pentateuch as law of state
400	Wisdom literature
THE GREEK PERIOD B.C.	
336	Alexander's conquests
285	Greek translation of Bible
168	Antiochus IV's persecution
	Seleucid dynasty
	Daniel
	Machabean revolt
162	Edict of Tolerance
143	Independence under Simon
	Machabee
	Hasmonean kings
124	Books of the Machabees

Approximate Dates   *Events of Importance*

THE ROMAN PERIOD

63	Romans capture Jerusalem
39	Herod the Great, a puppet king
27	Emperor Augustus
19	Herod's Temple built
6	Census by Augustus
	Birth of Christ
4	Rule by Herod Antipas, Philip, Archelaus

THE CHRISTIAN ERA A.D.

6	Roman procurator replaces Archelaus
30	Christ's death and resurrection
	Pentecost

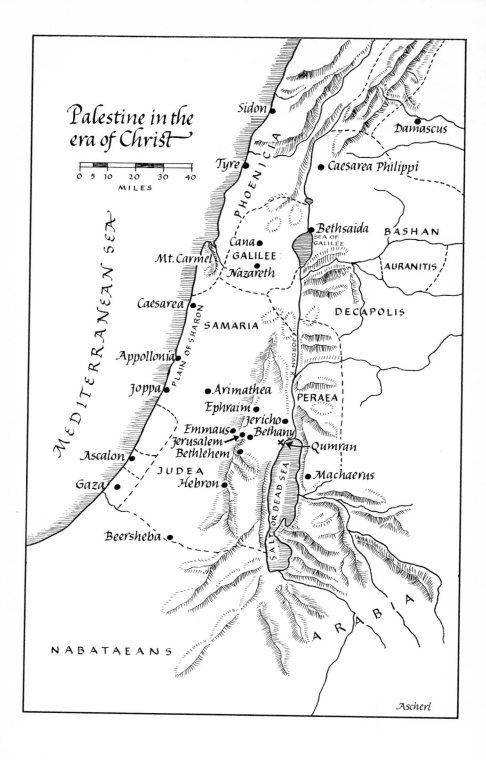

Palestine in the
era of Christ

0 5 10   20   30   40
MILES

MEDITERRANEAN SEA

Sidon

Damascus

Tyre

Caesarea Philippi

PHOENICIA

Bethsaida
SEA OF
GALILEE

BASHAN

Cana
GALILEE

AURANITIS

Mt. Carmel

Nazareth

Caesarea

DECAPOLIS

SAMARIA

PLAIN OF SHARON

JORDAN

Appollonia

Joppa

Arimathea

PERAEA

Ephraim

Jericho

Emmaus

Bethany

Jerusalem

Qumran

Bethlehem

Ascalon

Machaerus

JUDEA

Hebron

Gaza

SALT OR DEAD SEA

Beersheba

ARABIA

NABATAEANS

Ascherl

Part Two

CHRIST ON EARTH

Christ's coming marks the dawn of a new day for mankind. In God's Plan of Salvation we have already seen how the shadowy figure of the Messiah gradually came into the full light of the Incarnation. This was the part of our course which we called CHRIST PROMISED.

The wonderful thing about this next section is that in it God will no longer speak to us only through His friends and prophets. A new era in human history opens up. God will speak to man **through His own Son:**

God, who at sundry times and in divers manners spoke in times past to the fathers by the prophets, last of all in these days has spoken to us by his Son . . . (Heb. 1:1-2)

CHAPTER IX

CHRIST'S EARLY YEARS

History students stretch their imaginations to get back to Civil War days; yet the Civil War broke out only one hundred years ago. The Crusades of the Middle Ages seem off somewhere in a past so remote that they strike us almost as make-believe. What a strain upon our historical thinking to study the wars of the Romans two thousand years ago! But we saw in our preceding chapter that the Romans got to Palestine late in the history of the Jewish people. The Romans followed the Greeks of Alexander and his successors; and the Greeks followed the Persians, who went back to the time of Cyrus; and the Persians followed the Babylonians grown powerful under Nabuchodonosor, who in turn had rocked the Near East by toppling mighty Assyria. And just to stagger our imaginations, the historical fact is that in 1250 B.C., before the same Assyrians came to power, the Egyptians under Rameses II, Moses' adversary, were well into **their nineteenth dynasty of pharaohs.**

By locating our Lord in this fuller historical view, we can show that He did not live so long ago, after all. He goes back only to the time of the Romans, and it is no longer for us to look back upon His life that it was for Him to look back upon the twelfth of the Egyptian dynasties. When Christ appeared for the first time at the River Jordan, the monastery of the Dead Sea scrolls — the ruins of which you could still visit today — already had been in existence for a hundred years. To anyone walking along the monastery's porticoes today the centuries fall away.

With this chapter we begin to study the record of Christ's life on earth. First, look to the sources of our information, and then see what these sources tell us about Christ's early years.

Section 1. THE WITNESSES OF CHRIST

I. WE LEARN ABOUT JESUS CHRIST FROM THREE DIFFERENT SOURCES

A. Archaeology

Scientists go to work with pick and shovel to dig out the roads which knew Christ's tread and to locate the buildings which echoed to His voice, e.g., the road down to the Garden of Gethsemani and the site of Pilate's fortress-home.

B. Secular History

Non-Christian historians of the era immediately after Christ's time fill in some more historical details, e.g., the Roman historian Tacitus speaks in his Annales of the Jewish religious sect called "Christians" during the reign of Emperor Nero around 64 A.D. They are blamed for the great fire at Rome:

> *He (the Emperor) presented as the guilty ones and visited with the most refined punishments those whom the populace, hating them for their crimes, called "Christians." The author of this denomination, Christ, in the reign of Tiberius, had been condemned to death by Pontius Pilate; but, though checked for the moment, the deadly supersition broke out afresh, not only throughout Judea, where this evil originated, but also throughout the City (Rome), where all outrageous and shameful things gather from every region and are exalted. (Tacitus, **Annales** XV:44)*

The testimony of Tacitus is hardly laudatory; but it is all the more authentic and reliable coming from an unfriendly historian.

ANOTHER EXAMPLE The recorded death of Herod the Great, by our present calculations in 4 B.C., shows that the date of Christ's birth first estimated by monks of the sixth century was off by a few years. Christ was probably born, therefore, around 6 B.C. and returned from Egypt around 4 B.C. at Herod's death.

C. Sacred History

This literature divides itself into the Old and the New Testaments.

BUT NOTE WELL: This is not history of our modern type which seeks careful documentation and factual accuracy for the events it interprets. This is **religious history,** true history also, but more concerned to show only the essential aspects of the events and above all how they fit into God's Plan for man's salvation. The writers show little concern for careful detail and they allow their faith to shine through with an uninhibited enthusiasm that often led them to exaggeration of facts and glorification of events. As men of faith, they were writing for others who shared their Faith. (Review "A Searchlight on the Bible," p. 14, on "literary forms.")

1. THE OLD TESTAMENT may be divided into four sections:

a. THE PENTATEUCH: the books of the Hebrew Torah, a mixture of history, Jewish law, and traditions.

b. HISTORICAL BOOKS: largely accounts of early Jewish history.

c. WISDOM LITERATURE: literary efforts to form religious ideals.

d. THE PROPHETICAL BOOKS: often a combination of both history and religious ideals, an inspired look into the heart of the Hebrew people.

NOTE: For a full list of Old Testament books, see the appendix in the back of the book.

2. THE NEW TESTAMENT is most easily divided into two main parts:

a. THE GOSPELS: deserving of special attention because they record events and teachings from Christ's life on earth.

BUT NOTE WELL: The Gospels are not a biography in our modern sense. The evangelists never intended to write a day-by-day account of Christ's life. Rather, each of the Gospels is a collection of events and sayings from Jesus' life. The apostles hoped that these writings would acquaint the faithful as well as future converts with the Lord whom they themselves loved and wanted to make known. This gospel "good news" centered, of course, around our Lord's Passion and Resurrection.

- READ the Christian Message as presented orally at first by St. Peter, the first pope, in Acts 2:22-36. Can you pick out the heart of the message?

After about thirty years of this kind of oral and some written traditions, the evangelists thought it a very practical thing to bring together official editions of the Gospels, and particularly for these three reasons: 1. As convenient books of instructions, like our catechisms. 2. As source-books for liturgical readings at Mass, like our Missals. 3. As reliable accounts to counteract any false Gospel giving wrong ideas of the Lord they loved and served.

      b. THE EPISTLES: expanded letters from St. Paul and the other apostles to their different parishes all over the world.

NOTE: For a full list of the New Testament books, see the appendix in the back of the book.

Section 2. A CHILD OF JEWISH TRADITIONS

St. Luke and St. Matthew begin their Gospels with brief accounts of Christ's early years. Luke centers his facts around the Blessed Mother while Matthew also stresses St. Joseph's role.

Of Mary's and Joseph's upbringing we know little for certain, but one thing can be taken for granted: they were both raised in Jewish families strong in faith and piety. How could God have chosen anyone faithless to care for His Son on earth?

There was no doubt, therefore, that the child Jesus received the full initiation into the Jewish faith which any religious-minded parents would plan for their children. The Jewish practices of religious formation followed the pattern of the child's physical growth and were carefully regulated by centuries of tradition.

I. THE CIRCUMCISION

When God joined a covenant with Abraham, it was agreed that circumcision would serve as the physical sign to show that each believing Hebrew had pledged himself to a covenant with his Lord. The child became a true citizen of Israel on the day of the religious ceremony of circumcision.

The name a child received often denoted the special vocation expected of the child. The name Josue, or as we spell it, Jesus, was perfect for this child destined as the Messiah to save His people. Jesus means "Yahweh saves."

- CIRCUMCISION as a religious ceremony is "a type" of our Christian baptism. Is baptism also a sacrament of "vocation"? How?

Liturgy. The Circumcision is commemorated in the liturgy on January 1, the octave day of the Nativity.

The Sunday between Circumcision and Epiphany is a special feast in honor of the Holy Name of Jesus.

- COMPARE the Mass of the Holy Name of Jesus with the Mass for the Feast of St. Ignatius Loyola, the founder of the Society of Jesus. How did Ignatius in his life fulfill the spirit of the two introits, collects, and communions?
  Have a member of the class relate the story of the saint's vocation beneath the standard of Jesus.

II.   THE PRESENTATION AT THE TEMPLE

Jewish Law called for a religious ceremony at the Temple forty days after the birth of the first male child in a family. Just like the firstlings of the flocks and the first fruits of the fields, the first-born male child belonged to God. (See Exodus 13:2-16.) But now that the tribe of Levi tended the Lord's worship exclusively, parents could take back their child and give an offering of five shekels, about four dollars, in the child's place. Two doves or pigeons were sacrificed as a purification offering from the mother of the child. That Mary, she who was "full of grace," should have submitted to this purification ceremony gives us an insight into her humility and reverence for her Jewish faith.

There was certainly nothing extraordinary about the little group of three, parents and child, ascending the steps of the Temple. By an inspiration of the Holy Spirit, an elderly man named Simeon recognized them. Approaching Mary with respect, he asked to take the child in his arms; then from an overflowing heart he spoke:

> *"Now thou dost dismiss thy servant, O Lord, according to thy word, in peace; because my eyes have seen thy salvation, which thou has prepared before the face of all peoples: **A light of revelation to the Gentiles** and a glory for thy people Israel." (Luke 2:29-32)*

Simeon is the spokesman for countless generations of faithful Jews, "the remnant" who had prayed to see the day of the Messiah. This was "the Son of David," who would fulfill all their hopes and expectations.

● READ the full account of the Presentation in Luke 2:22-38.

Liturgy We commemorate the Presentation on February 2, forty days after our Lord's Nativity.

The feast is also called Candlemas Day. Read the third prayer for the blessing of the candles and point out a link with the underlined portion of Simeon's prayer above. Do you see any connection with the Introduction to our course?

III. LIFE AT NAZARETH

Once Herod the Great was dead, the Holy Family planned to return from exile in Egypt. Any hope they may have had of settling down in Bethlehem was shattered by the distressing news of the tyrannical rule which Archelaus imposed upon Judea. To beat down a riot at Passover time, Herod's son had three thousand Jewish pilgrims massacred. The only sensible thing for Joseph to do was to take Mary and Jesus back to the peaceful hills of Nazareth. They probably headed north along the coastline to avoid Judea, round the foot of Carmel, made famous by the prophet Elia, and through the Plain of Esdraelon into the foothills of Galilee.

A. Their Home

The carpenter's house, like many others in town, was made of mud and straw, square-shaped and flat-roofed, and usually painted white. You can still see similar houses in Nazareth today. An outside stairway climbed up to the roof, where on hot nights the family could enjoy cooler air. On the inside there was really only one big room, but with two different levels. The front part at street level housed the animals while the back part, raised somewhat on a platform, provided living quarters for the family itself. Furnishings were meager, but we might expect a few extra pieces in the house of a carpenter: a chest for clothes, a couple of stools to sit on, some water pots, and back to the rear of the platform often in openings cut out of the wall the family would stretch out their sleeping mats. The cooking of the simple meals of bread, grains, fruits, and — very rarely

— meats, might be done indoors, but more often the smoke of the fire would make outdoor cooking preferable.

B. A Young Man's Schooling

Actually there were no schools in our sense for Hebrew children. A boy depended a great deal upon his father and mother, who passed on to him whatever they had learned. The father would be most diligent to teach his son the trade which gave the family its livelihood. As carpenters, Joseph and Jesus spent hour after hour together in the workshop behind the house. They built wooden plows, window frames, tables, chairs, and even roofing. In a perfectly natural way Jesus listened and was eager to learn. His religious education was completed at the synagogue with the help of the rabbi.

- HOW does Christ's education bring out how perfectly human He was? He was truly man, even though He never ceased to be God.
  Christ's work as a carpenter gives new dignity to manual labor. Is this dignity of labor something new in God's Plan for men? Look back over the chapter on Creation before answering.

C. A Young Man's Prayer and Worship

1. Jesus learned to pray from earliest childhood. Just as Christian mothers teach their children to say "Our Father, who art in heaven . . . ," so Mary and the other Jewish mothers taught their families the favorite morning prayer:

"Hear, O Israel! The Lord is our God, the Lord alone! Therefore, you shall love the Lord, your God, with all your heart, and with all your soul, and with all your strength." (Deut. 6:4-5)

Moses had insisted upon this precious duty of parents:

"Take to heart these words ('Hear, O Israel, etc.') which I enjoin on you today. Drill them into your children." (Deut. 6:6-7)

Each morning, as head of the family, Joseph would pronounce the first few words of the prayer and then Jesus and Mary would join in. After Joseph's death Jesus led the prayer each day.

Jesus had a kind of prayerbook too — the Book of Psalms. In those days before printing presses, He may well have written out the Psalms long-hand. At key points in His life Jesus turned to those

prayers which He had first learned from Mary. They were a source
of strength and consolation to Him.

- LOOK UP the seven recorded utterances of Jesus while hanging
  on the cross. See how many of them are really parts of prayers
  He had learned as a boy from Mary. The footnotes in your
  New Testament will give you helpful clues.

2. Each Friday at sunset a loud trumpet pierced the silence; it
was the signal for all work to stop. This is how the Sabbath rest
would begin. Joseph and Jesus would leave their work benches and
enter the house, where they would find Mary just finishing preparations for the next day's meals. Mary would hasten to light the
Sabbath lamp.

On the Sabbath morning the Holy Family attended the synagogue.
Inside, the seating arrangements separated the men and women;
Jesus sat in front with Joseph while Mary stayed in the back behind
a screen with the other women of the town. A raised platform sup-
porting a desk and few chairs fixed the attention of all forward,
but there was no altar, nor were there any statues. Behind a curtain
to the rear of the platform stood the cupboard which enclosed the
Sacred Scriptures.

A prayer and hymn opened the service. Then the rabbi signaled
for the first of the seven readings from the sacred text. Any of the
male worshippers could be asked to read the chosen passages, usually
recounting God's gifts to Israel. It is highly probable that Joseph
and Jesus took their turns. Should another rabbi or a learned person
be passing through the town, he might give a short commentary
upon the passages read, much like our idea of a sermon. A final
blessing and prayer concluded the service. All then returned to their
homes for a day of rest and prayer.

- WHY do you think there would be neither altar nor statues in a
  Jewish synagogue?

3. There were four particularly big feast days:

a. PASSOVER: in April, recalling the deliverance from Egypt and
highlighted by the Paschal Supper.
b. PENTECOST: in May, reminding the people of the Sinai Covenant; also an opportunity to thank God for the spring harvest.
c. FEAST OF TABERNACLES: in October, commemorating the so-

journ of their ancestors in the desert, where they lived in tents; also in thanksgiving for the fall grape-harvest.

d. FEAST OF DEDICATION (Festival of Lights) : in December, recalling the reconsecration of the Temple after the victory of the Machabees over Greek rulers in 163 B.C.

The Jews were encouraged to go up to the Holy City for all these big feasts in order to participate in the Temple worship. However, Jews living outside Judea could be excused. Many tried to make at least one pilgrimage a year, for the feast of Passover. The Holy Family joined their Galilean friends each year at Passover. They traveled in caravans, keeping the tone of a religious pilgrimage along the way. They prayed together and sang psalms, particularly when they first caught sight of the Temple's towers gleaming in the sunshine. This was a great thrill for them. Just ahead was the Holy City of David, and within its walls was the meeting place of God and man, their beloved Temple.

> *I rejoiced because they said to me, "We will go up to the house of the Lord." And now we have set foot within your gates, O Jerusalem.... (Ps. 121:1-3)*

- CAN you think of anything in our Catholic customs which comes from this kind of Jewish pilgrimage? Do you remember any incidents in our Lord's life which bring out His great love of the Holy City and its Temple?

D. A Young Man's Pastimes

Outside of the reference in Luke 2:51-52, little is said in the Gospels of how Jesus spent the rest of His time at home in Nazareth. A careful reading, however, of much that He said in later life fills in the picture.

As a very young child He would often watch His mother at work baking bread (Mark 6:30), sweeping (Luke 15:8), mending clothes (Mark 2:21), grinding corn (Luke 6:38). He would skip along by his mother's side as she made her daily trip to the well, with her water pitcher balanced on her head. The well at Nazareth today is the same in use from Mary's time; it is the only well in the area. Pilgrims venerate the ground here, which often knew the tread of the feet of Jesus and Mary.

When Jesus grew older, He enjoyed good times with friends.

He probably climbed the nearby hills and watched with fascination as an eagle soared and circled overhead (Luke 17:31). He would track down foxes (Luke 9:58) or make friends with the neighboring shepherds (John 10:1-14). In more serious moments He may have helped out the farmers nearby (Mark 4:3) and He would be struck with the beauty of the wild flowers which bloom in the fields (Matthew 6:28).

Hiking was a welcome change for the young men of Nazareth. It was probably Joseph who first took Jesus to the flourishing city of Capharnaum, but after Joseph's death He probably walked the 18-20 miles frequently enough alone or with friends. He got to know the fishermen at the Lake of Galilee; they probably showed Him how to cast the little hand-net and how to set the huge drag-net tied to two boats (Matthew 13:47). The bargaining of caravan-traders and the haggling of merchants and money-changers at the market introduced Him to bustling city life (Luke 16:1-21). He never forgot the products of market: the oil (Matthew 25:9), the cattle (Luke 14:19), even weapons (Luke 22:36).

E. A Young Man's Thoughtful Moments

All young men, particularly those in their teens, dream of their future, of the worlds they hope to conquer. From the vantage point of a hill in Galilee, Jesus must have let His eye wander over the land His Father had promised to Abraham. In a few years He was to cover this Promised Land from north to south, from east to west. He caught a glimpse to the west of white-sailed ships creeping up the Mediterranean coast from Alexandria. To the north He spotted majestic Mt. Hermon, snow-capped against the blue sky. Over to the east mountains hid the Lake of Galilee, but the ten independent Greek cities glistened in the sun, with their temples of polished stone, their theaters, their gymnasia. How long it would be before these pagan peoples listened to His message! Off to the southeast zigzagged the deep gorge of the River Jordan which stretched out like a tremendous snake as far as the Dead Sea, 1286 feet below sea level. The hills of Samaria shut off the view to the south, but with His divine knowledge He knew that the Samaritans would not be completely deaf to His voice, even after so many years of bitter hostility to everything Jewish (John 4:28-30). But the beautiful view to the north, south, east, and west must have made Him sad more than anything else. God's People had waited so long for their Messiah, but as St. John put it later on, "He came unto his own, and his own received him not." (John 1:11)

A passing caravan on the road below might disturb His thoughts. Caravans often moved north to Damascus, around the crescent to Mesopotamia, or south to Egypt. They were symbols of the world He had come to save. He learned to recognize Roman legions kicking up dust in the distance as they marched along Galilean roads on their way to new assignments. The flash of the sun on their armor and the proud step of their horses must have thrilled Him as a boy, but in these later reflective moments the sight of Romans would stir up depressing pictures of what the Romans would do to His people and to Himself.

- WHAT thoughts do you think the sight of Roman soldiers stirred up in the mind of Christ with His special foreknowledge?

IV. AN INCIDENT AT THE TEMPLE

The age of twelve was a turning-point in the life of a young Hebrew boy. One of the privileges at this age was the yearly pilgrimage to Jerusalem at Passover time. Not that the trip was an easy one, but to a healthy young man the hardships brought adventure and even fun.

- READ Luke 2:40-45.

With the relaxed discipline usual with caravans of townspeople, it is not surprising that Jesus could have slipped away on the return trip without Mary and Joseph's realizing His absence. Upon arrival at the first night's caravan station, Jesus' parents suffered the shock of His loss. They rushed back to Jerusalem, but three days of search failed to solve the mystery. When they finally came upon Jesus with the doctors at the Temple, the brief exchange between them gives us a precious insight into the character of each.

- READ Luke 2:46-50.

The fact that Jesus showed Himself well read in the Scriptures and gave evidence of His razor-sharp mind did not surprise Mary and Joseph. After all, they had helped to educate Him and knew His special talents. What struck them speechless, however, was the cool statement of His Father's rights in His regard: "Did you not know that I must be about My Father's business?" Jesus was telling

Mary and Joseph that the mission willed by His Father had to come first always, even before their rights and feelings as parents. To this He was pledged; the circumcision and presentation at the Temple had been outward signs of this inner consent to His vocation according to God's Plan.

Mary felt her son slipping away from her. "She kept all these things carefully in her heart." She had only vague notions of this mysterious vocation to which her son referred, but she too, as on the day of the Annunciation, inwardly consented to all God asked of her.

V. FOLLOWING HIS VOCATION

After Joseph's death, Jesus became the head of the house. He carried on Joseph's carpentry work, took good care of Mary, and all in all lived the kind of peaceful life typical of a hilltown like Nazareth. The years were happy ones for Mary, but she knew they could not last. Around His thirtieth year Jesus told Mary that He must leave for good. She understood; though she did not know the details, she was confident of her son's final success at "His Father's business."

Coming down from the hills around Nazareth, our Lord undoubtedly headed east to follow the road south on the other side of the Jordan, thus avoiding unfriendly Samaria. A new phase of His life began as He drew near to the fording place just above the spot where the Jordan sinks into the Dead Sea. This so-called Public Life of Jesus will command our attention in the next few chapters of our course.

- DISCUSS the idea of "a vocation." Our Lord and the Blessed Mother knew that they had a special role to play in God's Plan for mankind. They both consented freely and gave themselves to the mission expected of them with full confidence in God's Providence.

  A Christian must discover the special role expected of him in God's Plan, too. An honest weighing of his talents will help: intellectual, physical, social, and above all spiritual. These talents should point to certain kinds of life work. Often a friend and counselor can be of assistance in reaching the right decision.

Section 3. TWO PERSONALITY PROFILES

When do you really know a person? The facts of experience tell us that it usually takes a good while. You must give yourself time to study a friend, his ways of acting, his response to different situations. Before you form a judgment, you should blend all the evidence into a well-balanced picture of the individual friend as an individual. But most of all, you should meet the friend as best you can, person to person, and share the mutual sympathies of what we call friendship. This is what we want to do now, first with our Lady and then with St. Joseph.

I. MARY

The data on Mary's character in the Gospel is rich. True, the sampling of texts picturing Mary will not actually bring her to life for us, but greater knowledge about her may encourage us to ask that she reveal herself to us more intimately.

A. **Genesis 3:15**

Mary was chosen by God as the New Eve, "the woman" whose offspring would "crush the serpent's head."

B. **Luke 1:29-31**

The Angel Gabriel rightly calls her "full of grace," because by her Immaculate Conception she was preserved free from original sin, never for the least moment deprived of the presence of God within her.

C. **Luke 1:39-40**

The unspoiled girl of fourteen or fifteen thinks with concern of her cousin Elizabeth, also with child in her old age; humility and charity leave no room for selfishness and pride.

D. **Luke 2:46-55**

Mary's song of joy, the "Magnificat," shows deep knowledge of Scripture. It catches the meaning of God's great Plan; its thoughts give us an inspired insight into Mary's heart.

E. Luke 2:6-7
Her courage shines through the uncomplaining experiences at Bethlehem, the physical weariness and the worry for the safety of the child.

F. Luke 2:34-35
At her purification in the Temple, Simeon tells her "thy own soul a sword shall pierce," but she does not back down from the pledge she gave at the Annunciation in her conversation with Gabriel, "Be it done to me according to thy word."

G. Luke 2:48-50
The painful experience of losing Jesus for a while, and then the hint in His words that she one day would lose Him for good, prepare her soul to sacrifice her son in God's mysterious designs.

H. Luke 2:51-52
The hardships of Nazareth life were constant opportunities for her to prove her love for Joseph, her husband, and for Jesus, her son.

I. John 2:3-5
Her complete confidence in Jesus is vindicated by His first miracle at her request. She will remain "the Mediatrix of all Graces."

J. Luke 8:19-21
A dramatic example of what Jesus meant by "His Father's business" always coming first. Mary accepts her son's decision to postpone seeing her.

K. John 19:25-27
The agonizing sorrow of seeing her son hanging on the cross has earned her the title "Mother of Sorrows." But do not forget that she chose this role freely in cooperating with man's redemption.

L. Acts 1:14
After sharing the triumph of her son's Resurrection and Ascension into heaven, she brings inspiration and encouragement to the young Church, even though she looks forward to joining her son through her own Assumption into heaven.

- SEE how many feastdays in honor of Mary you can list from the events and privileges of Mary recorded above. Add the correct dates.

  Type up or write out the brief texts above (excepting the "Magnificat") and, with the help of the little explanations given above, decide upon an appropriate title for each of the texts.

A SUMMARY

At the very beginning of the Gospels we meet the winning personality of Mary. Christians see in her God's most perfectly created person, free from any touch of sin. Mothers see in her all the ideals of motherhood, the love and sacrifice that went into the birth of her son and the hard years at Nazareth. Men see in her sharing of Christ's cross the courage and determination they like to claim for themselves; but in honest moments they frankly own up to cowardice in the face of temptation or the calling to a saintly life. Mary is many things to many people, but we love her most for her greatest prerogative: She is the mother of our Lord and our God.

- COMPOSE your own summary paragraph, trying to blend together the outstanding qualities of Mary's personality as you see them in the texts above.

II. JOSEPH

Think of the number of boys you call "Joe," and you will realize that Joseph is not a forgotten personality among Christians. But the trouble is that people too frequently pick up false pictures of this great man. To some Joseph is a kindly old fellow; to others he is young and energetic enough, but only a quiet partner riding along on the tide of great events. Better to fit together your picture of Joseph's personality from the precious little that the Gospels give us:

A. Luke 1:27
Joseph could be proud of his ancestry. He was of Juda's tribe and of the House of David, the religious nobility of the Jewish race.

B. Matthew 1:18-19
With the solemn betrothal to the maiden Mary, life promised Joseph great happiness, the joy of a devoted wife. Imagine the shock

of discovering that she is with child before they had begun to live together. As "a just man," he decides to "put her away quietly" rather than denounce her in disgrace.

C. Matthew 1:20

What first appeared to be the trial of his life turns out to be a special vocation from God. The angel explains all and Joseph consents to cooperate with God's Plan.

D. Luke 2:16

As the shepherds adored the child, Joseph stood by in wonderment at the great events of which he was part. This night he proved himself in a difficult situation.

E. Luke 2:33-34

Joseph heard Simeon's prophecy about the wife and child he cared for as his own. With them he generously offers himself to God's Plan.

F. Matthew 2:13

His quickness of action is put to the test when word reaches him of Herod's evil intention to kill the child. He does not panic; the flight to Egypt saves the child's life.

G. Matthew 2:19-21

Again unquestioning obedience before an order delivered by the angel. Egypt may have been pleasant; who knows what Judea or Galilee will bring?

H. Luke 2:40

Joseph was the ideal of Jewish faith and observance. Jesus modeled Himself after Joseph at prayer, in the synagogue, on pilgrimages; also in running the carpentry shop, working hard and well.

I. Matthew 13:55

It must have been a great joy to Joseph to hear Jesus spoken of as "Joseph the carpenter's son." The name stayed on in later life, too.

There is no mention in the Gospels of Joseph's death. It seems certain he died during Christ's life at Nazareth. To die with Jesus and Mary near is a happy death indeed. Joseph is the "Patron of a Happy Death."

- SEE how many feast days in honor of Joseph you can list with their proper dates.
  Type up or write out the brief texts above and, with the help of the little explanations given above, decide upon an appropriate title for each of the texts.

SUMMARY

Joseph was that manly type of individual who says little, but does much. You may be sure he spoke wisely when he wanted to, or he never would have survived so many crises in caring for Jesus and Mary. In any emergency Joseph took charge. He showed complete trust in God, yet intelligence, courage and energy as well in figuring out his every move. Time and again he was put to the test, but each time he responded with extraordinary faith. He was a man of vocation who had pledged himself to a mission, and who would never back down. All his life was wrapped up in complete devotion to Jesus and Mary because he knew that such was his mission from God. He worked hard and he prayed hard. Many saints followed his formula for sanctity.

- COMPOSE your own summary paragraph, trying to blend together the outstanding qualities of Joseph's personality as you see them in the texts above.

SUMMARY

For the facts of Christ's life on earth we turn to three sources of information: archaeology, secular history, and sacred history of both Old and New Testaments.

Mary and Joseph saw to it that Jesus received the same religious formation intended by tradition for all Hebrew boys. Jesus was circumcised, presented, and "bought back" at the Temple.

At Nazareth Jesus followed the pattern of life expected of any young man of His time. He was educated at home and in the synagogue; He learned Joseph's trade of carpentry; He enjoyed recreational pastimes with other young men; He participated in the Jewish life of prayer and worship. Though He never ceased to be God, Jesus showed Himself fully a man, too.

Jesus often thought of His special Messianic mission. He pledged Himself to His Father's Will, as is clearly brought out in the incident at the Temple when He was twelve years old. At about the age of thirty or more, He left His home at Nazareth in order to follow His vocation as planned by His Father. His Public Life began.

QUESTIONS

1. Explain the three different sources for our information on Christ's life.

2. How does sacred history differ from our modern notions of scientific history?

3. How are the books of the Old and New Testaments most simply divided?

4. What was the intention of the evangelists in writing the Gospels?

5. Describe the typical house at Nazareth.

6. What kind of an education did a Hebrew boy receive?

7. Discuss a typical synagogue service in which Christ would participate.

8. What prayers did Mary teach Jesus? Did Jesus ever use them in later life?

9. What did the four big Jewish feast days commemorate?

10. What were some of Jesus' pastimes while living at Nazareth?

11. Describe Jesus' view in each direction from a high hill in Galilee.

12. What was the meaning of Jesus' reply to Mary and Joseph when they found Him in the Temple?

13. Outline Jesus' probable route when He left Nazareth to begin His Public Life.

CHAPTER X

MISSION LAUNCHED:
THE FATHER CALLS

Two men set their course on foot for the ford over the Jordan near
Bethany. The one moved south from Galilee along the river road;
the other trudged north through the Judean desert. The first was
Jesus, just come from Nazareth to open the final stage of His life
on earth; the other was John, the son of Zachary and Elizabeth,
following the word of God which "came to him in the desert."
God the Father had called them both, each to a special mission in
His Plan for the salvation of men.

Section 1. THE NEW TESTAMENT
MEETS THE OLD

I. THE LAST OF THE PROPHETS

It is very possible that John came from the Essene monastery,
home of the famous "Dead Sea Scrolls," just to the northwest of
the Dead Sea's sunken waters; or perhaps he had lived a hermit's
life in one of the many caves which dot the area. His shaggy appearance in leather garments and cloak of camel's hair would not startle
the crowds at the ford too much; the traders had traveled the world
and grown used to strange people, even religious zealots, who were
common enough in Juda. But they were startled by John's message;
it stung them deeply, particularly those of Jewish faith:

"Repent, for the kingdom of heaven is at hand.

*". . . do not think to say within yourselves, 'We have Abraham
for our father'; for I say to you that God is able out of these
stones to raise up children to Abraham." (Mt. 3:2, 9)*

171

When John spoke, it was easy to see that he was a prophet. The listeners were spellbound at the wisdom of his words and the power of his message. Not for centuries had a real prophet's voice thundered through Israel. The souls of believing Jews hungered for spiritual food from another Elia. Or was this perhaps Elia himself come back to lead his people? (See John 1:21.) But to all John would only reply: "I am the voice of one crying in the desert, 'Make straight the way of the Lord.'" (John 1:23.) In the person of John the Baptist, who quoted the prophet Elia, therefore, **the Old Testament advanced to meet its Messiah.** John the Baptist is the last of the Old Testament prophets.

- READ Matthew 3:1-12 for a fuller picture of John the Baptist in action.

A. **John Meets Jesus**

One day a lone figure mixed in with the crowd awaiting John's baptism of repentance. He blended into the scene easily with His long-sleeved linen garment, woolen cloak, and head-covering to shade the hot Judean sun. Nevertheless, John recognized the Christ, whether from a previous meeting or special revelation. At Jesus' turn to enter the waters, these two men of destiny met face to face.

- READ the brief exchange of words between Jesus and John in Matthew's account, 3:13-15.

B. **Jesus Is Baptized**

Purification through the symbol of water was not something original with John. All the Essenes stressed ceremonial washings, and even pagan religions had seen in water the natural symbolism of a life-giving power and a force destructive of evil. But that the Son of God, the source of all life and the sinless one, should submit to John's rite of repentance, that is the extraordinary thing about Jesus' baptism. Two reasons stand out:

1. To pledge Himself again to His Father's Will, to His own Messianic mission.

2. To lay the groundwork for His own kind of baptism, which will be a true sacrament.

- JOHN's baptism is "a type" of the baptism instituted by Christ. Explain how. What are the big differences?

The River Jordan, the place of the Baptism of Christ by John the Baptist. THE MATSON PHOTO SERVICE

II. THE HOLY TRINITY

When Jesus had stepped out of the shallow water, He became conscious of an extraordinary experience, probably perceived by John the Baptist, as well. (See John 1:32) The Holy Spirit descended upon Jesus and the voice of God the Father shattered the stillness:

"This is my beloved Son, in whom I am well pleased." (Mt. 3:17)

- READ Matthew 3:16-17, and note it well for the revelation it gives us of the Holy Trinity.

A. The Revelation

Up to the time of Christ's coming, no Jew of the Old Testament could even have suspected the depths of the mystery presented in this dramatic scene at the Jordan: **The one, true God is three Persons, each equally God.**

- WHY do you think our Lord moved slowly and patiently in revealing the Trinity to His apostles and disciples?

B. The Plan of the Holy Trinity

Besides the revelation of the Holy Trinity itself, the scene at the Jordan has further significance. It pictures for us the three Persons of the Trinity giving approval and assent to the Plan of Salvation worked out from all eternity: **through redemption by the God-man, Jesus Christ, man was to be welcomed back into the inner circle of the Trinitarian Family.**

The first Adam through sin had thrown away the special gifts by which he and his descendants were meant to share God's life and power. The loss separated the entire human race from God. Jesus Christ, the second Adam, was to bring men back to God by joining them to His own mystical body. Once again God's life of sanctifying grace was to flow in men's souls; once again they were to be members of God's Family, the Family of the Holy Trinity.

- READ St. Paul's explanation of Christ's mission in his letter to the Romans 5:17-19.

- TRACE OUT from some book a good picture of the Jordan scene on the occasion of Christ's baptism. On another page sketch a similar scene with a baptismal font replacing the river, and a child being baptized instead of Christ Himself. In a paragraph or two explain the connections between the two scenes and their parallel religious meaning.

III. FOR AND AGAINST GOD'S PLAN

God's magnificent Plan for men naturally brought violent opposition from the forces of evil. From the beginning, Satan had leaped into combat. Under the guise of the serpent he had tricked Adam and Eve; he gloated near the altar of the golden calf, and must have played a major role in the corruption of the two kingdoms, Israel and Juda. Just as the prophets of old, this newcomer at the Jordan posed a serious threat. Although Christ's Plan was just beginning to unfold, Satan was alert and ready early in the Public Life; the two were to meet in spiritual combat, much like two warriors studying each other for the fight to the death, but the outcome was never in doubt.

A. Christ in the Desert

Refreshed by the support He received at the Jordan from the Father and the Holy Spirit, and pledged wholeheartedly to His

Messianic mission, Jesus might have been expected to go forth over the world in a sudden burst of activity. He surprised us. Instead of launching His mission with fanfare, He retired to a desert nearby for forty days. He chose to think things out for a while and, alone with the Father and the Spirit, He spent His time in prayer and penance. True, because of His divine nature Jesus did not need long reflection to form His plans, nor did He need to pray for His Father's support; and least of all would He need to do penance in order to train His body to serve God's purposes. And yet, all these things He did. Why? **Christ deliberately chose to experience what we would experience; He wanted to be like us in all things except sin.**

- IN ORDER to follow our Lord's lead, the liturgy calls us to a forty-day training period which we call Lent. Why do we need times like this for prayers, penance, and serious thought? Is there any parallel in the life of a soldier? of an athlete?

B. Enter Satan

The prince of evil had been keeping a careful watch over this carpenter from Nazareth. Satan was alert to goodness as well as evil; goodness was a constant threat. Who knew what harm this Nazarene might do? But was He the Messiah? The question tormented Satan's angelic mind, especially since the puzzling reception by that other troublemaker, John the Baptist. He had better find out. The prince of evil thought he knew how he might do it.

- READ the account of the temptations by Satan in Matthew 4:1-11. Because of the different ways of writing in those days, it is difficult to tell exactly how these temptations took place; perhaps they were all spiritual experiences of Christ, not physical at all.

C. The Battle Is Joined

And that was how the combat between the two leaders broke out into the open. Note that each of the temptations was fitted to the misguided Messianic ambitions of the Jewish people. "Give the people what they want," Satan argued. They wanted material comforts; they wanted eye-catching signs of power; they wanted to rule the world. If Christ would cooperate with him, he, Satan, "prince of the world," would help Jesus find shortcuts to this false kind of Messianic success.

Despite His weakened physical condition, Jesus replied swiftly and sharply. Satan was beaten back for a time, but, as it were, limped off; he had lost a skirmish, not the war. Now he knew the strength of his foe. He determined to plan his next attack more carefully still.

- IS THE devil a strong adversary for us in temptation? As an archangel, what special powers does he have? Where does our own strength lie? Listen to St. Paul's answer in his letter to the Ephesians 6:10-17.

The struggle between Satan and Christ will continue to the day of Christ's final triumph on Judgment Day. Every man must choose his own side. He may, with his freedom, choose to serve beneath Satan's flag, to his own damnation. Christians rally round the standard of Christ the King. In this choice lies the whole meaning of life.

- SEE how St. Ignatius Loyola in his Spiritual Exercises pictures the clash of Christ and Satan under their "Two Standards."

IV. MEETING THE FIRST APOSTLES

After His sojourn in the desert, Jesus returned to the Jordan one day. John the Baptist spied Him. For the benefit of his disciples, John pointed toward the approaching figure of Christ and startled them with the words:

"Behold the lamb of God, who takes away the sin of the world!" (John 1:29)

- READ John the Evangelist's account of this big day in his life in John 1:35-49. The evangelist was one of the Baptist's disciples who found Christ that day. Who were the others?

John the Baptist stood there watching his dearest friends and disciples, John and Andrew, approach Jesus, speak a word with Him, and then go off at Christ's side. He had accomplished his mission. "The one mightier than I is coming, the strap of whose sandals I am not worthy to loose." (Luke 3:16) Thus in the person of John the Baptist the Old Testament gave way to the New. In the person of Jesus the New Testament was launched; "the kingdom of God is at hand." Laying the groundwork for this Kingdom will hold our attention in the next chapter.

Section 2. THE HOLY SPIRIT SPEAKS THROUGH THE CHURCH

Through the first few centuries of the Church's life, Christians everywhere gladly gave worship to the three Persons of the Blessed Trinity, the Father, the Son, and the Holy Spirit. They directed their prayer **to the Father, through the Son, in the Holy Spirit.** Since Christ was their brother, what could be more natural than to pray to their common Father? "Our Father, who art in heaven" really held meaning for them.

Of course, at the same time those early Christians never doubted that there could be only one true God, "the God of Abraham, Isaac, and Jacob." Remember, many of them were Jews themselves, who never could have tolerated any other idea; only pagans worshiped more than one God. But did not those early Christians see something mysterious here? Certainly they did, and they marveled at the wonder of God, but they were not surprised that the secret of God's inner life should be beyond the power of their poor minds to understand. There were many things much simpler which they could not understand: What makes the grass green? Why doesn't the sun fall? But there was a better reason still for accepting the Trinity: Had not their Lord, the Son of God Himself, revealed the secret to them?

In the third and fourth centuries, however, some erroneous ideas challenged the wonderful faith of the Christian community. The Church reacted strongly. In a series of councils beginning with Nicea in 325 A.D., the assembled bishops solemnly reaffirmed and carefully defined the dogma of the Holy Trinity:

1. There is only one God.
2. There are three Persons in God, **each distinct and equal.**

In this way the three main heresies of that day were condemned:

I. That which denied the unity of the three Persons in one divine nature.

II. That which denied the distinction of the three Persons, each from the other two.

III. That which denied the equality of the three Persons.

The traditional dogma of the Church could be summed up by affirming only one "What," but three "Who's." The mystery of the three in one remains, but it remains precisely where it belongs, in the inner life of God Himself, which to our limited minds will always remain a mystery until God permits us to see Him as He is, "face to face." We must be grateful that by faith we now know all that we do about God.

- WHAT feast does the Church celebrate in her liturgy in honor of the Most Holy Trinity? When does it occur? How do we profess our faith in the Trinity in the simplest way of all?

SOME MEMORY HELPS:

1. The Trinity is the mystery of three Persons in one God, each distinct and equal.

2. A dogmatic mystery is a truth of revelation which is beyond the power of our human intellects to comprehend fully.

Section 3. A PERSONALITY PROFILE OF JOHN THE BAPTIST

The figure of John the Baptist towers over the first part of the Gospels. Try to know him as a real person because he combines the manly qualities which are the ideal of every Catholic youth:

A. Luke 1:13 and 66
The extraordinary circumstances of John's conception and birth pointed to a remarkable role in God's Plan.

B. Matthew 3:1 and 4
With a hidden life of his own, much like Christ's, John readied himself for his mission by the rugged existence of desert life.

C. John 1:22-23 and 3:30
John understood the limits of his mission; he heralded Christ's coming, then retired to the background.

D. Luke 3:16
A forceful picture of John's humility is given us here as he stood before his Lord and Messiah.

E. Matthew 3:7
But when faced with the enemies of Christ, John lashed out courageously in righteous anger.

F. John 1:32
The reward for his unshaken faith came in experiencing the presence of the Holy Trinity at the Jordan.

G. John 1:36 and Luke 7:20
The ultimate test of love and friendship is to sacrifice one's friends when it is for their good. John encouraged his disciples to leave him and follow Christ.

H. Matthew 11:7-11
Striking recognition of John's extraordinary character from the lips of Christ Himself.

I. Mark 6:20
Even John's enemies confessed admiration and respect for this extraordinary man.

J. Matthew 14:8-9
Nevertheless, John suffered death at Herod's order. The quiet resignation to God's Will was typical of the man's total dedication.

- LOOK UP the two big feast days of John the Baptist commemorating his birth and his death.

- TYPE or write out the brief texts listed above, and with the help of the little explanations given think out an appropriate title for each of the texts.

A SUMMARY

What precisely is "a manly character"? You could write books about manly qualities, but nothing is so convincing as the reality of a man before you. John the Baptist was this kind of a manly personality. There was nothing soft about him. He was strong of body and rugged of mind and will. Even his enemies respected him; his friends admired and loved him. And yet, instead of sending the Baptist out to convert the world with Christ, God sent John merely to announce Christ's coming, only to disappear from the scene as suddenly as he had arrived. With the strength and determination which we envy in the real men we know, John saw his job and did it. He is the perfect model for total dedication to one's vocation in life; he held back nothing. He did what God wanted him to do.

- GIVE a brief character sketch of John the Baptist.

SUMMARY

The ford at the Jordan near Bethany was the scene of the meeting of John the Baptist and Jesus of Nazareth. In their persons the Old Testament advanced to meet the New. John baptized Jesus just as he did the others who had heard his message of repentance.

The Holy Trinity, Father and Son and Holy Spirit, were present at the baptism, a striking sign of approval for the Messianic mission: to redeem all men through the God-man.

Christ retired to the desert for forty days of prayer and fasting in order to ready Himself for His mission. Satan seized the opportunity to find out more about this carpenter from Nazareth and, if He should be the Messiah, to induce Him to fit His mission to the material and political ambitions of so many Jewish people in those times. Christ was firm, a superb model for us when under temptation. But the battle to the death with Satan had only begun.

At a later date John again recognized Jesus at the Jordan and pointed Him out to some of his own disciples. Of these, the evangelist John and the future apostle Andrew followed Jesus. Christ quietly launched His mission.

QUESTIONS

1. What is the deeper significance of John's meeting with Jesus at the Jordan?

2. Why did Christ submit to John's baptism of repentance?

3. What was Christ's role in the Trinity's Plan of Salvation?

4. Why did Christ spend forty days in the desert?

5. How did Satan try to upset the Trinity's Plan?

6. Was this the only time Satan tried to upset the Plan of Salvation for men?

7. How did the first apostles come to join Jesus?

8. Express the mystery of the Holy Trinity with greatest accuracy.

9. What was the attitude of the earliest Christians to the three Persons of the Blessed Trinity?

10. What happened to cause the early councils of the Church to be convened?

The Liturgy of Septuagesima

When the priest comes out on the altar wearing violet vestments, we know that something new is coming up in the liturgy. The joy of the Christmas-Epiphany season gives way to another kind of spirit, the spirit of Septuagesima.

Septuagesima is something like the break between halves of a big football game. The football players huddle around their coach. He points out the serious weaknesses on defense which gave the opposing team repeated opportunities to score. He gets the team to face its weaknesses squarely. There is no sense in the false confidence of a lot of excuses; a big and decisive half is coming up. But no good coach will send his players back on the field discouraged, conscious only of their failings. He fires them up, too, and he gives them a new strategy to tighten up their weak defenses. The coach wants the team to win as much as the players do.

In a very similar way the Church tries to do three things of capital importance during the season of Septuagesima:

1. Remind us of the important goals in our lives.

2. Show us our weaknesses from the past.

3. Give us the needed strategy for the future.

This is the way the Church works these three ideas into her Septuagesima Masses:

A. **The goals** are in the Gospels.

B. **The weaknesses** are in the Introits.

C. **The strategy** is in the Epistles.

A. The Gospels: the Goals

The goals of a man's life are tightly linked to his vocation. This was true of John the Baptist, just as it was of Christ Himself. God never ceases to call specially picked men for special tasks. He called Abraham, Moses, David, and the prophets we studied last

181

"Go you also into the vineyard . . ." MT. 20:4

term. Neither did He always call the best men available; the apostles were as unpromising a crew of fishermen and local townspeople as you could find. Yet through them Christ founded His Church.

God has not changed His methods very much over the centuries. He is still picking special men for special jobs, and they do not always seem the most talented men around either. His call goes out to members of our generation this year and every year in the liturgy of Septuagesima. Let's see how:

1. SEPTUAGESIMA SUNDAY

The "Vineyard" is the vast field where God's work must be done. The laborers are the men chosen especially by God for different tasks. Just as Christ had called His apostles, so He searches out picked men to work at His side in His Father's vineyard. He looks at them earnestly and says:

"Go you also into the vineyard . . . ." (Mt. 20:4)

2. SEXAGESIMA SUNDAY

Christ's invitation to work with Him in the vineyard gets different kinds of reception. Some men respond at once enthusiastically, but others can't be bothered or don't want to be distracted from their own worldly ambitions:

". . . some seed fell by the wayside . . . And other seed fell upon the rock . . . And other seed fell among thorns . . . And other seed fell upon good ground . . . ." (Luke 8:5-8)

3. QUINQUAGESIMA SUNDAY

Our Lord does not try to fool anybody. He tells men just what to expect if they work at His side in the vineyard. The real test of their loyalty will be met by willingness to go through what He goes through Himself:

"For he (the Son of Man) will be delivered to the Gentiles, and will be mocked and scourged and spit upon; and after they have scourged him, they will put him to death; and on the third day he will rise again." (Luke 18:33)

Christ accepted His vocation, though He knew that suffering would accompany it. Men who follow Christ must do no less, but He assures them that all will share His final triumph.

- IN THE LIGHT of the invitation extended in the Septuagesima Gospel and the lengths to which it leads in the Quinquagesima

Gospel, discuss how different men might respond. Use the Gospel of Sexagesima as a guide.

- WHAT types of men would receive "seed by the wayside," "seed upon rock," "seed among thorns," "seed upon good ground"?

B. The Introits: the Weaknesses

In the early days of the Church the Christians used to enter for Mass singing a special procession hymn. These songs are preserved for us in our Introit prayers. "Introit" means making an entrance. These songs set the mood for the Mass, whether one of joy or one of sadness, or some other dominant emotion. Here are some examples:

1. SEPTUAGESIMA SUNDAY

We cry for help in our own weakness beneath the burden of sin:

. . . the cords of the nether world enmeshed me, the snares of death overtook me. In my distress I called upon the Lord . . . . (Ps. 17:6-7)

2. SEXAGESIMA SUNDAY

It is all too easy to get attached to the material comforts of this life. In this Introit we plead for God's help to rise to higher things:

Why do you hide your face, forgetting our woe and our oppression? For our souls are bowed down to the dust, our bodies are pressed to the earth. (Ps. 43:25-26)

3. QUINQUAGESIMA SUNDAY

When oppressed by our sense of weakness and sin, we can take courage in God's assistance:

In you, O Lord, I take refuge: let me never be put to shame. In your justice rescue me, incline your ear to me, make haste to deliver me! (Ps. 30:2-3)

- READ the full Introits for these three Masses and list the themes you find there. Can you tie in some well-known prayer to each of these themes?

C. The Epistles: the Strategy

Facing up to our weaknesses honestly, we should plot our strategy to obtain our goals despite them. We must be strong enough to take the necessary steps. St. Paul leads the way:

1. SEPTUAGESIMA SUNDAY

Like athletes entered in a race to win a champion's crown, we must train and keep in top condition:

Do you not know that those who run in a race, all indeed run, but one receives the prize? So run as to obtain it . . . I, therefore, so run as not without a purpose; I so fight as not beating the air; but I chastize my body and bring it into subjection. . . . (1 Cor. 9:24-27)

2. SEXAGESIMA SUNDAY

The willingness to follow Christ anywhere in "the vineyard," even at the cost to himself of hardship and suffering, was the glory of St. Paul:

Thrice I was scourged, once I was stoned, thrice I suffered shipwreck, a night and a day I was adrift on the sea;

Gladly, therefore, I will glory in my infirmities, that the strength of Christ may dwell in me. (2 Cor. 11:25; 12:9)

3. QUINQUAGESIMA SUNDAY

Here is the secret of all strategy in God's service. Only charity, the love of God, feeds the right kind of power for apostolic activity such as St. Paul's:

If I should speak with the tongues of men and of angels, but do not have charity, I have become as sounding brass or a tinkling cymbal.

Charity never fails . . . . (1 Cor. 13:1, 8)

St. Paul strikingly affirms that charity made him a man in the fullest sense of the word. It takes manly courage to be a man of charity in the steps of St. Paul:

When I was a child, I spoke as a child, I felt as a child, I thought as a child. Now that I have become a man, I have put away the things of a child. (1 Cor. 13:11)

- WRITE a brief sketch of some saint's life, one who in your estimation also exemplifies the courage of following a vocation for the love of God. How about St. Francis Xavier, St. John Baptiste de la Salle, St. Isaac Jogues, St. Francis Xavier Cabrini, St. Theresa of the Child Jesus, and the courageous Dominic Savio?

CHAPTER XI

HERALDING GOOD NEWS: THE KINGDOM

Together with His new friends, our Lord set out from the Jordan on the next stage of His Redemptive Mission. He was God the Father's ambassador-extraordinary appointed to a task which no one else could accomplish. John the Baptist had spoken truly when he summed up the significance of Christ's arrival:

"... *the kingdom of heaven is at hand.*" *(Mt. 3:2)*

This was the "kingdom" for which the Hebrew people had waited so long and so anxiously. This was the fulfillment of the promise made to Abraham, the dawning of the "Day of Yahweh" foreshadowed in so many prophecies, the triumph of the long expected "Anointed One," the Messiah, who would bring salvation to suffering Israel. No wonder John's announcement was good news. That is why the inspired authors of the New Testament called Christ's message the **evangelium,** which is derived from the Greek word meaning "good news."

Three particular questions interest us in this chapter:

  I. What is meant by the Kingdom of God?

 II. How does one recognize the Kingdom of God?

III. In what ways does a Christian live the Kingdom of God?

Section 1. THE KINGDOM OF GOD

I. WHAT IS MEANT BY THE KINGDOM OF GOD?

The first thing that usually comes to mind when we hear the word kingdom is some place over which a king or a queen rules, like the kingdom of Britain or the kingdom of Belgium. But that is not what the Scriptures normally mean by the idea. The biblical theme of the Kingdom rooted deeply in Hebrew traditions did not connote a place so much as a situation. For a Jew the Kingdom meant a very ideal situation, one in which **Yahweh would manifest His power and exercise His kingship and rule with full authority.**

What the coming of the Kingdom really meant for the Hebrews was the dawn of the day for which they had hoped and prayed, the "Day of Yahweh" which we noted earlier in connection with the prophets. On that day of Yahweh's triumph all the petty kingdoms of the world would fall beneath God's might and power. Israel's ancient enemies would topple and perish: the Egyptians, the Assyrians, the Babylonians, the Persians, the Greeks, and of course the formidable antagonists of Christ's day, the Romans. Then the Hebrew nation, the People of God, would know its day of glory, a glory surpassing that of David's prosperous age. This Kingdom of God was, therefore, the great Jewish dream for the future. The Messiah, "the anointed one," would fulfill these hopes and prayers; He would lead his people into a new era of political and economic, as well as religious prosperity.

The Christian understanding of the Kingdom, on the other hand, as transmitted to us through the Gospels, is different and still more remarkable. The Christ, Lord and King, has already come. As John the Baptist proclaimed when he saw Jesus at the Jordan, "the Kingdom of heaven is at hand". (Mt. 3:2). God's Plan has begun its final stage with the presence among men of God's Son.

In a few of Christ's parables, like that of the mustard seed (see Mt. 13:31-32), it is clear that God intended the Kingdom to grow. Christ's triumph at the end of time will bring the final harvest, but at each stage of the growth God will give more and more of Himself as He is present in the sharing of sanctifying grace. This ever deepening union with God is the heart of the Kingdom. Few men saw the privileged status of those who live the Kingdom more clearly than did St. Paul:

> *For this reason I bend my knees to the Father of our Lord Jesus Christ, from whom all fatherhood in heaven and on earth receives its name, that he may grant you from his glorious riches . . .* **to have Christ dwelling through faith in your hearts:** *so that, being rooted and grounded in love, you may be able to comprehend with all the saints what is the breadth and length and height and depth, and to know Christ's love which surpasses*

knowledge, in order that you may be filled unto all the fullness of God. (Eph. 3:14-19)

St. Paul, of course, was already filled with the spirit of the Resurrection when he wrote. The Hebrews of the Old Testament would have little suspected the true grandeur of God's designs for the Kingdom. Dazzled as they were with visions of earthly prosperity, they would never have sought nor even suspected as possible the privilege to join God's family, to serve Him as adopted sons and to share His Kingdom as heirs for eternity. It was Christ's mission to tell them about God's most extraordinary Plan. If they listened to Him, He would bring them the first of the Kingdom's gifts and He would help these gifts grow to their fuller maturity.

II. HOW DOES ONE RECOGNIZE THE KINGDOM OF GOD?

In retrospect it is very easy for us to see how false some of the Jewish notions were about the Kingdom. It is true that the Hebrews of Christ's time were slow to learn, but perhaps we can be more understanding toward their failure now that we know of the misguided notions and false interpretations of Sacred Scripture which were continually fed to the ordinary man-in-the-street by their leaders. Who can say how much of the true nature of the Kingdom even the apostles truly understood after being instructed by the greatest of teachers, Christ Himself?

- ON THIS same point do you remember the question the apostles asked our Lord even *after* His resurrection from the dead? Look up Acts 1:6 and judge for yourselves whether they understood very much about the Kingdom.

From our present vantage point as we look back, we can see that the Kingdom of God is set apart by certain characteristics:

A. **Unity in the Kingdom**

While preaching along the shores of Lake Genesareth one day, our Lord was so pressed by the crowds that He asked His friend Peter if He might use his fishing boat for a pulpit. Peter rowed a few strokes away from the shore and Jesus preached from there, projecting His magnificent voice out toward the hills which rose from the lake. After the talk Peter was rewarded with the miraculous

catch of fish from the very waters where he had labored without
success the night before.

The point which interests us the most here is the remark our
Lord made in answer to Peter's astonishment at the miracle: "Hence-
forth, thou shalt catch men." Our Lord's sudden turn from fish to
men starts one of the Church's oldest traditions, the custom of
looking upon Peter's fishing bark as an image of Christ's Church.
The picture brings out the unity of all men who live the Kingdom
within Christ's Church with Peter at its head. It is only in this one
boat that men can be saved, the boat of the Church. Do you see why
the reigning Holy Father wears a fisherman's ring?

- READ the full account of the miraculous catch of fish in Luke
  5:1-11. Compare this account with the parable of the fishing
  net in Matthew 13:47-50 and show what new point is brought
  out by the parable.

- READ also the parable in John 10:6-18, especially v. 17, and
  discuss what special pertinence these parables on Church unity
  have for our modern times. What is the Ecumenical Movement
  among Christian Churches today? Do you think that God intended that the Jewish people should be included?

CONCLUSION

Christians form but one family, the family of the children of
God. Christians belong to one kingdom, the Kingdom of Christ the
King. Christians must belong to but one church, the Church of
Christ's mystical body.

B. Holiness in the Kingdom

1. THE SERMON ON THE MOUNT

Crowds followed Jesus just about wherever He went. One day
on a plateau somewhat removed from the lakeside in Galilee, Christ
chose to address the crowds and give them a fuller picture of what
was expected of them in God's Kingdom. This is the stirring
Sermon on the Mount.

In view of the worldly traditions of national power and prosperity
which were current among many of the Jews, imagine their shock
to hear Christ tell the listeners who had flocked to hear Him:

*"Blessed are the poor in spirit . . . Blessed are they who suffer
persecution for justice's sake . . . Blessed are you when men*

reproach you, and persecute you, and, speaking falsely, say all manner of evil against you, for my sake." (Mt. 5:3, 10-11)

"Poor in spirit"? What future could there be in the deadening poverty known in Israel since immediately after Solomon's time? "Suffer persecution"? Had not Israel suffered enough?

As is clear, this was not a popular message our Lord was proclaiming to the Hebrew multitudes.

- READ chapters 5-7 in St. Matthew's Gospel slowly and reflectively, and in several sittings. In all probability, our Lord did not say all of this in one talk. The sacred author edited a collection of Jesus' ideas gathered from many different talks. Some things Jesus said can be understood properly only in their Hebrew context.

Clearly, the Kingdom was not for people looking for an easy way to a this-world contentment and prosperity. The Kingdom was and is still a challenge for men and women of strong purpose. They are called to be "the salt of the earth," bringing the flavor of Christ-like lives to their own little worlds, and living thus not so as to win favor and reputation among their fellow men, **but for love of their Father,** "who sees in secret." They are to "love their enemies, do good to those who hate them," just the way God Himself loves all men and "makes his sun to rise on the good and the evil, and sends rain on the just and the unjust." This is the kind of **holiness in practice** which marks off the citizens of the Kingdom of God on earth. Who but real men, men of courage and determination, could live such a high ideal? But that is precisely what our Lord called for: men of courage, even of heroism. No wonder He was so pleased with the manly personality of John the Baptist. Listen to what He said to the crowds about John, the man who went all out in living the Kingdom:

> *"What did you go out to the desert to see? A reed shaken by the wind? But what did you go out to see? A man clothed in soft garments? Behold, those who wear soft garments are in the houses of kings. But what did you go out to see? A prophet? Yes, I tell you, and more than a prophet . . . Amen I say to you, among those born of women **there has not been a greater than John the Baptist.** . . . ." (Mt. 11:7-11)*

But our Lord did not only list the exacting demands upon those who wished sincerely to follow Him. He knew that his Jewish listeners were shocked and disappointed because they concluded that this new Kingdom which He proposed shattered all their dreams for a rosy future. So He went on to assure them that their future in the new Kingdom would be rosier than they dreamed:

> *"Do not lay up for yourselves treasures on earth, where rust and moth consume, and where thieves break in and steal: but lay up for yourselves treasures in heaven, where neither rust nor moth consumes, nor thieves break in and steal." (Mt. 6:19-20)*

> *"But seek first the kingdom of God and His justice, and all these things shall be given to you besides." (Mt. 6:33)*

2. HOLINESS AS UNION WITH GOD

The Sermon on the Mount teaches most beautifully what holiness in practice should be. But the practice of holiness is not the essence or the deepest meaning of holiness. Even an irreligious person can love his neighbor. Philanthropists may give generously of their wealth, doctors and teachers may dedicate their lives to health of body and mind, and yet God may never have entered their motivation. **True holiness is union with God through God's grace.** Unless good deeds for one's fellow men flow from hearts at one with God in love and grace, they fail to measure up to the standards of holiness in the Kingdom of God.

- READ John 17:20-23 and explain the deeper meaning of holiness in the words of the text. What is the connection between this deeper holiness and the practice of good deeds and good life on the part of parents, teachers, doctors and other people of true dedication? Could you say that the two aspects of holiness nourish one another? How? Explain.

CONCLUSION

Sincere Christians make Christ's Sermon on the Mount, when correctly understood, the blueprint of their lives. When practice of such ideals is founded on life-sharing union with God and membership in God's family, we see true holiness.

The Commandments guide men in their quest of Christ's ideals. Holiness would be a sham without careful observance of their guidelines.

> *"If you love me, keep my commandments." (John 14:15)*

C. Universality of the Kingdom

Our Lord spoke in parables so that the simple and uneducated people might better understand the truths of the Kingdom. One day He told of a great supper to which many guests had been invited. When a good number made excuses for not attending, the master sent his servants out into the streets to invite anybody and everybody willing to come in so that his house might be filled with guests.

To Jewish ears talk about mixing with strangers like this, with Gentiles and "the unclean," was the equivalent of denying their Jewish faith. The Pharisees in particular reacted sharply to Christ's clear suggestion that **all peoples would be welcome in the Kingdom of God.** They had refused to accept the warning of John the Baptist:

> "... and do not think to say within yourselves, 'We have Abraham for our father'; for I say to you that God is able out of these stones to raise up children to Abraham." (Mt. 3:9)

- READ this parable of the "great supper" as recorded in Luke 14:15-24. Do you see any relevance and significance here for problems in modern times? For the problem of race relations? International cooperation? Interfaith understanding?

CONCLUSION

God intended His Kingdom for all men of all time.

D. A Kingdom by Choice, Not Force

Once while spreading Christ's Gospel on a missionary journey, some of the disciples were treated roughly by Samaritan townspeople. The apostles James and John became indignant and were all for bringing immediate punishment down upon the heads of the culprits:

> "Lord, will thou that we bid fire come down from heaven and consume them?" (Luke 9:54)

Jesus calmed them down and taught them a much-needed lesson in missionary patience: No one can be forced to accept the Christian message. The Kingdom, **as a free gift, must be freely accepted.** Perhaps the missionaries may be able to reach the hearts of these stubborn Samaritans some other time:

> "... for the Son of Man did not come to destroy men's lives, but to save them." (Luke 9:56)

- READ the full account of the incident in Luke 9:51-56. What was behind all this ill feeling between the Jews and the Samaritans? Refer back to the fall of the northern kingdom of Israel in 721 B.C. for the answer. What are your views about this kind of prejudice? Are there any such prejudices evident in America today? Discuss.

CONCLUSION

God's invitation to the Kingdom is a free gift which must be freely accepted.

E. A Kingdom Looking Beyond This World

When face to face with Pontius Pilate, you would think that our Lord looked like anything but a king. His face was bruised and His hands were tied. But Pilate had heard Jesus spoken of as a king and he was impressed with Christ's royal bearing. And so he asked Christ pointblank: "Art thou the king of the Jews?" Christ's answer gives us one more insight into God's Kingdom:

> *"If my kingdom were of this world, my followers would have fought that I might not be delivered to the Jews. But, as it is, my kingdom is not from here." (John 18:36)*

- READ the rest of this revealing conversation between the Roman politician and the Lord of History, as recorded in John 18.

In earlier preaching our Lord had left no doubt about the meaning of this life as the preparation and proving ground for the life that is to come, life in the Kingdom of God of the future. And yet at the same time He never stopped emphasizing that the Kingdom was already at hand because of His presence among them.

- READ the parable of the servants waiting for their master, as recorded in Luke 12:35-41; also of the virgins with their oil lamps as they watched hour after hour for the coming of the bridegroom and his bride, as recorded in Matthew 25:1-13.

But the Jews had not understood at all. At the time of the multiplication of the loaves and fishes, Christ had to flee to the mountains lest they try to make Him a king, the kind of this-world king they wanted more than anything else. At long last they had found someone powerful enough to lead them against the Roman tyrants.

> *"This is indeed the Prophet who is to come into the world." (John 6:14)*

• DOES anyone recall the Old Testament foreshadowings of this reference to the Prophet who is to come? Check back to Deuteronomy 18:15-18 and look ahead to Acts 3:22.

But no king's crown of gold and diamonds was destined for the savior of mankind. In fulfillment of His Redemptive Mission, Christ would only accept a crown of thorns. As He explained to Pilate:

"This is why I was born, and why I have come into the world, to bear witness to the truth." (John 18:37)

CONCLUSION
Christ intends the Kingdom to begin and to grow in men's hearts through sanctifying grace, but Christ will take final and complete possession of His Kingdom only in the glory of the last day.

III. HOW DOES A CHRISTIAN LIVE THE KINGDOM OF GOD?
Now that we have a fair idea of what Christ meant by the Kingdom of God and how men can recognize it, the logical and very practical question arises, "How does one live it?"

Since the Kingdom which Christ preached took on the aspects of a **new** kind of kingdom, we should not be surprised to find **a new law** for life in the Kingdom:

A. The Law of Love
At the Last Supper the night before He died, Jesus opened His heart to His apostles. Knowing full well that this would be the last time He would talk to them before His death, the things He told them took on a certain urgency. The Law of the Kingdom figured most prominently in His thoughts and words that night:

"A new commandment I give you, that you love one another; that as I have loved you, you also love one another. By this will all men know that you are my disciples, if you have love for one another." (John 13:34-35)

The New Law of Love should not have been a complete surprise to the apostles. Christ had spoken of it before:

• READ the parable of the Good Samaritan in Luke 10:30-37. Discuss how this New Law of Love exemplified in the parable goes *beyond* the law of love taught by Moses in Deuteronomy

6:5 and Leviticus 19:18. Both of these passages so far as they go are quoted approvingly by Christ in Luke 10:27 as the motivating force which inspires both the Mosaic and the New Covenants. Note the words "as I have loved you" as a hint to help find the something extra in the New Law.

The apostles were amazed at the lengths to which such a love in imitation of their Master would lead. Here are two of the startling things they heard from our Lord, even though at the time they may not have completely grasped their significance:

1. WHEN PETER once wanted to know how often he should forgive those who wronged him, our Lord showed him a new dimension to the notion of forgiveness.

- READ Matthew 18:21-35.

2. FOR JEWS who were brought up upon the Law of Talion, "an eye for an eye, a tooth for a tooth," the Sermon on the Mount commanded a change of attitudes toward enemies.

- READ Matthew 5:43-48.

The New Law of Love is not, therefore, to be confused with natural affection for relatives or the easy kind of charity in behalf of those one likes particularly. Rather the New Law demands that Christians love everyone **as God Himself loves all men and because God loves them.**

- COULD it be possible to *feel* a friendliness and affection toward relatives and a few close friends, and still not have the charity of Christ's New Law? Discuss your answers.

- COULD it be possible to have the charity of Christ's New Law and still not *feel* the affection and friendliness toward some people we know and the many we don't know? Discuss.

- CARRY your discussion over into the pressing social problems of our times: racial tensions, religious differences, international disputes, labor-management relations. In what way should this New Law of Love exercise its impact upon your school? Upon your family life? Within your parish?

CONCLUSION

A Christian follows the New Law of Love when he loves God above all things, and loves his neighbor just as God Himself loves them **and because** God loves them. All men will be judged according to the New Law of Love.

- READ Matthew 25:31-46 for a preview of our own Judgment Day according to the Law of Love.

B. The Counsels in the Gospels

Our Lord never deceived people into thinking that life according to the Kingdom's Law of Love was easy. The Kingdom's standards are high, and the obstacles resulting from man's fallen human nature are often difficult to surmount. Here are three people, each of whom heard the call of the Kingdom from the lips of Christ Himself; each failed to respond. The first two stayed paralyzed by their sins; the third rejected, possibly without any sin at all, the highest of vocations, the call to the priesthood. First note the particular obstacle in the way of each, and then the counsel of Christ which could have swept the obstacle away if heeded in time:

1. KING HEROD ANTIPAS, chained by the pleasures of the flesh.

- READ Luke 9:7-9 and Matthew 14:3-12.

BUT our Lord had said:

*"If anyone wishes to come after me, **let him deny himself, and take up his cross, and follow me** . . . for what does it profit a man, if he gain the whole world, but suffer the loss of his own soul?" (Mark 8:34-36)*

2. CAIPHAS THE HIGH PRIEST, drugged by pride and power.

- READ John 11:45-53 and Matthew 2:62-68.

BUT our Lord had said:

*"Amen I say to you, whoever does not accept the kingdom of God **as a little child** will not enter into it." (Mark 10:15)*

3. THE RICH YOUNG MAN, weighed down by the spirit of riches.

- READ Matthew 19:16-26.

BUT our Lord had said:

"If thou wilt be perfect, go, sell what thou hast, and give to the poor, and thou shalt have treasure in heaven; and come, follow me." (Mt. 19:21)

P. Joubert

The attraction of pleasure, power, and riches is strong in every man. Look what uncontrolled tendencies like these did to Herod and Caiphas, and what a wonderful opportunity was lost for the rich young man who might have become an apostle. That is why our Lord, in order to protect us from sin and dispose us for higher things, planned a new way of life called "the life of the counsels." This is an invitation, not a command, but any man who follows the way of poverty of spirit, self-denial, and humble submission to God's Will has a far better chance of sweeping away the obstacles to the full living of Christ's Law of Love. This is the way of life our Lord Himself chose. Christ, therefore, urges **all men,** according to their individual vocations in life, whether clergy or lay people, to strive for the perfection of this "life of the counsels."

"You, therefore, are to be perfect, even as your heavenly Father is perfect." (Mt. 5:48)

- DO YOU think it possible for a millionaire to follow "the life of the counsels"? Discuss.

Within the varied life of the Church today, there are men and women who dedicate themselves by profession to special efforts in living up to the standards of the Kingdom. They do so by "the life of the counsels." These priests, brothers, and nuns bind themselves by vow to these counsels of poverty, chastity, and obedience as encouraged by Christ in the Gospels. They are called "religious."

- ELECT a few members of the class to search out the facts concerning the foundation of the best known religious orders of men and women.

CONCLUSION

Christ in the Gospels offered to all men a way of life called "the counsels." Thus they would better surmount the obstacles to a fuller living of the Kingdom.

C. Strength from Prayer

The high ideals of the Kingdom can sometimes leave men discouraged. Christians are rightly conscious of their weaknesses. If success depended upon themselves, there is no doubt that they would fail miserably in their efforts to live up to Christ's ideals. But the happy fact is that no one is asked to work alone; Christ is with him every inch of the way. A Christian makes this contact with his Lord **through prayer and the sacraments.** Here are four unlikely candidates for the Kingdom who made the contact that changed their lives:

Before	*After*
St. Peter	
Peter was selfish. Read Mt. 19:27.	Peter was repentant. Read Mt. 26:75.
Peter was proud. Read Mt. 26:33.	Peter loved much. Read John 21:15-17.
Peter was cowardly. Read Mt. 26:56.	Peter preached fearlessly. Read Acts 4:8-14.
Peter was disloyal. Read Mt. 26:69-75.	
St. Mary Magdalene	
Mary led an evil life. Read Luke 8:2.	Mary braved the crowds at the cross. Read John 19:25.
	Mary spread word of the Resurrection. Read John 20:18.
Nicodemus	
Nicodemus was fearful. Read John 3:1-2.	Nicodemus openly professed his faith. Read John 19:39.
St. Paul	
Saul persecuted the Church. Read Acts 9:1.	Paul was converted and set about converting the world. Read Acts 9:4-7.

In each of these cases it was a contact with our Lord and His grace which brought about a total change in these weak human beings. This contact which is possible to all men, normally **begins in prayer,** whether one's own prayer or another's in one's behalf. Man's prayer should be:

1. HUMBLE
● READ of the contrasting kinds of prayer in the story of the Pharisee and the Publican. Luke 18:9-14.

2. PERSEVERING
● READ of the persistent favor-seeker in Luke 11:5-10.

3. CONFIDENT
● READ of the centurion's confidence in Luke 7:1-10.
Let each member of the class select a saint of his own choice, and write a brief biography to bring out the way each saint reformed his life after some contact with Christ.

But how should man go about communications? Surely the best communication of all is through the Mass and sacramental life, but what about other forms of prayer? How should we pray?

D. Different Ways to Pray

We could read books and books about prayer and never learn to pray. One learns to walk by walking; one learns to pray by praying. Nevertheless, there are a few things that we should remember regarding the theory of prayer.

First of all, it should be noted that just as there are different kinds of communication in our everyday life, there are different ways to communicate with God by prayer, too. In our correspondence we might send a telegram, short and to the point; or we might choose a form letter, not at all personal, but adequate for conveying the ideas we intend; or we might write a personal letter, or better still phone our friend and thus share the pleasure of a voice to voice encounter.

In a somewhat similar manner our communication with God in prayer can take different forms, too:

1. WE CAN TALK WITH GOD IN SET WORDS
Sometimes a set prayer like the Our Father or the Hail Mary or even a terse ejaculation may suit the spirit or need of the moment. This is particularly true when under stress we are at a loss for words or when we seek to blend our prayerful spirit with others. Remember how Christ in His agony on the cross recited Psalm 21, and how at the Last Supper He prayed the traditional psalms of Passover with the apostles?

2. WE CAN TALK WITH GOD IN OUR OWN WORDS

This may well be the most effective kind of private prayer in that it rises freely and spontaneously from our hearts. Remember how Christ conversed with His Father in the Garden of Olives?

3. WE CAN TALK WITH GOD WITHOUT ANY WORDS AT ALL

This may seem a contradiction at first, but a little reflection will show how sincere an act of worship a genuflection could be, or how eloquently one could speak to God just kneeling quietly in His presence.

4. WE CAN THINK ABOUT GOD, ABOUT OUR LORD ON EARTH AND ABOUT THE INSPIRING TRUTHS OF OUR FAITH

This is the kind of prayer called "meditation," a helpful way to keep contact with God, thus inspiring a heartfelt response of love, gratitude, worship, and sorrow for sin.

But let us not forget:

5. WE MUST ALSO LISTEN TO GOD

In conversation with friends no one likes constant chatter. God must wonder sometimes why we talk so much and listen so little. God speaks to us in the quiet of our hearts; we must keep still at times to hear Him. Or God may speak to us through a slow, thoughtful reading of His sacred Word from Scripture or of the prayers, hymns, and readings in the liturgy of the Mass and the sacraments.

- IS IT possible that some of our prayer may employ combinations of these forms of communication listed above? Discuss some possibilities. At Mass? At benediction of the Blessed Sacrament or a Holy Hour? For the Stations of the Cross? For the rosary?

Section 2. THE APOSTLES

I. MISSION OF THE APOSTLES

In His few years of preaching, Christ had fulfilled His mission from the Father to bring to men "the good news" of their redemption. When the time came to return to His Father by His ascension into heaven, the mission to spread "the good news" of the Gospel fell to the apostles. "Apostle" means "one who is sent," and that is precisely what happened. Christ sent them out into the whole world:

"Go, therefore, and make disciples of all nations, baptizing them in the name of the Father, and of the Son, and of the Holy Spirit, teaching them to observe all that I have commanded you; and behold, I am with you all days, even to the consummation of the world." (Mt. 28:17-20)

• CAN the word "apostle" ever be applied to a layman? In what sense? Give some examples. In what areas of life in America today do you think there is real need for lay apostles? Discuss.

It is interesting to follow the long training period of the twelve, though only eleven persevered to the end. From uneducated, timid, and at times irresponsible fishermen and townspeople, Jesus had formed the first bishops of His Church.

". . . I have called you friends, because all things that I have heard from my Father I have made known to you." (John 15:15)

• FOLLOW the development of the apostles in these stages:

1. Their final calling:
READ Mark 3:13-19.

2. Their first missionary efforts.
READ Matthew 10:1-23.

3. Their darkest hour.
READ Matthew 26:50.

4. Their coming of age as fearless preachers.
READ Acts 2:1-14.

II. POWERS GIVEN TO THE APOSTLES

Christ had given the apostles many powers to help spread the Kingdom even during His own lifetime. (See again Matthew 10:1). However, if the apostles were to carry on the work of Christ as the first bishops of His Church, they required other essential powers:

A. The Power to Govern God's People, the people of the Kingdom on Earth

• READ the promise to appoint Peter the first Pope as recorded in Matthew 16:17-19. Also, the right to exercise this power as often as needed, explained in Matthew 18:17-18.

B. The Power to Teach and Convert the Whole World

- READ in Matthew 28:19-20.

C. The Power to Sanctify by bringing the grace of God to men whereby they become sons of God, as recorded in the institution of the sacraments

- READ Luke 22:19-20, John 20:21-23 for the institution of the Eucharist and of the sacrament of penance.

These then are the principal powers which the apostles were to exercise in the youthful Christian Church, the community of the Kingdom, the people of God. Just before He ascended into heaven, our Lord once more made it clear to them that they were commissioned to use these powers throughout the world:

> ". . . *you shall receive power when the Holy Spirit comes upon you, and* **you shall be witnesses for me in Jerusalem and in** *all Judea and Samaria and* **even to the very ends of the earth."** *(Acts 1:8)*

- HOW does Christ's Church respond to the challenge of being witnesses to the ends of the earth in the world today? What role do lay people have, either directly or indirectly, in this apostolate of the mission? Do some research on the missions and find some examples of lay participation in this challenging work of the Mystical Body of Christ.

- SEE how St. Ignatius Loyola in his Spiritual Exercises highlights "the call of the King," as the invitation to spread the Christian message.

In the world today, the Church continues the mission of Jesus Christ. The Church is really **"Christ living on."** The Church governs, teaches, and sanctifies only through the life of Christ which is in her. And it is in this way that she lives and communicates the riches of the Kingdom. Along an unbroken line of bishops down from Peter's day to the present, Christ still works in the world in spreading His Kingdom, in bringing "the good news" of man's salvation to all who will listen. And such will be the mission of the Church until the end of time, the final stage of God's Plan, when the triumphant Christ will bring His Kingdom on earth into the glory of His eternal Kingdom in heaven.

SOME MEMORY HELPS:

1. **The Gospel or "Good News"** which Jesus announced was the coming of the Kingdom which all men are invited to share.

2. **The Kingdom for Hebrews** was the triumphant time in which Yahweh would manifest His royal power and rule the world with full authority.

3. **The Kingdom for Christians** is the God-given Plan present by which we join God's family even now and as children of God live and grow with the very life of God our Father.

4. **Membership in God's Family** is bestowed upon us through the "new birth," i.e., being born again through baptism to a new life in the People of God, the Church.

5. **The "New Birth"** effects a union with Jesus Christ that is most preeminently achieved in the Eucharist, i.e., our dying to sin and rising to glory with Christ in the Mass.

6. **The Law of the Kingdom** is the Law of Charity: God loved men first and men respond by loving God and loving their fellow men for God's sake.

SUMMARY

After the incidents at the Jordan, Jesus set out to preach the Kingdom. This was His mission from the Father. The Kingdom to the Jews meant God's complete triumph and the rise to power and prosperity of God's Chosen People, the Hebrews themselves.

Christ, however, startled the Jews by picturing the Kingdom in a different light. The Kingdom was to be unified, but universal, holy in the traditional sense of nearness to Yahweh, but calling for new and challenging ways of life which are called "the life of the counsels." There was only the one Kingdom of God, but it had to be accepted by man's free choice, not by force, and it looked beyond this life to the world to come. And supreme in the Kingdom was the New Law of Love. Strength to live this New Law of Love came from contact with Christ through prayer and the sacraments of His Church.

After the ascension, Christ left the task of spreading the Kingdom to His apostles. He gave them special powers: to govern, to teach, and to sanctify. These powers come down to our bishops today.

QUESTIONS

1. What is meant by the Kingdom of God in the Bible?

2. What did Christ add to the Jewish notion of the Kingdom of God?

3. Explain how Jesus used Peter's fishing boat and the miraculous catch of fish as images of the Church.

4. Enumerate some of the aspects of holiness which Christ developed in the Sermon on the Mount.

5. Though not developed in the Sermon on the Mount, what religious truth is the foundation of all holiness?

6. What lesson did our Lord teach the apostles after the mistreatment of some missionaries by Samaritan townspeople?

7. Did our Lord teach that the Kingdom was of this world or of the next or of both? Explain.

8. Distinguish the New Law of Love from the earlier Jewish ideas of love; also from a merely natural kind of human affection.

9. What two examples of the Law of Love startled the Jews, the apostles included?

10. What way of life did our Lord suggest in order the better to surmount obstacles to the Law of Charity?

11. What do you mean by the term "religious orders" in the life of the Church?

12. What encouragement is held out to men striving to live the high ideals of the Kingdom?

13. What are the qualities of effective prayer? Give an incident from the Gospels illustrating each of these qualities. What are some different ways to pray?

14. What were the four principal stages in the apostles' formation?

15. What were the special powers given to the apostles for their task of carrying on Christ's work and where is the transference of these powers recorded in the Gospels?

16. What precisely do you mean when you say that the Church is "Christ living on"?

LITURGY OF LENT

We compared Septuagesima to the half-time of a football game, a time for sizing up our strengths and weaknesses. Lent is the resumption of actual play, and the pace can be hard and heavy. Lent is a time of intense spiritual combat, but always looking forward to the final victory. Just as the slow grinding out of yardage reaches its victorious climax in a score, so the self-discipline and hard work of Lent are directed with confidence to the victorious climax of Easter. A touchdown gives meaning to the struggle for down-by-down yardage; only the Paschal Victory can light up the significance of Lent.

Three questions are of particular interest here:

I. What is this Paschal Victory?

II. By what means do men attain it?

III. How does Lent prepare for it?

I. THE PASCHAL VICTORY

The Pasch (or Passover) recalls for faithful Jews the deliverance from slavery in Egypt. The eating of the Paschal lamb and the sprinkling of its blood upon the Israelite door-posts figured prominently, as we saw in an earlier chapter, in the saving events of that night of nights. The angel of death "passed over" the homes marked with the blood of the lamb, but it slew the first-born of each Egyptian family. The miraculous passage through the Reed Sea would provide another dramatic proof of Yahweh's saving action in behalf of His people.

In Israel's passage from slavery to freedom the sacred authors of later eras in the History of Salvation would see a striking typology for more wonderful saving events still. For all time the Exodus would be a type of man's redemption. **Jesus Christ is the Paschal Lamb sacrificed for the sins of men.**

Christ, our passover, has been sacrificed. (1 Cor. 5:8)

It is this Christian Pasch that we celebrate and relive each year of our lives at Easter. We commemorate man's passage from slavery to freedom, really from death to life because of sin to a new life of glory as children of God.

At the heart of this Christian Pasch is the contact with Christ Himself. **Man meets his Lord personally** when through baptism he dies to sin and is resurrected to grace. Christ's presence begun in baptism reaches its supreme fulfillment in the Eucharist. To some this may sound too much to expect. Humanly speaking, it is too much to expect. And yet that is exactly what the saving action of God means.

How grateful we would have been to have shaken Christ's hand when He walked the earth, or by the custom of earlier times to have embraced Him as friend to friend. How much more has been given to us! Through the Paschal Mystery we are one with Christ, one in His death, resurrection, and ascension to glory. Even now we share His Paschal Victory, though only in part; when He comes again we shall share it in full.

Our paschal victory is our death to sin and new life in Christ. St. Paul reveals this Paschal Mystery:

> *Do you not know that all we who have been baptized into Christ Jesus have been baptized into his death? For we were buried with him by means of Baptism into death, in order that, just as Christ has arisen from the dead through the glory of the Father, so we also may walk in newness of life.* ***For if we have been united with him in the likeness of his death, we shall be so in the likeness of his resurrection also.*** *(Rom. 6:3-5)*

II.   THE MEANS TO VICTORY

In the early Church the new converts who had completed their preliminary instruction met Christ and shared His Paschal Victory for the first time on the night of the Easter vigil. At the height of the Paschal liturgy on Holy Saturday night the new converts were baptized. For the first time they shared the full life of Christ in His Church; with Christ as their brother they joined God's family. Then a little later that same night they were gifted with a special presence of the Holy Spirit through the sacrament of confirmation. Finally, to complete their share in the Paschal Victory, at least as far as such is possible in this life, the converts participated in their first Mass-sacrifice and received the Body and Blood of Christ in their first Holy Communion. This was indeed the big day in their lives. The only bigger day will be their own triumphant entrance into heaven according to the pattern of Christ's bodily resurrection and ascension into heaven. The life of grace now is a pledge of this total victory to come.

- LOOK back over the section covering the Advent liturgy. Does Advent's "triple coming of Christ" have any special pertinence here as well?

III. THE LENTEN PREPARATION

No victory is won without a combat. The Paschal Victory is no exception. Lent is an intensive effort of forty days' duration. It is a hard struggle to keep in spiritual training, but somehow the demanding routine of training for victory takes on some of the glow of the victory itself. Ask the halfback who has just scored his team's winning touchdown. How worthwhile the long practice and training program seem in that triumphant moment!

Here are some of Lent's main ideas. Because they keep repeating themselves all through the Lenten liturgy, we'll call them "themes":

A. **The Desert Theme**

When the Hebrews crossed the Reed Sea to escape the slavery of Egypt, they journeyed forty years **in the desert** before reaching the Promised Land. So a Christian by baptism becomes free, free of sin and the slavery to Satan which sin brings with it. But the inclination to sin remains, and so he too must struggle **across the desert** before he reaches the eternal Promised Land of heaven.

Our Lord deliberately chose **a desert** for his forty days of prayer and penance before setting out upon His Public Life. (See Matthew 4:1-2) Just like Moses, who was "a type" of our Lord (see Exodus 34:28), Jesus wanted to prepare Himself for the fulfillment of His mission by spending the days and nights in solitude close to His Father.

Lent serves the same purpose. It is **our sojourn in the desert.** Like Moses and Christ, we learn to contact God in prayer, and prepare ourselves to share God's life of grace now, even before we have entered God's Kingdom for good.

"Begone, Satan!" MT. 4:10

- PICK out some examples of this desert-theme in the Lenten liturgy and summarize them in a few well-chosen words.

- HERE are a few leads:
  the Gospel for the 1st Sunday of Lent,
  the Gospel for the 4th Sunday of Lent,
  the Epistle of Friday in 3rd week.

- CAN you find any others?

B. Baptism Theme

In the early centuries the Church used the forty days of Lent, as noted above, for the final intensive course of convert instructions. The entire Catholic community on the night of the Easter Vigil welcomed the converts into the family of God, and then in a most impressive way repeated their own baptismal vows.

We are not surprised, therefore, in view of these ancient customs that many references to baptism are found in the Lenten Masses. The readings are often taken from the Old Testament to show how God prepared the way for the sacrament itself by types and prefigurements of baptism, and then from the New Testament as well to bring out how these types and prefigurements were fulfilled.

- FIND and summarize in a few words some examples of the baptism theme in the Lenten Masses.

- HERE are a few leads:
  the Epistle for Monday in 3rd week,
  the two Epistles for Wednesday in 4th week,
  the Gospel for Friday in 3rd week,
  the Gospel for Wednesday in 4th week.

- CAN you find any others?

C. Penance Theme

Lent was also a special time for another group of early Christians, the publicly known sinners. For serious and public sins known to the Christian community, the public sinners were expelled until public penance followed by absolution could bring them back into the family of God. Lent was judged the perfect time. Reconciliation came through the absolution granted by the bishop or his representative on Holy Thursday. The lost sheep were welcomed back into the fold so that they might again share the Paschal Victory of Christ along with their friends.

The practice of sprinkling the public sinners with ashes at the beginning of Lent was a carryover from Hebrew customs. The story of Jona and the people of Ninive tells how the prophet counseled the sinful Ninivites to acknowledge their sinfulness by dressing in sack-cloth and sprinkling themselves with ashes. But, of course, as the prophet made clear, all of this meant nothing unless it was inspired by a real change of heart. In later years, since everyone must admit his sinfulness before God to one degree or another, **all** Christians began to accept ashes on Ash Wednesday as a symbol of their sorrow and penance for sin.

The New Testament also stresses the call to penance. John the Baptist (Matthew 3:2) preached repentance, as did our Lord Himself (Matthew 4:17). The apostles did nothing more than to re-echo this message when they spread the gospel around the world (Acts 2:38). The Church continues the same mission from Christ when in Lent she pleads with sinners in a motherly fashion that they show a change of heart in true repentance and a change in their lives by avoidance of sin.

- FIND and summarize in a few words some examples of this Penance theme in the Lenten liturgy.

- HERE are some leads:
  the Epistle of Friday after Ash Wednesday,
  the Epistle of Monday in Passion week,
  the Gospel for Ash Wednesday,
  the Gospel for Saturday of the 2nd week.

- CAN you find any others?

D. Jerusalem Theme

At the very outset of Lent, on Quinquagesima Sunday, the Gospel introduces a Lenten theme which is packed with meaning. Christ is breaking the news of His coming death to the apostles:

> *"Behold, **we are going up to Jerusalem**, and all things that have been written by the prophets concerning the Son of Man will be accomplished." (Luke 18:31-32)*

In the Lenten liturgy, the phrase "going up to Jerusalem" represents everything that is going to happen to Christ on His Redemptive Mission. The Jerusalem theme, therefore, is a symbol of all that the apostles, and we too, are invited to share with Christ. If we "go up to Jerusalem" with Him, as the apostles had courage enough to do, then we too will share in His resurrection and glorious entry into His kingdom, which lies beyond the immediate prospect of suffering and death. St. Paul sums up this idea best of all:

> *"But if we are sons, we are heirs also; heirs indeed of God and joint heirs with Christ, provided, however, we suffer with him that we may also be glorified with him." (Rom. 8:17)*

- FIND in your Missals and then note down some examples of this Jerusalem theme.

- HERE are some leads:
  the Gospel of Thursday in the 4th week,
  the Gospel of the 2nd Sunday in Lent.

- READ and reflect upon Psalm 121. This was a song our Lord Himself may well have sung as He climbed up the hill to Jerusalem on a pilgrimage to the Holy City. It sums up the meaning of Lent:

> *"We will go up unto the house of the Lord." And now we have set foot within thy gates, O Jerusalem —*
> *May those who love thee prosper. (Ps. 121:2, 7)*

CHAPTER XII

SIGNS AND WONDERS:
WHO IS THIS MAN?

Just as they were with John the Baptist, the Jews were at first fascinated by this new preacher from Nazareth. He spoke "as one having authority" (Matthew 7:29), and with His vast knowledge of the Hebrew Scriptures He struck a responsive chord in the hearts of faithful Jews. They had been without a prophet's voice all too long. Now Yahweh had sent them two prophets in short succession; truly He still loved His Chosen People.

But the early fascination began to wear thin. Jesus preached a message hard to take. He said nothing of Israel's triumph over the nations of the world, but kept speaking of humility and suffering. And yet like John the Baptist, He too announced that "the Kingdom of God is at hand."

"Who is this man?"

"By what authority does he speak?"

These were the questions the Jews asked. Jesus began His long and patient course of instruction. He tried to educate them to understand the meaning of His mission; as part of this educational process He worked miracles. This was the kind of language the simple, uneducated people could understand.

In this chapter we shall first follow the education by miracles, and then we shall answer the two pointed questions the Jews kept asking.

Section 1. SIGNS AND WONDERS IN
THE GOSPELS

On the day of the Church's birth, Pentecost Sunday, St. Peter won his first converts by using the appeal of miracles:

214

"Men of Israel, hear these words. Jesus of Nazareth was a man approved by God among you by miracles and wonders and signs . . . ." (Acts 2:22)

God intended miracles to help men of all times in their religious searchings and strivings. **Miracles are perceptible signs of God and of His Revelation.** Here is a more technical definition:

Miracles are startling events beyond scientific explanation which God brings about for special religious purposes.

Here are some of the special purposes which miracles achieve:

I. To show God's goodness and mercy.

II. To give divine authority to Christ's Redemptive Mission.

III. To teach spiritual truths through visible signs.

IV. To foreshadow and preview life after death.

Each of the miracles in these categories throws out a challenge to man and his faith. **Man freely accepts or rejects what the miracle represents.** Even miracles do not force assent. Remember the Pharisees saw Jesus perform miracles too, **but they never believed.**

In order to illustrate each of God's purposes, here are some miracles from the Gospels fitting each of the categories just listed:

I. TO SHOW GOD'S GOODNESS AND MERCY

A. **While a guest at a marriage banquet,** Jesus revealed the goodness of God at Mary's request by helping the young couple to escape the embarrassment of a wine shortage

- READ the account of the miracle, Christ's first, in John 2:1-10.

B. **While passing through the town of Naim,** about eight miles southwest of Nazareth, Jesus and the apostles met a funeral procession. A sorrowing mother walked behind the stretcher which bore the body of her son. Christ's generous heart was moved to sympathy and He brought the boy back to life. Picture the amazement on the faces of the crowd

- READ the account in Luke 7:11-17.

II. TO GIVE DIVINE AUTHORITY TO CHRIST'S RE-DEMPTIVE MISSION

A. Encouragement for the Apostles

1. WHEN A typical lake storm funneled down the Jordan valley from snow-capped Mt. Hermon in the north, the boat transporting Jesus and the apostles tossed about at mid-lake like a toy. The experienced fishermen cowered in fear. They awakened Jesus and stared in awe as the Lord of the World quieted the storm with a word.

- READ Mark 4:35-40 for the account, and particularly note v. 40. The apostles are asking the right question, too.

2. ANOTHER TIME when Jesus had sent the apostles back across the lake without Him, He came to them in mid-lake walking on the waters. So well was Peter's confidence bolstered that he tried to join Christ out upon the waters.

- READ Matthew 14:22-33 for the full account of what happened to the daring Peter.

B. Signs of God's Power in Christ

Of the more than thirty miracles recounted with some detail in the Gospels, the majority deal with the healing of the sick. It was not by chance, therefore, that Jesus could point to the cures when the disciples of John the Baptist came asking just who He was:

> "Go and report to John what you have heard and seen: the blind see, the lame walk, the dead rise, the poor have the Gospel preached to them." (Luke 7:22)

The Jews who were well versed in their Scriptures would catch the echoes of Isaia in Christ's words. It was with words like these that the great prophet of the coming of the Messiah had spoken of the day of Israel's salvation and final triumph.

> Then will the eyes of the blind be opened, the ears of the deaf be cleared; then will the lame leap like a stag, then the tongue of the dumb will sing. (Isa. 35:5-6)

The curing of the sick by miraculous healings, therefore, was **a clear sign of the Messiah's coming,** just as Isaia said it would be.

It marked the beginning of the Messianic age. So effective was this sign that at times Jesus had to flee lest the people make him their earthly king. (See John 6:14-15)

Here are some of these miraculous cures:

1. PETER'S MOTHER-IN-LAW was cured when Jesus visited her house after a hard day of preaching. As the sun set, scores of the crippled and diseased crowded around Peter's house begging for help. Christ laid the hand of God's mercy on all of them.

   • READ Mark 1:29-31.

2. THE DEAF-MUTE Christ healed by external gesture and word, "Epheta," giving thereby an early model for the sacraments' gestures and words which would be formulated in the early Church.

   • READ Mark 7:31-37.

3. THE BLIND MAN AT BETHSAIDA Jesus cured with the external sign of rubbing saliva upon his eyes. He enjoined the man to "tell nobody," undoubtedly at a time when miracles only fanned the flame of Jewish hopes for an earthly kingdom.

   • READ Mark 8:22-26.

4. THE LEPER who called to Jesus must have sent the people nearby scurrying for cover. Lepers had to live outside the city in little colonies of misery and were made to carry a bell to warn passersby along the road. Picture the startled faces as they watch the Savior walk up to the loathsome creature, touch the sore-ridden body, saying, "Be thou made clean."

   • READ Luke 5:12-14.

5. THE CENTURION'S SERVANT was healed in a remarkable manner, not by the touch of Christ's hand, but from a distance. The power of faith as exemplified in the centurion works wonders.

   • READ Luke 7:1-17.

6. THE PARALYTIC AT THE POOL OF BETHSAIDA never asked for help from Jesus, though his pitiable appearance must have entreated for him. Jesus made the first move by approaching him, then cured the old man of his malady.

   • READ the account in John 5:1-9.

John the Evangelist, who had walked up and down Palestine with his Lord, summed up the meaning of these striking signs:

Many other signs also Jesus worked in the sight of his disciples,
which are not written in this book. But these are written that
you may believe that Jesus is the Christ, the Son of God, and
that believing you may have life in his name. (John 20:30-31)

John's lesson is clear: miracles are signs of God's revelation. They
lead us to believe that Jesus is the Son of God, and, from this belief,
to believe all that Jesus has taught.

III. TO TEACH SPIRITUAL TRUTHS THROUGH VISIBLE SIGNS

Our Lord took the Jewish people just as they were, poor and
uneducated, easily led this way and that. Just as He had patiently
taught them in parables, little stories which they could follow easily,
so also He used miracles to teach truths which their untrained minds
were slow to comprehend.

Here are some miracles clearing the way for difficult truths:

A. The Curing of the Withered Hand

The Pharisees had harassed Jesus on violations of the Sabbath.
Jesus defied them. On this day at the synagogue, their own home
grounds, He humiliated them before the assembled congregation.
He cured the man with the withered hand when everybody knew
that the Pharisees had gone on record as condemning all Sabbath
cures. No wonder these evil men, set on revenge, "began to discuss
among themselves what they should do to Jesus." At the cost of
His own safety, Christ taught sane attitudes toward the Sabbath rest.

- READ the account in Luke 6:6-10.

B. The Man Born Blind

As we saw in the Introduction, the physical miracle symbolized
the opening of the new eyes of the soul, the eyes of faith.

- READ in review John 9:1-41.

C. The Miraculous Catch of Fish

Remember how we saw that Jesus used the miracle to tell the
future apostles about their life's work. They would be "fishers of
men." Thus He also set up the symbolism of Peter's boat as representing the Church.

- READ in review the account in Luke 5:1-11.

D. The Multiplication of the Loaves and Fishes

In his account of this extraordinary miracle and its aftermath, John underscored how Christ prepared the people for His prediction of the Holy Eucharist by feeding the thousands with bread for their bodily strength. What He had done physically with ordinary bread He would do spiritually with the Bread of His Body.

- READ the miracle first in John 6:1-15 and then follow up with part of the discourse on the Eucharist in John 6:26-27, 32-35, 48-52.

E. A Paralytic at Capharnaum

Quick-thinking friends of the paralytic managed to get the helpless cripple to Christ in a seemingly impossible situation. The house where Christ was staying was packed, and crowds spilled over into the street. But the stretcher-bearers were determined men, undoubtedly urged on by the cripple. They carried the old man onto the roof, using the outside stairway so common in the East. With wonderful resourcefulness they lowered the stretcher through the opening in the roof which was easily uncovered during heat spells. The people in the house were aghast at the sight of the stretcher. Our Lord was unperturbed, but He was probably smiling to Himself. Yes, He would cure a man of such faith. What sign did He use to work the cure? "Son, thy sins are forgiven thee." He used the physical miracle to teach a spiritual truth, this time the forgiveness of sins. In seeing the crippled limbs loosened before their eyes, the onlookers could more easily grasp and more readily believe in Christ's power to forgive sins within men's souls.

- READ the full account of the miracle with its meaning in Mark 2:1-12.
- HOW do you explain the reaction of the Pharisees? Does the incident bring out an important aspect of miracles? Discuss and apply the same point to some scientists who witness a miracle at Lourdes.

IV. TO FORESHADOW AND PREVIEW LIFE AFTER DEATH

For a people who were tied down by earthly ambitions, talk about an after-life, Judgment Day, heaven and hell, meant little. Our Lord had to give them visual glimpses into the reality of life after death, some foretaste of the resurrection of the body. This is precisely what He did by bringing back the dead to life before the very eyes of the startled Jews. He proved to them that He had power over life and death, thus encouraging confidence in His preaching about man's eternal destiny.

Numbered among the miracles of life after death (besides that of the Naim widow's son) are the following:

A. The Raising of the Daughter of Jairus

The quiet majesty of the Lord of History, the Lord of life and death, contrasted sharply with the scene at the young girl's wake. In keeping with oriental custom, professional mourners, hired for the occasion, wept and wailed to the accompaniment of high-pitched flutes. When Jesus said that "the girl is asleep, not dead," the hirelings laughed at Him, but Jairus told them to leave. "Girl, I say to thee, arise." And before the eyes of the relatives present, the twelve-year-old maiden lifted herself from her bed and walked into the arms of her parents.

- READ the full account in Mark 5:21-43.

B. The Raising of Lazarus

Lazarus had been one of Jesus' closest friends. So moved was He by His friend's death that He wept at Lazarus' tomb. But the sad occasion gave Him the chance to put death once and for all in its proper place.

"I am the resurrection and the life; he who believes in me, even if he die, shall live: and whoever lives and believes in me, shall never die." (John 11:25-26)

With a prayer of thanks to His Father for having heard His request, Jesus cried out with a loud voice: "Lazarus, come forth!"

- READ the full account in John 11:1-44, noting especially the faith of Martha in v. 21-27.

C. Christ's Own Resurrection

One miracle stands forth in a class by itself, containing elements of the last three of the four purposes listed earlier. **By His divine power** Christ raised **Himself** from the dead. This was the pinnacle of His triumph, the miracle of miracles. All the extraordinary events of His lifetime led up to this climax. Christ's Resurrection was the clearest sign for all to see that He was truly the Lord of History, the Lord of life and death, the Son of God who He said He was. His new life is the guarantee of the new life awaiting all who love Him.

*"He who eats my flesh and drinks my blood has life everlasting and **I will raise him up on the last day**." (John 6:55)*

- READ about the full power Christ had over His life in John 10:17-18.

Section 2. SIGNS AND WONDERS IN OUR TIMES

God has never stopped manifesting His power and goodness in the world. Men of every generation see God in nature as created and preserved by God. The earth continues to revolve around the sun in perfect order; the galaxies of stars keep on spinning at unimaginable speeds and yet manage to avoid collision; the rain falls and the grass grows. But the trouble is that men grow hardened to these wonders of God's creation and take them for granted. Men run about pursuing petty things, often too busy to read the signs in large letters by which nature tells us of God's magnificence and glory. In a word, God still works miracles, and for the same reasons we studied above in the Gospels. Like a teacher who must stir his listless students, God still speaks in the language of startling signs. Men of all generations are forced to look — and think.

- SEARCH out some miracles from the lives of your favorite saints. As individual assignments, recount a few to the class. Are miracles necessary for canonization? Discuss.

I. MIRACLES TODAY
When Christians visit a place like Lourdes today and stand beside the miraculous baths, they can sense the power of Christ spanning the ages. Just as the Church is the extension of Christ in the world, so too, miracles like those recorded at Lourdes are continuations of Christ's power in the world of our day. What Christ once did in history He wills to continue till the end of time. Miracles cross all boundaries of time and space.

Here are two among the many miraculous cures at Lourdes which have withstood the demanding tests of science:

A. The Case of John Traynor

John Traynor was a British soldier in World War I. A bullet had severed the large nerves in his upper arm making movement and sensation in the arm impossible. Four operations failed to tie the nerves together again. The medical men counseled amputation because there was no hope of ever using the arm again.

John Traynor as a devout Catholic went to Lourdes to ask our Lady's help. When the bishop at the shrine paused in front of the confident soldier to bless him with the Blessed Sacrament, suddenly the injured right arm burst its bandages and moved freely in a startling cure. The man was taken to the team of scientists for examination. The medical report: cure beyond scientific explanation.

B. The Case of Francis Pascal

At the age of three, a French child by the name of Francis Pascal was stricken with a severe case of meningitis. The doctors managed to save his life, but the boy was left paralyzed and completely blind. In 1937 the case was officially pronounced hopeless, that is, hopeless to all except the mother of deep religious faith who carried the child to Lourdes and personally plunged him into the miraculous baths. The same doctors who had declared the case incurable examined the boy after the trip to Lourdes. The medical report: cure beyond scientific explanation. Each signed the official report.

- AN EXCELLENT study of the miracles at Lourdes is available in English, *The Miracle of Lourdes,* by Ruth Cranston. One of the most interesting things about the book is that the authoress is a non-Catholic.

C. The Greatest Miracle of All at Lourdes

During the one hundred years of the existence of Lourdes as a shrine to our Lady over fifty cures have been thoroughly documented by scientists on the scene. All carry the same conclusion: **cure beyond scientific explanation.** There are hundreds of other cases under scientific study. The authorities move very slowly to confirm a miracle, so thorough are they to check every least detail of each case.

But the greatest of all miracles at Lourdes, of much more importance than the physical cures, is **the gift of faith which millions have carried away with them.** Many of these miracles of faith are known to God alone, but thousands of persons have also given testimony to God's gift by reforms in their lives and generous sacrifices. God continues to startle men into listening to Christ and His message, and one of His most effective means remains the extraordinary physical and spiritual occurrences we call miracles.

This brief study of miracles, particularly as they figure in Christ's teaching strategy in the Gospels, brings us to the point of answering the big questions posed by the Jews, questions which remain so critical for men of all time.

Section 3.   WHO IS THIS MAN?

I. PETER'S REPLY

With his new strength from the coming of the Holy Spirit at Pentecost, Peter faced the indifferent crowds of Jerusalem. His opening words went right to the heart of the Christian Message, and answered the question so long raised in the minds of all who heard Jesus: "Who is this man, Jesus of Nazareth?" This was Peter's reply:

> *"Men of Israel, hear these words. Jesus of Nazareth was **a man approved by God** among you by miracles and wonders and signs, which God did through him in the midst of you, as you yourselves know. Him, when delivered up by the settled purpose and foreknowledge of God, you have crucified and slain by the hands of wicked men . . . This Jesus God has raised up, and we are all witnesses of it . . . Therefore, let all the house of Israel know most assuredly that God has made **both Lord and Christ,** this Jesus whom you crucified." (Acts 2:22-23, 32, 36)*

NOTE HERE TWO RELIGIOUS TRUTHS OF CAPITAL IMPORTANCE:

1. Jesus was a **man** whom the apostles had known and whom the Jews and Romans had crucified.

2. This Jesus was also "Lord," a term used with great precision by the Jews to refer **only to divinity,** the God whom they worshipped. **He was the Son of God.** See Romans 10:12-13, and compare with Joel 2:32.

- IS THERE any difference at all to be pointed out between speaking of God and speaking of Jesus Christ? between speaking of the Son of God, the Second Person of the Blessed Trinity, and speaking of Jesus Christ? Explain.

- HINT toward the correct answer: Did Jesus Christ exist as Jesus Christ before His conception at Nazareth and birth at Bethlehem?

II. A FULLER PORTRAIT

Over many months our Lord had educated Peter and the other apostles. Through the instruction by miracles which we followed in this chapter, particularly by the greatest of all miracles, the Resurrection, Peter and the rest came around to see the true identity of their Master. With the coming of the Holy Spirit, everything fell into place with a fresh clarity. The many faces of the Messiah as prophesied in the Old Testament now blended into the apostles' fuller portrait of the Risen Savior.

A. Jesus of Nazareth Was the Messiah Prophesied in the Old Testament

1. THE SON OF DAVID and King of Israel awaited so long by the prophets.

- SEE Luke 1:30-33.

2. THE VICTIM OF SUFFERING as portrayed by Isaia.

- SEE Luke 18:31-34.

3. THE TRIUMPHANT SON OF MAN of the Book of Daniel, who will come with God's power to judge the world.

- SEE Matthew 26:64.

- REVIEW the summary at the end of our Old Testament study of "the many faces of the Messiah." See once again how the foreshadowings from the prophets are fulfilled in the person of Jesus Christ.

B. Jesus of Nazareth, the Messiah, Was the Son of God

In the beginning was the Word, and the Word was with God; ***and the Word was God.***

And the Word was made flesh, and dwelt among us. And we saw his glory — glory as of the only-begotten of the Father — full of grace and of truth. (John 1:1, 14)

Section 4. THE HOLY SPIRIT SPEAKS THROUGH THE CHURCH

That the early Church proclaimed the dogma of the Incarnation to the scattered lands of the known world there is no doubt. The greatest missionary of all, St. Paul, expressed the Incarnation this way, when writing to his converts in the Greek town of Philippi:

*Have this mind in you which was also in Christ Jesus, **who though he was by nature God,** did not consider being equal to God a thing to be clung to, but emptied himself, taking the nature of a slave and being made like unto men. And **appearing in the form of a man,** he humbled himself, being obedient to death, even to death on a cross. (Phil. 2:5-8)*

But the words of Sacred Scripture can at times be misinterpreted and misunderstood. When, years later, erroneous ideas began to challenge the true faith, the Church had to clarify the expression of the dogma of the Incarnation. A series of councils, especially the Council of Ephesus in 431 A.D. and the Council of Chalcedon in 451 A.D., defined precisely the terms used in explaining the Incarnation and thus clarified the position of our Catholic faith.

The bishops assembled at these councils solemnly affirmed:

A. Jesus Christ has the nature of true man
- LOOK back through the Nazareth chapter and see again how clearly this is brought out. Does Jesus have a human soul?

B. Jesus Christ has the nature of true God
- REVIEW the testimonies of Peter, John, and Paul above. A still fuller treatment of Christ's divinity will be taken up later in another year's course.

C. Jesus Christ is only one Person
- LOOK for this point in the text of St. Paul to the Philippians 2:5-8. This also will receive further scrutiny later.

It is in the joining of these two natures in one Person that we have the mystery which is beyond our minds to comprehend fully.
THESE ARE THE HERESIES WHICH WERE CONDEMNED BY THE COUNCILS:

1. That which denied that Jesus was true man: called the Apollinarist heresy after its leading thinker, Apollinaris, whose position was condemned in 381 A.D., at the Council of Constantinople.

2. That which denied that Jesus was true God: called the Arian heresy after its leading thinker, Arius, whose position was condemned in 325 A.D., at the Council of Nicea.

3. That which denied that Jesus was one Person: called the Nestorian heresy after its leading thinker, Nestorius, whose position was condemned in 431 A.D., at the Council of Ephesus.

● HOW would these heresies affect the dignity and the worth of every human being? Discuss.

SOME MEMORY HELPS:

1. Jesus Christ is God because He is the only Son of God with the same divine nature as His Father.

2. Jesus Christ is man because He was born of the Blessed Virgin Mary by the power of the Holy Spirit, with a body and soul like ours.

3. By the Incarnation is meant that the Son of God, never surrendering His divine nature, took to Himself a human nature with a body and soul like ours.

4. Jesus Christ is only one Person, the Second Person of the Blessed Trinity.

SUMMARY

As an important part of His teaching strategy, Jesus made use of "signs and wonders," miracles of all kinds. Miracles are startling events beyond scientific explanation which serve as signs of God's revelation. The purpose of the different miracles differed in emphasis: some were intended to show God's goodness and mercy; others to encourage the apostles and support Christ's Messianic mission; still others to teach spiritual truths through visible signs; or finally to give a preview of life after death.

In our own time God continues to use miracles for the same purposes, as for example the miracles at our Lady's shrine in Lourdes.

After seeing Christ's "signs and wonders," many asked, "Who is this man?" After the coming of the Spirit on Pentecost, Peter answered that question with a fresh clarity: Jesus of Nazareth was the Messiah expected by the prophets; but more important still, He was the Son of God. John, Paul, and the other apostles proclaimed this message throughout the known world.

When heresy threatened to distort the truth of the Incarnation, the Church in her early councils exposed the errors and defined the accurate words to express the mystery.

QUESTIONS

1. What are miracles and what purposes do they serve?
2. Give one example to illustrate each of these different purposes.
3. Why does God continue to work miracles in modern times?
4. Of all the miracles at Lourdes, what is really the one most outstanding?
5. What two truths did St. Peter emphasize in his sermon as recorded in Acts 2?
6. What are the three principal faces of the Messiah as prophesied in the Old Testament? How were they verified in Jesus Christ?
7. Where does St. John clearly affirm Christ's divinity?
8. Point out the dogma of the Incarnation in the text of St. Paul, Philippians 2:5-8. Where is the mystery?
9. What were the main heresies which developed around the truth of the Incarnation?
10. When and where were they condemned?
11. Memorize the precise statements of the Incarnation dogma.

CHAPTER XIII

THE HEART OF CHRIST: LOVE AND REDEMPTION

In previous chapters we have heard Christ's Message and seen the miracles which supported it. "What manner of man is this, that even the wind and the sea obey him?" asked the apostles (Mt. 8:27). Peter answered the big question in the minds of all when on the first Pentecost he proclaimed to the crowds:

> *"Therefore let all the house of Israel know most assuredly that God has made both Lord and Christ, this Jesus whom you crucified." (Acts 2:36)*

In the present chapter we shall try to probe beneath the external signs, beneath the words and deeds of Christ. With all reverence we hope to look into the very Heart of Christ.

THE INNER LIFE OF CHRIST'S HEART WAS DIRECTED:

1. Above all to His Father.

2. But also to His brothers, the sons of Adam.

Section 1. JESUS AND HIS FATHER

Throughout Christ's entire life concern for the Father was a dominant theme. The truth Jesus preached came from the Father; the miracles He performed gave glory to the Father; the person He was most anxious to see loved by all men was the Father. His own love for the Father was truly at the center of Christ's Heart. Here are some further manifestations of this relationship between the Father and the Son:

I. CHRIST WAS SENT BY THE FATHER

At the Jordan baptism we stood with John the Baptist and witnessed the special dedication of Christ to His Father's mission with the signs of the Trinity's approval. Repeatedly, throughout His public life Jesus made it clear that He had been sent by His Father for this special assignment.

> *"For I have come down from heaven not to do my own will, but the will of him who sent me." (John 6:38)*

- WHAT were the special signs of the Father's satisfaction on the occasion of Christ's baptism?

II. CHRIST AND HIS FATHER WERE ALWAYS CLOSE TO ONE ANOTHER

A. Through Christ's Divine Nature

The Incarnation in no way interfered with the union of God the Father and God the Son. Christ spoke of this union often:

> *"And he who sent me is with me: he has not left me alone, because I do always the things that are pleasing to him." (John 8:29)*

At the Last Supper He spoke further of this "oneness" with the Father, and in words which most probably mystified the apostles at that time:

> *"And the glory that thou (the Father) hast given me, I have given to them (the apostles), that they may be one, even as we are one: . . . ." (John 17:22)*

- WHAT is the explanation of this "oneness" between the Father and the Son? Were They always united this way? What then was added by the Incarnation?

One day during His public life, this divine nature shared with the Father in the glory of the Trinity shone through in a particularly impressive manner. Jesus had taken Peter, James, and John with Him that day up to the summit of Mt. Thabor. Before the startled eyes of the three apostles, Jesus was "transfigured," i.e., the divine glory was permitted to shine through Christ's human body.

- READ the account of this remarkable occurrence in Luke 9:28-36. Why didn't Jesus always let His divinity shine through like this? Why did He allow it on this occasion? As a hint, read the next incident in Luke's Gospel, especially verses 44-45.

B. Through Christ's Human Nature

Besides enjoying unity by the divine nature, Christ as man also kept in constant touch with His Father **in prayer.** It was in perfect accord with His human nature to converse with His Father in prayer, and He undoubtedly wanted to teach us this key to intimacy with God:

> *"Father, I have given thee thanks that thou hast heard me. Yet I know that thou always hearest me. . ." (John 11:41-42)*

And as encouragement for the right kind of prayer, on another occasion He counseled:

> *". . . when thou prayest, go into thy room, and closing the door, pray to the Father in secret;*
>
> *"But in praying do not multiply words, as the Gentiles do; . . .* **for your Father knows what you need before you ask him.** *In this manner, therefore shall you pray: 'Our Father who art in heaven, hallowed be thy name.' " (Mt. 6:6-9)*

- READ Luke 11:1-13 for an insight into prayer from God's point of view, especially the confident and persistent prayer recommended by Christ. Can you think of any examples of this kind of confident prayer in the lives of the saints? of St. Monica? of St. Francis of Assisi?

Jesus would often slip away from His friends for a night of prayerful communication with His Father. It was after nights like these that He made some of the most important decisions of His life, as for example, the final choice of the twelve apostles. (See Luke 6:12-16)

Finally, Christ as man was united to the Father with a particular intimacy, inasmuch as He enjoyed the Beatific Vision while on earth.

- DURING the Middle Ages knights-to-be would keep an all-night vigil before the Blessed Sacrament on the eve of their elevation to knighthood. What is the aim of Nocturnal Adoration Societies in our parishes today?

III. CHRIST DID HIS FATHER'S WORK

As early as His twelfth year, Jesus let Mary and Joseph know that he must be "about His Father's business." When He had reached His early thirties, He left His widowed mother behind in Nazareth and traveled south in order to launch the Messianic mission planned by His Father. Nothing, neither home ties nor the frightening events He knew to be ahead of Him, could turn Him from His set purpose.

"I have come to cast fire upon the earth, and what will I but that it be kindled? But I have a baptism to be baptized with: and how distressed I am until it is accomplished!" (Luke 12:49-50)

By His "baptism" here, Christ meant His baptism in blood, the suffering of the Passion which He was to offer to the Father in sacrifice in behalf of sinful men.

And yet when the fateful moment came on that first Holy Thursday night, as if to convince us once and for all of His completely human feelings, He shrank from the horrible prospect of taking all men's sins upon Himself. His human nature buckled under the load and He fell to the ground in an agony of sweat. The emotional clash of human fear against the unbending determination to do His Father's Will caused the very blood to ooze from His pores and trickle down His stricken body.

- READ Matthew 26:36-41 and see our Lord writhing beneath the strain of this emotional conflict.

The violence of the temptation to throw over the entire Redemptive Plan indicates the relentless pressure from Satan. The lord of Hell must have applied every pressure on Christ on this occasion, as with panic he sensed approaching defeat. This man must be stopped, or men might once again know God's friendship. Christ's response to Satan's onslaught took the form of a prayer to His Father:

"Father . . . yet not as I will, but as thou willest." (Mt. 26:39)

With these words Satan had been defeated. The Savior Jesus Christ was determined to carry out His mission. Christ was willing to take the sins of all mankind upon Himself and He prepared His soul for the bloody sacrifice on the Cross including the suffering which preceded it.

IV. CHRIST LOVED HIS FATHER

The only way to understand the complete dedication of Christ to His Father's Will is to realize its motivation. No son ever loved His Father with so complete a love. It is this love which explains the total obedience, "obedience even to the death on a cross."

While actually hanging from the cross, Jesus gave expression to this loving obedience with two of His final utterances:

> *"It is consummated!" (i.e., my mission is accomplished) (John 19:30)*
>
> *"Father, into thy hands I commend my spirit." (Luke 23:46)*

- READ also John 17:1-26 and note down the passages which best bring out Christ's love for and union with His Father.

V. CHRIST RETURNED TO HIS FATHER

According to many Catholic theologians, Christ returned to His Father immediately after His Resurrection. **He took possession of His glory at once,** although He returned on several occasions to visit His apostles. On Ascension Thursday, forty days after His Resurrection, He returned to His Father for what seemed the final time; but He had promised at the Last Supper that at some unknown date in the future He would come again:

> *"If you loved me, you would indeed rejoice that I am going to the Father . . . ."*
>
> *"In my Father's house there are many mansions. Were it not so, I should have told you, because I go to prepare a place for you. And if I go and prepare a place for you,* ***I am coming again,*** *and I will take you to myself: that where I am, there you also may be." (John 14:28; 2-3)*

What would that precise date be? Christ never told us, but at the trial before the High-Priest Caiphas He did give us a symbolic picture of that last day:

> *". . . I say to you, hereafter you shall see* ***the Son of Man sitting at the right hand of the Power*** *and coming upon the clouds of heaven." (Mt. 26:64)*

- WHAT prophecy is Christ here applying to Himself? Look back over what you learned from the Book of Daniel.

With this triumphant return of Christ on Judgment Day, history will have turned full cycle. The Christ who was promised in the Old Testament, who after many centuries lived among men in fulfillment of that promise, will take possession of the world as Lord and King. On that final Judgment Day all who loved their Lord and who proved it by their loyalty in life will rise from their graves and take possession of "the mansions" the Lord had promised them.

Section 2. JESUS AND THE MEN OF HIS TIMES

In the course of His lifetime Christ met all kinds of people. In dealing with them He revealed Himself in word and action. When we study His ways of approaching people in varying circumstances, His different reactions to different classes of people, we catch glimpses of the Savior's personality, each of which is a little insight into the true Heart of Christ which we want to know and love.

I. THE HEART OF CHRIST AND THE POOR

More than to anybody else, our Lord seemed to be drawn to the poor and needy. In a world which made idols of political power and brute strength, Christ chose to stand by the side of the weak and the defenseless. Everyone was assured of a gracious welcome, provided that they opened their own hearts to His.

> "*Come to me, all you who labor and are burdened, and I will give you rest.*" (Mt. 11:28)

One day He saw that a large crowd had anticipated His trip across the Lake of Galilee. As His boat glided into shore, the sight of the multitudes assembling on the hills beyond the shoreline made His Heart well up with pity.

> . . . *they were like sheep without a shepherd. (Mark 6:34)*

His Heart went out to these sons of Israel, weak and defenseless, but worse still, deprived of all leadership within their nation. Why was He so concerned? Because he saw in each of them, beneath the shabby clothes and behind the anxious faces, the image of His Father. Just as we can recognize the features of parents in the faces of their children, so too Christ saw God the Father in the poor of Palestine. No wonder His Heart went out to them.

- WHAT saints can you recall who showed special charity toward the poor? Where in the world today would you say that men of this Christ-like spirit are most needed? Where in this country of ours? What ways are open to Christians to help the poor of their community? Do you think almsgiving is enough?

- HAVE two members of the class give reports on the careers of the famous Dr. Albert Schweitzer and the inspiring young American, the late Dr. Tom Dooley, careers dedicated to the poor and infirm.

II. THE HEART OF CHRIST AND CHILDREN

It is not easy to catch the wavelength of children in an audience. The price of their attention comes high, if you want to teach them anything. Children, of course, took to Christ magnetically. The Gospels on several occasions picture the mighty Lord of History concerning Himself with the young:

- READ the incident in Mark 10:13-16.

Don't for a moment think that this is a case of some cute children playing upon Christ's human emotions. Christ had a serious purpose in paying such attention to children, and He explained to all the adults standing around what the purpose was:

> *"Amen I say to you, whoever does not accept the kingdom of God **as a little child** will not enter into it." (Mark 10:15)*

- DISCUSS what our Lord could mean here.

On another occasion the apostles were probing for some information about the Kingdom of heaven and who would have the highest place there. Our Lord again used children to make His point:

> *"Amen I say to you, unless you turn and **become like little children,** you will not enter into the kingdom of heaven. Whoever, therefore, humbles himself as this little child, he is the greatest in the kingdom of heaven." (Mt. 18:3-4)*

While giving warm encouragement to all who influenced the young for good, our Lord was strong in condemning corrupters of youth:

"And whoever receives one such little child for my sake, receives me. But whoever causes one of these little ones who believes in me to sin, it were better for him to have a great millstone around his neck, and to be drowned in the depths of the sea." (Mt. 18:5-6)

- WHO ARE some of the people in line for Christ's special blessing? What kind of people fall under the condemnation as corrupters of youth? Discuss the kinds of business in which evil men try to victimize youth in America today. What can be done to oppose these evil schemes?

III. THE HEART OF CHRIST AND REPENTANT SINNERS

Sinners saw in Christ a friend who would forgive and help them. The Pharisees, on the other hand, looked down on sinners with nothing but contempt. Remember how they despised Christ too, when at dinner He allowed a sinful woman to bathe and anoint His feet?

"This man, were he a prophet, would surely know who and what manner of woman this is who is touching him, for she is a sinner." (Luke 7:39)

- READ the entire account of this clash between Christ and the Pharisees as recorded in Luke 7:36-50.

Christ's answer to the Pharisees:

"It is not the healthy who need a physician, but they who are sick. For I have not come to call the just, but sinners." (Mark 2:17)

And just so that the people would not miss the lengths to which Christ's mercy would go, He told them the parable of the Prodigal Son:

- READ the parable in Luke 15:11-32. Do you think the older brother's objections had any force?

But perhaps the most dramatic of the meetings Jesus had with sinners took place just outside the Temple one day. The Pharisees at the head of an angry mob had dragged before our Lord a woman caught in the sin of adultery. By Mosaic Law she should be stoned

to death. The Pharisees smirked with satisfaction, thinking they had Jesus trapped by His own softness toward sinners. A silence fell over the mob as Jesus stooped, wrote something on the ground, and then stunned the crowd with these words:

> "Let him who is without sin among you be the first to cast a stone at her." (John 8:7)

Thus forced to face their own hypocrisy, the crowds of Jews melted away. Turning to the woman kneeling in fright before Him, Jesus must have smiled to quiet her fears:

> "Woman, where are they? Has no one condemned thee? . . . Neither will I condemn thee. Go thy way, and from now on sin no more." (John 8:10-11)

- READ the entire account in John 8:1-11. What dispositions are necessary for such a sinner to win forgiveness?

Finally, even on the cross mercy continued to overflow from the Heart of Christ. He prayed for His persecutors:

> "Father, forgive them, for they do not know what they are doing." (Luke 23:34)

When the thief on His right showed some sign of repentance and belief, He met the man more than half way with as generous a promise as has ever been recorded. He assured this common robber, perhaps even a murderer, of a place among the saints of God.

> "Amen I say to thee, this day thou shalt be with me in paradise." (Luke 23:43)

For all who are speechless as they marvel at the Lord's mercy the Psalmist is the perfect spokesman:

> "Give thanks to the Lord, for he is good, for his mercy endures forever." (Ps. 117:1)

IV. THE HEART OF CHRIST AND THE PROUD

In marked contrast to repentant sinners were the proud and defiant Pharisees, who were sinners too, but in their self-sufficiency, hardened to grace. The wonder is that Jesus kept His patience with the Pharisees and Sadducees as long as He did. These unscrupulous men played the power game of politics for all it was worth and used religion as a springboard for their own ambitions. Our Lord saw right through them, their pride, and their selfishness. But many of the simpler folk were deceived by their external fidelity to the Law of Moses and their apparent dedication to Temple worship. Recall how, with the passing of the prophets, the Law and the interpreters of the Law had usurped the leading roles in Jewish religious life. It followed, therefore, to simple minds at least, that the Pharisees, as interpreters of the Law and champions of Temple worship, were thereby most pleasing to Yahweh. Our Lord set the record straight:

> "Now you Pharisees clean the outside of the cup and the dish, **but within** you are full of robbery and wickedness." (Luke 11:39)

But the most scathing denunciations are recorded in St. Matthew's Gospel:

> "But woe to you, Scribes and Pharisees, hypocrites! because you shut the kingdom of heaven against men. For you yourselves do not go in, nor do you allow those going in to enter.

> "Woe to you, Scribes and Pharisees, hypocrites! because you are like whited sepulchres, which outwardly appear to men beautiful, but within are full of dead men's bones and of all uncleanness.

> "Serpents, brood of vipers, how are you to escape the judgment of hell?" (Mt. 23:13, 27, 33)

- READ through Matthew 23:1-35 to get the full impact of Christ's condemnation of the Pharisees. Describe the kind of person you would consider a modern day Pharisee. What would by contrast be the Christian ideal?

Christ had treated with kindness every sinner who had come to Him with a repentant heart: an adulteress, a woman of the street, a thieving tax-collector, a robber on the cross. But He did not move the hearts of the hardened Pharisees. Spiritual pride is perhaps the most solid wall that resists the merciful Christ.

V.   THE HEART OF CHRIST AND ALL MEN

If there is any image which could sum up the attitudes of Christ's Heart toward men, it is that of "the Good Shepherd." We already saw that Christ's heart went out to the ordinary people

A shepherd tending his flock. Bethlehem is seen in the background. THE MATSON PHOTO SERVICE

because "they were like sheep without a shepherd." Sheep by nature are helpless creatures, and a herding people like the Jews realized how dependent they were upon the shepherd. They were easy prey to wolves, and if separated from the flock they became hopelessly lost. But they got to know their shepherd well, and what is more, he knew them. They responded to his call and had complete confidence in him. These were the ideas that our Lord stirred up in the minds of His hearers with the image of "the Good Shepherd."

Recall that it was the prophet Ezechiel who had developed this shepherd theme in the Old Testament in order to portray the goodness and mercy of God. (See Ezechiel 34:5-6, 11-16, and 23-24). Now Jesus applied this prophecy of Ezechiel to Himself:

> "I am the good shepherd, and I know mine and mine know me . . . I lay down my life for my sheep. And other sheep I have which are not of this fold. Them also I must bring, and they shall hear my voice, and there shall be one fold and one shepherd. For this reason the Father loves me, because I lay down my life that I may take it up again." (John 10:14-17)

- READ the full revelation of Christ as the Good Shepherd in John 10:1-18, and then compare it with the parable of the lost sheep in Luke 15:3-7.

- WHAT does our Lord mean by "one fold" and "one shepherd"? Discuss the divisions among Christians in the modern world. What is the Ecumenical Movement?

Section 3. THE HEART OF CHRIST AND THE REDEMPTION

I. THE TRINITY'S LOVE FOR MEN

The love of Christ for His Father and love for His fellow men merge in the great work of man's redemption, and for a very good reason. When Christ died for men, He fulfilled out of love the mission given Him by His Father. He did His Father's Will, as we saw above, because He loved His Father with a perfect love. The Redemption was God's great act of love; each of the three Persons of the Blessed Trinity shared in both the work itself and in the love which inspired it:

A. **The Father Loved Men**
For God so loved the world that he gave his only-begotten Son, ...(John 3:16)

B. **The Son Loved Men**
"Greater love than this no one has, that one lay down his life for his friends." (John 15:13)

C. **The Holy Spirit Loved Men**
"And I (Christ) will ask the Father and he will give you another Advocate to dwell with you forever, ... and be in you." (John 14:16-17)

The Redemption is **the triumph over sin of the love of the Blessed Trinity.**

But what, more exactly, did the Redemption accomplish?
Above all, the Redemption accomplished these two things:

1. THE LIBERATION FROM SIN

Man was enslaved by sin, unable to help himself. Christ was the great liberator who freed men from the bonds of sin.

- WHAT "type" from the Old Testament foreshadowed this Redemption by Christ?

2. THE COMMUNICATION OF TRINITARIAN LIFE

When God created man, He endowed him with a gift which was in no way due to his human nature, but entirely above nature, a "supernatural gift." This was the most precious gift of all, the sharing of His own Trinitarian life, which we call **sanctifying grace.** This gift was lost through Adam's sin. Christ restored the gift of sanctifying grace through His Redemption of mankind.

- WHEN was this Trinitarian life first communicated to man? In virtue of redemption by Christ, how do we come to share in it?

II. MAN'S RESPONSE TO THE TRINITY'S LOVE

God, however, does not force Himself and His gifts upon men. Man is a creature endowed with freedom of choice. It is up to him to accept God's gifts. His acceptance takes the form of cooperation with God's designs in behalf of his happiness. It is an extraordinary thing to think about: **All God asks in return for so much is man's cooperation.**

What is the cooperation expected of man?

Man's cooperation comes down to living "the Jerusalem theme" which we study in the Lenten liturgy, i.e., **joining himself with Christ totally.** Thus man joins Christ in giving worship to the Father, in keeping the Commandments, the terms of the Covenant, and in accepting from God's hand whatever cross he is given to bear.

> *"And he who does not take up his cross and follow me, is not worthy of me."* (Mt. 10:38)

But, as you remember from the "Jerusalem theme," Christ never asks men to follow Him in any kind of suffering just for the sake of suffering itself. Suffering and death are only passageways to a new life, as Christ Himself demonstrated in His glorious Resurrection from the dead.

*. . . we are heirs also: heirs indeed of God and joint heirs with Christ, provided, however, we suffer with him **that we may also be glorified with him.** (Rom. 8:17)*

- SINCE Christ was both priest and victim-offering in the original redemptive sacrifice, can Christians of today be the same? Explain how.

Section 4. THE HEART OF CHRIST IN CHURCH TRADITION

After studying the Heart of Christ in relation to His Father and to His fellow men, especially in the great work of the Redemption, we should expect the Scriptures to have made references to Christ's Sacred Heart. Even back to ancient times people have looked upon the heart as the center of the human personality, the symbol of love, the focal point of man's relationship to God and to his fellow men. No heart ever deserved to be remembered more than this Sacred Heart of the Messiah, the Son of God.

I. THE SACRED HEART FORESHADOWED

Many centuries before the coming of Christ the Psalmist had prepared the way for devotion to the Sacred Heart. Church tradition has applied these words to the Messiah and His obedience to His Father's Will:

*". . . to do your will, O my God is my delight, and **your law is within my heart.**" (Ps. 39:9)*

Thus Christ gave Himself completely to the Father's Will "even to death on a cross."

And in another place, the Psalmist refers to God's Plan for mankind as "the design of his heart":

*But the plan of the Lord stands forever; **the design of his heart,** through all generations. (Ps. 32:11)*

This is the Plan of God which would be brought to men and fulfilled by the Messiah. In His Redemptive Mission the Heart of

Christ would speak to the hearts of all men, and in that way the knowledge and love shared by the Trinity would pass "from heart to heart," from the Sacred Heart of Christ to the hearts of all men who will choose to listen.

- REVIEW a prophecy noted earlier in our course, that of Jeremia 31:31-33. Do you see any connection between that prophecy of Jeremia and the redemptive work of Christ's Sacred Heart?

II. THE SACRED HEART OF CHRIST IN FULFILL-MENT

Did our Lord ever speak of His Sacred Heart? Yes, He did call attention to His Heart, but indirectly, not always in the words familiar to us from the Sacred Heart devotion today. On one occasion He extended this invitation to His listeners:

> "Come to me, all you who labor and are burdened, and I will give you rest. Take my yoke upon you, and **learn of me, for I am meek and humble of heart:** and you will find rest for your souls. For my yoke is easy and my burden light." (Mt. 11:28-30)

And another time, in words rich with symbolism, He added:

> "If anyone thirst, let him come to me and drink. He who believes in me, as the Scripture says, **'From within him** (the Messiah) there shall flow rivers of living water.' " (John 7:37-38)

Church tradition sees these words of symbolism fulfilled in the coming of the Holy Spirit sent by Christ. Thus the Holy Spirit, the Spirit of Love, descended upon men at Pentecost, with the flow of precious graces continuing for all time. According to the symbol contained in Christ's words just quoted, these graces flow from Christ Himself, **"from within him."** From where else would they flow but from the love of His Sacred Heart? That is why one of the details in St. John's account of the death of Jesus ties in here with the Sacred Heart devotion:

> ". . . but one of the soldiers **opened his** (Jesus') **side** with a lance, and immediately there came out blood and water." (John 19:34)

The "blood and water" symbolize the flow of grace that comes with the presence of the Holy Spirit, all symbolically coming from the

Heart of Christ. In the tradition of the Church the blood and water also frequently symbolized the two sacraments, Holy Eucharist and baptism.

- WHAT are some of the special graces which come with the Holy Spirit? The best summary is that of St. Paul in his letter to the Romans 8:14-17. List as many of God's gifts as you can find in this text.

The Church re-echoes these symbolisms in much of her liturgical and private prayer. As an example, the Church addresses Christ:

"O Thou who pourest forth grace from Thy Heart . . . ."

III. THE SACRED HEART AND ST. MARGARET MARY

Our Lord gave special visions of His Sacred Heart to a Visitation nun at Paray-le-Monial in France, beginning with the year 1673. With her canonization she became known as St. Margaret Mary. As a result of her visions, the devotion to Christ's Heart took on a new impetus in the Church. Among the things Christ is reported to have told Margaret Mary were the following:

Behold this Heart which has so loved men that it has spared nothing in order to give them proof of its love. In return I receive from the greater number nothing but ingratitude, contempt, sacrilege, and coldness in this sacrament of my love . . . Therefore, I ask of thee that the first Friday after the octave of the Blessed Sacrament (Corpus Christi) shall be kept as a special feast in honor of my Heart . . . I also promise that my Heart shall shed in abundance the influence of its divine love on all those who shall thus honor it or cause it to be thus honored.

- LOOK UP the special Mass for the Feast of the Sacred Heart. Does this Mass include any of the scriptural texts treated above?

Margaret Mary fulfilled her special mission in relaying Christ's message. The Feast of the Sacred Heart was officially proclaimed for the entire Catholic world by Pope Pius IX in 1856. In 1899 Pope Leo XIII consecrated the entire world to the Sacred Heart.

- WHAT other features of the Sacred Heart devotion do you know? The League of the Sacred Heart? First Friday devotions? Family

consecrations to the Sacred Heart? Anything else in your home
or school? Discuss each.

In conclusion, we might take time out again to think over the
special prayer of St. Paul in behalf of his friends in the town of
Ephesus:

> . . . *and to have Christ dwelling through faith in your hearts:
> so that, being rooted and grounded in love, you may be able
> to comprehend with all the saints what is the breadth and length
> and height and depth,* **and to know Christ's love** *which sur-
> passes knowledge, in order that you may be filled with all the
> fullness of God.* (Ephesians 3:17-19. As found in the Epistle
> for the Feast of the Sacred Heart.)

The words, "to know Christ's love," sum up the meaning of the
Sacred Heart devotion to Catholics today.

SOME MEMORY HELPS:

1. **Redemption** is the liberation from sin accomplished through
the death and resurrection to glory of the Redeemer, Jesus Christ,
which regained for men their privileges as children of God and
heirs of heaven.

2. **The Sacred Heart Devotion** is the special honor given to the
physical heart of Christ as the symbol of Christ's redemptive love.

SUMMARY

The inner life of Christ was dominated by love for His Father
and for men. The Father sent Him on His Redemptive Mission,
and the Son obeyed out of love. Until His return to heaven after
the Resurrection, Christ and the Father stayed united with one
another through Christ's human as well as His divine nature.

Christ's love for His fellow men reached out particularly to the
poor and needy. Christ loved children, too, and went out of His
way to help sinners. But with the proud He could do nothing. The
image of the Good Shepherd more than any other seems to sum up
Christ's concern for men.

The Heart of Christ as the symbol of divine love best brings out
the true meaning of the Redemptive Mission. Love conquered sin
in the Redemption. Each Person of the Trinity shared this redemp-

tive love which brought about the liberation from sin and the communication of the Trinity's life of grace.

All God asks of men is cooperation. Man cooperates by joining himself to Christ so that they share together the cross and the glory that will follow.

The Sacred Heart Devotion attempts to bring men into closer contact with the love of Christ. From that Sacred Heart of Christ all graces flow, as St. Margaret Mary Alacoque helped us to understand.

QUESTIONS

1. Show how our Lord stayed close to His Father both in His divine and human natures.

2. What was the conflict within Christ which brought on the bloody agony in the Garden?

3. How did Jesus best prove His love for His Father?

4. Why did Christ show particular concern for the poor and needy of Israel?

5. What point did our Lord emphasize through the example of little children?

6. Relate briefly three incidents where Christ showed a special kindness toward sinners.

7. What did our Lord criticize so sharply in the conduct of the Sadducees and Pharisees?

8. Explain why the image of the Good Shepherd is so effective when applied to Christ.

9. Show how the Redemption manifests the love each Person of the Trinity has for men.

10. What two things did the Redemption accomplish?

11. How can men best cooperate in their response to the Trinity's love?

12. Give two foreshadowings of the Sacred Heart Devotion as found in the Psalms, and two references made by our Lord Himself to His Sacred Heart.

13. Briefly sketch the role of St. Margaret Mary Alacoque in fostering devotion to the Sacred Heart of Jesus.

CHAPTER XIV

MISSION FULFILLED: THE PASSION AND RESURRECTION

The last week of Christ's life approached. His friends grew fewer and fewer, His enemies more and more determined. The love of Christ's Sacred Heart was soon to express itself in the extraordinary events of this pivotal week in God's Plan for man's salvation. First, study the people involved, then the events themselves. When the people are known, events take on true meaning.

Section 1. THE PEOPLE INVOLVED

The teachings and miracles of Christ provoked different reactions among the people who heard His Message and witnessed His deeds. Some minds opened immediately to the Light of the World; others shut out the light, preferring the darkness of their ignorance, and clinging to their own ideas. Still others, almost in the manner of children, opened their hearts enthusiastically for a while, only to close them complainingly when they didn't get their own way. Here are some samples:

I. THE DISCIPLES OF CHRIST

We have no way of knowing how many of those who heard Christ's call recognized Him as the Messiah and pledged themselves as loyal followers. Of the twelve in Christ's inner circle of friends, one turned traitor, but the others were faithful to His love. All but St. John the Evangelist eventually sealed their love with martyrdom. We know that the holy women, Nicodemus and Joseph of Arimathea, Lazarus with his sisters, Martha and Mary, and most of all, His own

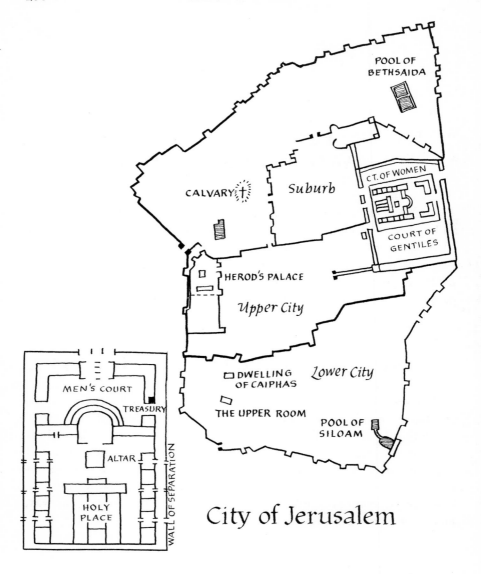

City of Jerusalem

mother, Mary, stayed faithful to Him. Surely there must have been others among the Jews of whom we have no record, but there appears to be little reason for believing that the faithful "remnant" prophesied in Isaia was very numerous at the time of Christ's death. Those who persevered in loyalty to Christ cherished the never-to-be-forgotten tribute of faith expressed by Peter when much of the crowd had gone off grumbling at the promise of the Eucharist:

Christ asked:

"Do you also wish to go away?"

Peter replied:

*"Lord, to whom shall we go? Thou hast the words of eternal
life, and we have come to believe and to know that thou art
the Christ, the Son of God." (John 6:68-70)*

II. THE PHARISEES AND THE SADDUCEES

The earlier pioneers of the Pharisee tradition were priests of
courage and dedication to ideals. Recall the role they played in the
struggle of the Machabee brothers for independence from foreign
oppression. How far the Pharisees of Christ's time had fallen from
those ideals became evident in our previous chapter. Christ failed
to win them over. When torn between this world's renown on the
one hand, and the humility, charity, and self-sacrifice demanded by
this Messiah on the other, they fell victims to Satanic pride. In their
minds, therefore, they were determined that this Messiah must be
destroyed.

III. THE COMMON PEOPLE OF PALESTINE

When our Lord spoke of the masses of Jews as "sheep without
a shepherd," He knew what He was talking about. This He knew
from His divine knowledge, of course, but even His human dealings
with the badly confused and misled Jews would have led Him to
the same conclusion. The inconsistency of the Jewish masses ran
true to form all through Christ's Public Life. This is the cycle of
their relations with Christ:

A. Initial Enthusiasm

- READ Luke 5:15-16 and Matthew 7:28-29. It would seem
  obvious that the Jewish masses first flocked to Him for the
  authority of His Message and the power of His miracles.

B. Disappointment and Unbelief

- READ Luke 4:16-30 and John 6:61-67. The crowds at Nazareth
  and Capharnaum became disillusioned with Jesus. He simply

failed to measure up to their Messianic expectations. The
Messiah was supposed to bring political power and might in
war, not the kind of ideals counseled in the parables and the
Sermon on the Mount.

C. A Final Break with Jesus

- READ Matthew 11:20-24. Our Lord directed hard words to the
  impenitent towns which refused to accept His Message. In
  His last hours He warned the women of Jerusalem of the
  tragedies that awaited their people. They had hardened their
  hearts to the Christ. (See also Luke 23:27-31)

IV. THE SAVIOR HIMSELF

The spotlight now narrows to Jesus Christ Himself, and it
goes without saying that He is the central character in the unfolding
drama. After the pledge of faith made by Peter in the name of the
other apostles at Caesarea Philippi (see Matthew 16:13-20), Christ
gave the apostles the first inkling of what they could expect of the
future:

- READ Matthew 16:21-23 where Christ predicts His own death,
  and then in Matthew 16:24-28 the all-important doctrine of the
  cross as applied to all men. Discuss some of the frequent crosses
  that men must bear in union with Christ in this life. Are
  sufferings such as these good things in themselves or must they
  be seen in some particular light? What is the link to Christ's
  Resurrection?

On another occasion our Lord spelled out more in detail just
what suffering lay in store for Him in fulfilling His Redemptive
Mission:

> But Jesus taking to himself the Twelve said to them, "Behold,
> we are **going up to Jerusalem,** and all things that have been
> written through the prophets concerning the Son of Man will
> be accomplished. For he will be delivered to the Gentiles, and
> will be mocked and scourged and spit upon: and after they have
> scourged him, they will put him to death: and on the third day
> he will rise again." (Luke 18:31-33)

- LOOK back over the Jerusalem theme as it is developed in the

Lenten liturgy. Do you think the apostles understood this theme at this time? Read Luke 18:34 for your answer.

But Jesus made it very clear that when He chose "to go up to Jerusalem," He did so by His own free decision. Even the timing of His surrender to the forces of evil was set by His own choice.

- BRING out this point of free choice with the help of the following texts: Luke 4:30, John 11:15-16, and John 10:17-18.

The final clash between Christ and Satan was at hand. Good met evil head on. All of us, Christian as well as Jew, even non-believers were involved.

It would be easy to place the blame for Christ's conviction and death solely upon Pontius Pilate, upon the Pharisees, upon the Jewish people. A moment's serious reflection, however, should demonstrate the hypocrisy of such a charge. All mankind must bear responsibility for the death of Jesus Christ. With the exception of her alone who was without sin, all men stand accused. True, a number of the Jews of Christ's time, especially the leaders, clearly rejected Christ; but they are not the entire nation, nor the descendants of Israel for all time to come. It is certainly equally true to say that many Christians since have rejected their Lord. Sin and pride know no distinction of race or creed. All mankind can pray with the Hebrew prophet Isaia:

> . . . it was our infirmities that he bore, our sufferings that he endured . . . he was pierced for our offenses, crushed for our sins . . . . (Is. 53:4-5)

- LOOK back over the biblical record of this momentous clash between the Messiah and Satan:
  Genesis 3:15 – the combat foreshadowed.
  Matthew 4:1-11 – the combat in the desert.
  Mark 14:32-38 – the combat in the Garden.
  Luke 24:3-8 – the combat decided in Christ's Easter Victory.

Section 2. THE LAST WEEK OF OUR LORD'S LIFE

When our Lord received the news that Lazarus had died and He made the decision to return to Bethany, the apostles sensed that something disastrous might happen. Bethany was in the vicinity of

Jerusalem and they had been avoiding the city for some time. The apostles knew one reason: Christ's enemies had been intensifying their scheming against Him. Jesus alone knew the other reason: "His time had not yet come." As they now turned their steps in the direction of Jerusalem, Thomas spoke for all of them when he said: "Let us also go, that we may die with him." (John 9:16)

I. PALM SUNDAY: 30 A.D.

Jesus delayed His actual entrance into the city until "six days before the Passover" (John 12:1). It was in springtime when He prepared to celebrate the greatest of the Jewish feasts with His apostles. A last meal at the home of Lazarus preceded the extraordinary day which we observe yearly as the Second Sunday of the Passion or "Palm Sunday." It was to be the day of Christ's triumphal entry into Jerusalem.

A. The Foreshadowing

This day, too, had been foreshadowed many centuries before in the writings of the prophet Zacharia:

"Rejoice heartily, O daughter Sion, shout for joy, O daughter Jerusalem!"

"See, your king shall come to you; *a just savior is he, meek, and riding on an ass, on a colt, the foal of an ass." (Zach. 9:9)*

B. The Fulfillment

On the first Palm Sunday Christ's entrance into Jerusalem was received with palms and the joyful Hosannas, but behind the smiles and shouts of praise our Lord saw hearts fickle and confused: they did not understand the real designs of God in their regard. Some who did understand them rejected them. No wonder that St. Luke recorded that Jesus "wept when He drew near and saw the City." (Luke 9:41)

- READ the full account of Palm Sunday in St. Luke 19:29-44, and note particularly Christ's feelings as revealed in verses 41-44.

C. The Symbol

The triumphal entry into the Holy City of David is a striking symbol of the final stage in God's Plan for mankind. Christ will

come in triumph on that day to take possession of "the New Jeru-salem," the symbol of His eternal Kingdom. The Lord of History will then reign as King forever.

- LOOK back over the Old Testament chapter on King David and review the symbolism of "the City of David."

II. HOLY THURSDAY

NOTE: We follow here the traditional order of the **Thursday Passover meal,** but it is well to note that there is some possibility that a double Passover was celebrated during that era. According to this theory the Last Supper was held on **Tuesday,** while Christ was put to death on Friday.

As the final week of Christ's life progressed, the Hebrew Passover was at hand. As loyal sons of the Mosaic Law, Jesus and the apostles were obliged to go into the Holy City to celebrate the Supper of the Paschal Lamb, as so many generations had done before them. The threat to His life from the plotting Sadducees and Pharisees did not keep our Lord from His religious observance. He called Peter and John and gave them instructions:

"Go and prepare for us the passover that we may eat it." (Luke 22:8)

- READ Christ's full instructions in Luke 22:7-13. The house chosen for the supper belonged to one of Christ's wealthier friends, possibly one of the parents of young Mark the Evan-gelist.

A. **The Passover Meal**

The historical origins of the Passover go back to Mosaic times. Every faithful Jew proudly celebrated this glorious day of liberation from Egypt. God had come to the defense of His People; He had freed them from slavery. As on that first fateful night, God's instruc-tions were carried out to the letter. The lamb was sacrificed and its meat eaten at a special supper, which was food for a long and arduous journey. A feeling of confidence and complete dependence upon Yahweh filled the people's hearts, just as it did with their ancestors, 1,300 years before.

Peter and John hastened to their task. They purchased the lamb, brought it to the Temple to be offered in sacrifice to Yahweh, and then prepared it for the supper meal. They gathered the other dishes of food also traditional for this solemn occasion: the herbs, the special sauce, the rolls of unleavened bread, and the cups of wine.

- SHOW how the lamb first sacrificed in Egypt around 1250 B.C. prepared the way for the true Lamb of God, the Messiah.

- EXPLAIN the connections between the Exodus and the Redemption, the Passover and the Mass. Review the diagram in Chapter V.

With the preparations for the Paschal Supper now completed, the stage was set for the transition from the Old to the New Covenant.

1. THE NIGHT OF THE LAST SUPPER

When evening came and all the apostles were assembled with Jesus at the supper-room, a new reason for sorrow burdened the heart of Christ. The apostles were bickering with one another about where they would sit for the meal. Of all the nights to quarrel! Rather than scold them, Jesus in His own patient way gave them a lesson in humility which they would never forget. He took the place of the slave who in rich men's houses bathed the dusty feet of the guests. Christ girded Himself with a towel and went from one apostle to the next, washing the feet of each. He must have washed Judas' feet, too!

- READ the account in John 13:1-17 and try to picture the astonishment of the apostles.

- HOW is this remarkable event commemorated in the Holy Thursday liturgy? Why is it commemorated thus, even at the Holy Father's Mass in Rome?

2. THE SACRIFICE OF THE NEW COVENANT

It was during this Passover meal that Jesus took one of the small round loaves of unleavened bread, broke it apart, and gave a portion to each of the apostles, saying:

"Take and eat: this is my body." (Mt. 26:26)

Then reaching for one of the cups of wine, Jesus went on:

*"All of you drink of this: **for this is my blood of the new covenant,** which is being shed for many unto the forgiveness of sins." (Mt. 26:27-28)*

Just how well the apostles at this time understood the rich significance of what Christ had said and done we cannot know for sure. Christ's intention, however, when taken in the total picture of the Old Covenant's Paschal Meal, is clear: **A New Covenant was being born, and toward that purpose Christ's blood would be shed.**

The Paschal Lamb is a type of Christ, whose Body and Blood in sacrifice sealed the New Covenant.

Just as the lamb in the time of the Exodus was offered in sacrifice for the Hebrews' liberation from Egyptian slavery, so now in the New Covenant Christ offered Himself as the victim of sacrifice **for men's liberation from sin.** Christ offered Himself in this bloody manner on Good Friday.

- WHAT dogma of our Catholic faith comes out of Christ's words, "unto the remission of sins"?

3. COMMUNION IN CHRIST'S SACRIFICE

By God's command to Moses (see Exodus 12:8), the Hebrews on the first Paschal night ate of the lamb which had been offered in sacrifice. They nourished themselves as part of the sacrificial rite, thus uniting themselves with the sacrifice in a striking symbol of oneness. In that oneness they saw their complete dependence upon God and found there the strength and confidence they sought and needed so desperately.

In the New Covenant sacrifice Christ fulfilled the Old Testament's foreshadowings. "Take and eat . . . All of you drink this," He had said. By their Lord's directive, therefore, the apostles nourished themselves, and thus in the same striking symbol of oneness they united themselves with the sacrifice of Christ's cross and the glorious resurrection that followed. In this oneness with their Lord they found — and all Christians after them find — the strength and confidence each seeks and needs so urgently to live the full Christian life on earth.

Christ's Body and Blood unites men to the Paschal Sacrifice and nourishes them for life in the New Covenant.

- IN HER pastoral concern for the good of the faithful, does the Church ever allow Communion outside of Mass? Discuss the advantages and disadvantages. By what reflections can those communicating link their Communion to the Mass of the day?

4. A FINAL COMMAND

When He had thus completed the institution of the Eucharist

and the apostles had received of His Body and Blood, Jesus looked around at His chosen eleven and spoke these significant words:

". . . do this in remembrance of me." (Luke 22:19)

What Christ had just done, **they were to do, too.** They were to take bread and wine in the same way, offer them to the Father in sacrifice, and share the sacrificial offerings as nourishment for the faithful. Under these signs of bread and wine (later to be called sacramental signs) the Lord's sacrifice **would be made present** to all generations in an unbloody manner. Holy Communion would seal the union. In this way the faithful are united with their triumphant Savior until the end of time.

By giving the apostles this special power which was His alone to give, Christ ordained them His first priests. The Last Supper marked the night of their ordination.

- HAD the apostles any ideas at all about the Eucharist prior to this night? Clear ideas? Confused ideas?

- READ John 6:48-60. Why do you think our Lord waited until this day in Capharnaum to make His promise of the Eucharist? The event recorded in John 6:1-15 should give you the answer.

- DO YOU remember any other foreshadowing in the Old Testament? Read Exodus 16:4, 13-15, and 31-35.

B. Gethsemani: after 11 P.M.

After singing a traditional Hebrew hymn, the group left the supper room in the direction of the city gates looking out to the east. Once they had passed through the gates, they made their way down the hill along a rocky path until they reached a tiny brook called Cedron. Crossing the bridge, they moved part way up another hill until they reached an olive garden. The garden was a favorite place of prayer within a half-hour's walk of the supper room. Mark's parent may well have owned the garden, also. Undoubtedly our Lord had often taken the apostles there before. But this night was different; they recalled it vividly to the end of their lives.

The apostles were tired that night. In typical oriental fashion eight of them stretched out upon their cloaks and fell asleep. Jesus took His three special friends, Peter, James, and John, with Him a little farther into the garden. Then He went off "a stone's throw" by Himself and prayed. It was during this experience of prayer that

Tree of Agony in the Garden of Gethsemane. THE MATSON PHOTO SERVICE

He suffered the inner conflict which changed His sweat into a bloody agony. He allowed His human nature to feel the full revulsion of the events the next day would bring. By one last assault Satan tried to swerve Him from the mission His Father had given Him. A flow of ideas clouded His mind until He felt lost and abandoned:

1. **He saw the real evil of our sins,** the revolt against the generous Creator and the betrayal of the Father's love.

2. **He saw the horrible details of the Passion,** the physical suffering and the deeper psychological agony.

3. **He saw the ingratitude and hardness of sinner's hearts,** the refusal of men to cooperate in their own Redemption.

No wonder His human will cried out:

> *"Abba, Father, all things are possible to thee. Remove this cup from me: yet not what I will, but what thou willest." (Mark 14:36)*

III. GOOD FRIDAY

A. **The Arrest:** about 2 A.M.

The traitor Judas guided the squad of soldiers assigned to arrest Jesus. He too knew the garden well. With torches blazing in the night they searched around in the darkness until they saw a majestic figure striding resolutely toward them. Judas motioned to the band to halt and moved forward to meet his Lord with a traitorous kiss. The soldiers marked the signal identifying Jesus and rushed forward, as they had done so many times in capturing notorious criminals. Satan took over. He whipped up the evil spirits in men in order to take revenge upon this Messiah who would "take away the sins of the world." Christ revealed Satan's wicked designs:

> "... **this is your hour,** and the power of darkness." (Luke 22:53)

- READ the full account of the arrest in Matthew 26:47-56. What is brought out clearly by verses 53-54?

The apostles fled in terror, just as Christ said they would. The Lord of History freely gave Himself over into the hands of evil men.

B. **Before Annas and Caiphas:** between 3 and 6 A.M.

They dragged Jesus back into the city after stopping at the homes of Annas and Caiphas, the instigators of the plot against our Lord. Caiphas was the ruling high-priest, while Annas, his father-in-law, remained a strong power behind the scene. Since the hour was too late for convening the Sanhedrin at the Temple, the usual meeting place, Caiphas summoned to his own home a group of the lay and priestly aristocracy — even including some Pharisees. They intended to make short work of this troublemaker.

We saw before that Sadducees like Annas and Caiphas were political opportunists of the most unscrupulous kind. In order to advance their own selfish interests, they had compromised with the Romans. The Pharisees, on the other hand, as proud patriots seeking to overthrow this Roman tyranny, detested the ruling Sadducee aristocracy, particularly their fellow members of the Sanhedrin. And yet in this one venture, the elimination of the Nazarene troublemaker, the Pharisees readily joined common cause with their deadliest enemies.

- REVIEW from an earlier chapter the characteristics of the Sadducees and Pharisees. They are important for their role in Christ's execution.

Caiphas was careful to observe at least the form of legality. There was to be no slip-up. When witnesses contradicted one another, Caiphas played his final card. He asked Christ pointblank:

"I adjure thee by the living God that thou tell us whether thou art the Christ, the Son of God." (Mt. 26:63)

If Jesus answered, "Yes, I am," to the mind of Caiphas and the others He would have blasphemed, making a mockery of sacred Messianic beliefs. Thus Caiphas intended to trap our Lord. Christ did not dodge the insolent challenge. He answered Caiphas. Using the Messianic prophecies of Daniel and the psalmists, He replied:

"Thou hast said it. Nevertheless, I say to you, hereafter you shall see the Son of Man sitting at the right hand of the Power and coming upon the clouds of heaven." (Mt. 26:64)

- READ the rest of the trial account in Matthew 26:59-66 and then the horrible aftermath in verses 67-68. Do you see any connection of the latter with the Agony in the Garden?

C. Before Pilate: beginning about 8 A.M.

Jewish law prescribed punishment of death for blasphemy, but the puppet Sanhedrin had no authority to pass sentence of death. Hence it was necessary to induce Pontius Pilate, the Roman procurator, to serve their ends by condemning Jesus to death.

Pilate, however, was no friend of the Sanhedrin. In fact, he detested the Jews, and most of all their hypocritical leaders. The massacre of Jewish pilgrims at the Temple during the Passover a few years earlier remained an ugly symbol of the bad feeling between the Sanhedrin and the Roman procurator. And now another potential riot was brewing, much like the menacing crowds which had refused to disperse at the procurator's orders on that shocking day at the Temple. This miracle-working Nazarene, he mused, might stir up another hornets' nest, and around Passover time, too. Even if he himself were harmless, he stirred up crowds; and crowds were dangerous. Pilate had received full reports on the Palm Sunday triumph, that alarming display of power which brought out the fanaticism of the Jewish mobs at their worst. One thing was sure: Pilate could not

afford another riot; this kind of thing was frowned upon at Rome. Peace and prosperity filled the Roman coffers, not riots. And so, Pilate had to give the Sanhedrin a hearing, whether he liked it or not.

Caiphas and his conspirators dragged the Nazarene before the judgment-seat of the pagan procurator. The charge? Not blasphemy alone, with which Christ had been condemned at the Jewish trial, for a purely religious charge would never stand up in a Roman court. Rather, in a burst of hypocrisy the Jewish leaders charged Jesus with a political crime, "stirring up the people" against the emperor Caesar. This man had called Himself "the King of the Jews."

> *"If thou release this man, thou art no friend of Caesar: for everyone who makes himself king sets himself against Caesar."* (John 19:12)

1. PILATE AND THE KING

The face-to-face meeting of the petty politician and the Lord of History gives us as we noted before, another deep insight into the Heart of Christ the King.

- READ the revealing account of this meeting in John 18:33-38.

- LOOK back over the king-theme in the David chapter. David is a type of Christ the King. Despite the marked similarities, what notable differences would you point out between the kingship of David and that of Christ?

2. THE KING AMONG ROMAN SOLDIERS

Pilate gave the prisoner over to his Roman soldiers for scourging. Perhaps he thought the sight of blood might placate the Jews, and they would then let this man of obvious innocence go free. Pilate sensed all along that the priests were using him to take revenge upon one of their own rivals, and he resented it. He wanted to be resolute in his determination to set Jesus free, but there was always that complication with headquarters at Rome. He could not risk another black mark on his record.

a. **The Scourging** The thought of Roman scourging horrifies and sickens civilized men of today. Soldiers stripped the criminal, bound him to a post, and thrashed away with rods and chain-like cords linked with bone and lead. In a matter of seconds the flesh hung in bleeding shreds, but the heartless Romans put no legal limit to the number of blows.

When they dragged the bleeding Christ to a stool, a comic among the soldiers must have suggested a game of "Kings," actually a popular pastime of that day, as we know from archaeological discoveries. The game quickly slipped into a sacrilegious outrage which is unequaled in history.

- READ the account in Matthew 27:27-31 and recall two things:

  1. Behind the Roman soldiers are Satan and sinful men *of all time.*

  2. Christ chose this suffering *freely.*

The Psalmist in prophecy had looked into the Heart of Christ:

But I am a worm, not a man; the scorn of men, despised by the people. All who see me scoff at me; they mock me with parted lips, they wag their heads . . . . (Ps. 21:7-8)

b. **Ecce Homo** Even Pilate was shocked by the sight of Jesus. "Behold the man!", he said with perhaps even a gesture of sympathy. But the cry from the priests and their professional rabble-rousers swelled all the louder: "Crucify him! Crucify him!" Pilate weakened. He spoke with Christ again, tried one last time to talk the priests out of their madness: "Shall I crucify your king?" The answer of the Jewish leaders has rung down through history. With it they signed their own condemnation before the eyes of men of all time:

"We have no king but Caesar." (John 19:15)

How many in the crowds seconded that cry of final rejection, we will never know in this life. But it is clear that the leaders of the Jewish people had rejected "the holy one of God." The Messianic Age that had been promised to their people from Abraham's time, prophesied again and again by their holy men, had begun. Whatever their guilt before God may have been, many failed to accept their Messiah.

- READ this sad chapter in Jewish history in John's account 19:4-16, and remember that John is writing as a believing Jew who is horrified at the rejection of the Messiah.
  "He came unto his own, and his own received him not." John 1:11.

Pilate surrendered. He yielded to the pressure of the priests and their followers. In a symbolic washing of hands he tried to disown the conviction, but the same hands picked up pen and officially signed the papers of execution. The Roman seal ratified the document. Jesus stood by, ready according to His Father's Plan to suffer for the sins of men.

- WOULD you excuse Pilate from the guilt of Jesus' death? Discuss. Note John's record of Christ's words in chapter 19:11. Would you hold the Jewish people responsible for Christ's death? In what way are all men responsible?

D. The Death-march to Calvary: 11 A.M.

Already a broken man physically, Jesus was now compelled to shoulder the cross-bar for his own execution. With a manful effort He kept His feet beneath the load and then staggered along the narrow streets behind the squad of executioners led by the mounted Roman centurion in charge.

- RELIVE Christ's Way of the Cross in the fourteen Stations of the Cross.

E. The Crucifixion: 12 Noon

Golgotha, "the place of the skull," was a small knob of rocky ground just outside of the city to the northwest. The road edged the base of the hill and then swung around through the city's gates. Workmen on Calvary had earlier dug holes to support the upright beams for the executions. Pilgrims flocking to the city for the Passover probably stopped to stare at the three beams, finger-like against the sky. Some may even have waited, lining up for the promised spectacle of Roman horror.

The Romans did not disappoint the curious crowds. The centurion snapped his orders as the procession reached the hill. Professional executioners leaped to their tasks and in just a few moments were driving nails through the hollow wrist bones of Christ's arms into the sturdy wood of the crossbeam. Next they got Jesus to His feet, dragged Him over to the upright beam, and then pushed the crossbeam up, until it caught with a thud in the joint carved out at the top. Jesus hung there helpless and in excruciating pain. His legs dangled free only for a moment; two of the executioners grabbed them at the calf and began the most delicate job of all, nailing the right foot over the left, thus pinning both to the upright beam itself. The cross now stood there intact, and to its beams were pinioned the arms and legs of the Son of God made man. The Lord of History, the mediator between God and man, offered Himself in bloody sacrifice. Little

did the pious Jews from the diaspora realize that the true Paschal
Lamb of God was being sacrificed before their very eyes.
NOTE: People familiar with the prophetic books of the Old Testament recognize in this moment of Christ's suffering the fulfillment
of the prophecies in Second-Isaia, chapters 40-55:

> . . . there was in him no stately bearing to make us look at him,
> nor appearance that would attract us to him.

> He was spurned and avoided by men, a man of suffering,
> accustomed to infirmity, . . .

> Yet it was our infirmities that he bore, our sufferings that he
> endured, while we thought of him as stricken, as one smitten
> by God and afflicted.

> **But he was pierced for our offenses, crushed for our sins; upon
> him was the chastisement that makes us whole, by his stripes
> we were healed.**

> We had all gone astray like sheep, each following his own way;
> but the Lord laid upon him the guilt of us all.

> Though he was harshly treated, he submitted and opened not
> his mouth; like a lamb led to the slaughter or a sheep before
> the shearers, he was silent and opened not his mouth.

> . . . he was cut off from the land of the living, and smitten
> for the sin of his people . . . . (Isa. 53:2-9)

- REREAD the emphasized sections and then discuss their meaning
  in the light of our redemption. Note how much more fully we
  can understand some of these passages only in the light of their
  fulfillment in the New Testament.

- COUNT in this passage from Isaia the references to the theme of
  the Paschal Lamb. Can you think of any other references to the
  Paschal Lamb in any other parts of the Bible, either Old or
  New Testament? Remember, a biblical theme is an idea which
  keeps coming up in biblical history with increasing clarity of
  meaning.

Some suggested places to search:

1. Genesis 4:4 – Abel's sacrifice.

2. Genesis 22:13 – Abraham and Isaac.

3. Exodus 12:1-14 – The Exodus from Egypt.

4. Isaia 53:7 – The suffering Messiah.
5. John 1:35-37 – The "Lamb of God."
6. Hebrews 9:11-14 – St. Paul's explanation.
7. I Peter 1:18-19 – St. Peter's explanation.
8. Apocalypse 5:6-14 – Triumph of the Lamb.

• IN A written assignment show how the one main theme of *the lamb to be sacrificed* runs like a thread through all of these biblical passages. What is the meaning of this Paschal Lamb theme in God's Plan for man's salvation? Bring out the full force of the final stage of Christ's triumph, as symbolized in the passage from the Apocalypse.

F. The Death of Jesus: 3 P.M.

Death through severe shock could come quickly to the crucified, or it might drag out for hours, even days. Sometimes the Romans left the bodies to hang on the cross indefinitely as a harsh lesson for all passersby. But they could not leave Jesus and the two thieves on the cross too long because of the Jewish Sabbath. The Romans, shrewd conquerors that they were, respected for political reasons the religious customs of their conquered peoples. That is the reason why the executioners broke the legs of the two thieves; thus they hastened their death. But when they turned to Jesus, they found Him already dead. Instead of breaking Christ's legs, the centurion plunged his spear into Jesus' side, a routine stroke insuring death.

What had been the actual cause of Christ's death in medical terms? Medical men in studying the details given us in the Gospels judge death to have come by suffocation, largely due to the extreme shock which Christ's agonizing posture on the cross brought to the lungs. Circulation failure also would develop as the crippled body ceased to function.

At the moment of His death (and, as God, He Himself decreed the hour), Christ cried out **in triumph,** as triumph His death indeed was:

"Father, into thy hands I commend my spirit." (Luke 23:46)

His final words emphasized again the freedom of decision which Christ exercised first in becoming man, and then in taking upon Himself the sufferings of the Passion. His Passion, as His Incarnation, was **an act of perfect love.** The Redemption is a mystery of love, God's love for men. Christ made this freedom of decision perfectly clear:

". . . I lay down my life that I may take it up again. No one takes it from me, but I lay it down myself." (John 10:17-18)

- WE ARE most accustomed to the kind of crucifix which brings out forcefully Christ's physical suffering. Did anyone ever see a crucifix which brings out *the triumphant aspect* of Christ's death? Discuss the merits of each type of crucifix. If available, bring in some crucifixes or pictures of them to illustrate the different types.

The evangelists report startling things occurring at the moment of Christ's death. (See Matthew 27:51-54). The symbolism in the rending of the curtain veiling the Temple's Holy of Holies is of special interest. Just as the Temple had always been a sacred symbol for the Hebrews (see the David Chapter), so now there is deep meaning in the shattering event at the Temple's very heart, the Holy of Holies. The Temple had symbolized God's presence among men, among His Chosen People. The rent curtain strikingly symbolized God's departure from the Temple, the end of Temple sacrifice in His honor, and the transition from the Old to the New Covenant. A new temple replaced the old. The new temple is the Temple of the Holy Spirit which we call the mystical body of Christ. God is present among His children, but not merely in a building of mortar and stone. He is present in the mystical body of His Son, the Church, and He will stay with Christ's Church until the end of time.

Old Covenant	New Covenant
Yahweh	God the Father
dwells among men	
in the Temple.	in the mystical body of His divine Son.

- READ St. Paul's explanation of the transition from Old Testament sacrifice to New Testament sacrifice. Compare Hebrews 9:1-10 with 9:11-15.

G. The Burial: around 6 P.M.

The crowds dispersed with the threatening darkness mentioned in the Gospels (Matthew 27:45). A small band of loyal men and women hovered around the Blessed Mother as she held her Son's bruised body in her arms.

• THIS is the scene depicted in the famous Pietà of the great
sculptor Michelangelo. Try to find a picture of this impressive
work of art.

Joseph of Arimathea obtained permission from Pilate to bury
Jesus in a nearby tomb which he had purchased for himself. It is
here that they put the body of Jesus. They rolled in place the rock
which sealed the tomb. Darkness filled the tomb and the darkness
of death fell over the entire Jerusalem countryside. The body of
the Son of God made man lay stretched out lifeless upon the shelf
cut out as a niche in the rock wall. Jesus' dearest friends withdrew,
with much the same darkness in their hearts.

IV. THE GLORY OF EASTER: Christ rises from the dead – around 6 A.M.

At what precise moment the glory of the resurrected Christ
dispelled the darkness of the tomb we do not know. But sometime
before the morning sunrise broke over the Jerusalem countryside,
Jesus Christ, the Son of God, rose from the dead. With His divine
power He brought human soul and human body together again.
A newly glorified human nature passed through the stone confine-
ment of the tomb. Christ went to His Father and in that moment
crowned His Redemptive Mission with magnificent victory.

A. The Discovery

The Sabbath was now over. The faithful women hurried back
to the tomb to complete the burial preparations. The April morning
was probably bright and clear as the sun rose over the city's rooftops,
but little did these still saddened friends of Christ suspect the day's
true splendor:

> And when the Sabbath was past, Mary Magdalene, Mary the
> mother of James, and Salome, bought spices, that they might
> go and anoint him. And very early on the first day of the week,
> they came to the tomb, when the sun had just risen and they
> were saying to one another, "Who will roll the stone back from
> the entrance of the tomb for us?" And looking up they saw that
> the stone had been rolled back, for it was very large. But on
> entering the tomb, they saw a young man sitting at the right
> side, clothed in a white robe, and they were amazed. He said

Ancient Palestinian rock-cut tomb with a rolling stone at the entrance. This is similar to the tomb in which Christ was buried. THE MATSON PHOTO SERVICE

to them, "Do not be terrified. You are looking for Jesus of Nazareth, who was crucified. He has risen, He is not here. Behold the place where they laid Him. But go, tell His disciples and Peter that He goes before you into Galilee; there you shall see Him, as He told you." (Mark 16:1-7)

God's Plan for man's salvation had reached its high point. Love had triumphed over sin. "The anointed one," the Christ, had redeemed His people just as God had promised in the Garden of Eden after Adam's fall from grace. Satan's head was crushed beneath the Savior's heel.

The Lord of History reigns now and forever.

St. Paul captures the true dimension of this central event of all history when he exalts the Resurrection of Christ and its meaning for all of us:

> *But if we have died with Christ, we believe that we shall also live together with Christ; for we know that Christ, having risen from the dead, dies now no more . . . . (Rom. 6:8-9)*

> *Therefore, if you have risen with Christ, seek the things that are above, where Christ is seated at the right hand of God . . . When Christ your life, shall appear,* **then you too will appear with him in glory.** *(Col. 3:1-2, 4)*

SOME MEMORY HELPS:

1. **The Passover** or Pasch is the Jewish liturgical feast commemorating the Exodus from Egypt.

2. **The Mass** is the sacrifice of the New Covenant in which under the sacramental signs of bread and wine at a meal the Glorious Christ in union with His Mystical Body offers Himself to the Father in behalf of men.

SUMMARY

Christ met with varying responses from His hearers: the disciples loved and followed Him, the Pharisees and Sadducees plotted to kill Him, as a threat to their personal ambitions; the common people flocked to Him early, but then fell away when He failed to make their dreams of riches and power come true. The clash of Christ and Satan reached its peak in this final week.

The last week started off with a day of triumph on Palm Sunday, but Holy Thursday found our Lord seated around a secluded Passover table with just His innermost circle of friends. In the framework of the Hebrew Paschal liturgy, He instituted the Holy Eucharist, and then imparted to the apostles the priestly powers of ordination.

After the disquieting prayer and agony of blood in the Garden of Gethsemani, events moved swiftly: the arrest, the religious trial before the Sanhedrin, the hours of mockery and outrage. In the morning Christ was dragged before Pontius Pilate for civil trial. Against his own judgment, Pilate yielded to the pressures of the

Jewish leaders, had Jesus scourged, then finally signed the decree of execution.

Jesus carried the crossbar to Calvary and there was crucified between two thieves, but His death was a triumph amid seeming defeat. The Old Covenant died with Him, and a New Covenant was joined with God as Christ rose gloriously from the dead.

QUESTIONS

1. What was the response to Christ and His Message on the part of the Jewish leaders? of the common people?

2. In the Lenten liturgy what has the theme "going up to Jerusalem" come to mean?

3. Sketch briefly at least four stages of the clash between Christ and Satan.

4. What was the prophetic foreshadowing of Christ's triumphal entry into Jerusalem? its symbolism?

5. What is the connection between the historical events of the Exodus and of the Redemption? between the Jewish liturgy of the Passover and the first Mass at the Last Supper? Explain.

6. How does Holy Communion fit into the sacrifice of the New Covenant?

7. How did Christ institute the sacrament of Holy Orders?

8. What brought on the bloody agony which Christ suffered at Gethsemani?

9. What was the principal charge brought against Christ at the religious trial? at the civil trial before Pilate?

10. Describe the Roman torture by scourging.

11. What would you say about the guilt of the Jews in crucifying Jesus?

12. Describe each successive stage in a routine Roman execution by crucifixion.

13. Why was Christ's death on the cross really a triumph?

14. What is the symbolism of the split curtain in the Temple's Holy of Holies?

15. What is the new temple of God's presence in the world?

16. What is the real significance of the Resurrection and why is it so essential for Christ's Redemptive Mission?

The Liturgy
of Passiontide and Easter

We are approaching the very heart of the Church's liturgical year, the Paschal Mystery. Just as in the actual history of Christ's final weeks of life, things are moving to a swift climax.

I. THE FIRST SUNDAY OF THE PASSION

Passiontide begins with the first Sunday of the Passion. The faithful are forcefully alerted to the concluding weeks of Lent when they find the statues and other religious objects in church veiled in purple. This recalls that Christ hid Himself from His enemies when they took up stones to cast at Him for seeming to claim equality to God Himself:

> *"Amen, amen, I say to you, before Abraham came to be, I am."* *(John 8:58)*

- READ and reflect upon the Epistle of this Mass. Notice how *"Christ offered Himself"* unto God the Father," thus reminding us that all the events of the next two weeks were *freely chosen for the love of us.*

II. THE SECOND SUNDAY OF THE PASSION

But on the second Sunday of the Passion, often called Palm Sunday, the ceremonies begin on a triumphant note. The priest wears red vestments during the blessing of the palms, and psalms of joy burst upon what might have been another day of sorrowful foreboding, had not a remarkable event occurred. The triumphant entry of Christ into Jerusalem cleared the skies of threatening clouds to let the sun of final victory shine through. In the liturgical procession planned for this day, we can give full expression to our confidence in this final victory of our Savior:

276

"Hosanna to the Son of David! Blessed is he who comes in the name of the Lord!" (Mt. 21:9)

Even though the Mass itself requires a change back to violet vestments, the complete confidence in Christ's victory will never desert us through the darkest hours of Holy Week. In the triumphant entry we have an early glimpse of Christ's total victory.

- READ the magnificent Epistle of Second Passion Sunday. Pick out the words which best bring out the double theme of Lenten sorrow and Paschal victory.
  The solemn reading of the Passion is according to the Gospel of St. Matthew.

III. TUESDAY AND WEDNESDAY IN HOLY WEEK

The Masses for these days include the reading of the Passion according to St. Mark on Tuesday, St. Luke on Wednesday. The stage is now set for the central event of all human history, and, therefore, the central action of the Church's liturgy.

IV. HOLY THURSDAY: an evening liturgy between 5 and 8 P.M.

Holy Thursday is like a hinge between the lengthier part of Lent and the three days of the Paschal Triduum, thereby connecting the time of penance with the special days of grace. It is the day of several important liturgical events:

A. Confessions

The public sinners of the Church were accepted back into the Christian community after their weeks of public penance with fasting, ashes, and sackcloth. They received the Paschal Communion with family and friends.

Today too, sinners should not wait until Holy Saturday to make their peace with God. At least by Thursday they should feel united again to their Savior so that through Paschal Communion they may join him more fully in His Passion and glorious Resurrection.

B. The Mass

The Mass for Holy Thursday is a reliving of the Last Supper of Christ with His apostles. This is the night of the Eucharist and the first ordinations to Christ's priesthood. All Christians gather around Christ's Eucharistic table just as the apostles did 1,900 years ago.

- READ the Epistle for St. Paul's account of the institution of the Holy Eucharist.
  What is the mood set in the Introit of the Mass? One of Paschal joy or one following the usual Lenten themes? or perhaps both?

A special feature of the Mass is the re-enactment of the external sign used by our Lord to teach His apostles the virtues of charity and humility. Like Christ Himself, the celebrant, be he pope or parish priest, will perform the washing service for his brethren. The gesture puts the words of the Gospel immediately into practice: "For I have given you an example, that as I have done to you, so you also should do." (John 13:15). This act of charity prepares the way for **the sacrament of charity, the Eucharist.**

- READ the Antiphons sung during the washing of the feet. Memorize Antiphon 8 as the perfect summary of the spirit of Holy Thursday.

C. **After the Evening Mass**

A procession is formed, in which the hosts which the faithful will receive on Good Friday are transferred to the "repository." Since no Mass-sacrifice is permitted on Good Friday, the hosts are consecrated on Holy Thursday. By watches during the night at the repository, the faithful will pay reverence to our Blessed Lord in the Eucharist. The main altar of the church is stripped bare while the deeply moving Psalm 21 is recited.

- OF WHAT is the altar a symbol?

The night is shrouded with sorrow at the knowledge that Christ has fallen into the hands of the enemy and even now is dragged to the homes of Annas and Caiphas.

D. **The Bishop's Mass**

In the Mass of Holy Thursday morning at the cathedral, the special oils for use in the sacraments during the year are consecrated.

V. GOOD FRIDAY: an afternoon liturgy between 3 and 6 P.M.

No Mass-sacrifice is offered on Good Friday. Christians join themselves with Mary beneath the cross on Calvary. These are the high points of the liturgical service:

A. Liturgy of the Word

Sacred texts are solemnly read.

1. THE LESSON FROM THE PROPHET OSEE: expresses sorrow for sin with hope in our final victory in rising with Christ.

2. THE LESSON FROM EXODUS 12:1-11: develops the theme of the Paschal Lamb, the type of Jesus Christ. The Lamb's blood will bring deliverance, while eating of the Lamb's flesh will nourish the Hebrews on their journey to the Promised Land.

- REVIEW the typology which was more fully developed in the earlier chapter on Moses and the Exodus.

3. ST. JOHN'S ACCOUNT OF THE PASSION: Notice the reference to the Pasch. The Christian Pasch replaces the Hebrew Passover and the New Covenant fulfills the Old.

B. The Solemn Prayers

Many of the Church's most pressing needs are recommended to God. In the early days of the Church, intentions like these were often read out at the Offertory of the Mass.

- LOOK UP in your Missals the special nine intentions chosen for prayer at this sacred moment.

C. Veneration of the Cross

This is a particularly stirring manifestation of Christian faith, as all the participants of the service approach the altar in order to pay their respects to Christ's cross, the symbol of His victory over Satan. The tradition goes back to the fourth century, after St. Helena's discovery of the true cross.

Behold the wood of the cross: on it hung the Savior of the world.

The cross of Christ is the standard of a victorious king.

"Truly he was the Son of God." MT. 27:54

- READ the famous and most moving of chants, called "The Reproaches." In response to the accounts of God's many kindnesses to the Hebrews listed in Psalm 135, the choir sings the following refrain as if coming from the heart of Christ Himself:

"O my people, what wrong have I done you? . . . What more should I have done for you that I have not done?"

These "reproaches" from the suffering Christ pierce deeply into the heart of every repentant sinner.

D. **Holy Communion**

By uniting ourselves with Christ in the Eucharist we join Him in His Passion, but always with confidence in His Paschal Victory. Like Mary, we would not wish to be any place else but at His side on Calvary; like her too, we shall share His glory.

- READ Psalm 21, which is sung during the distribution of Communion. Pick out the prophetic foreshadowings. Christ Himself prayed this psalm in His dying moments, just as we might pray the Our Father and Hail Mary in ours. Our Lady probably taught Him this Hebrew prayer in His boyhood.

VI. HOLY SATURDAY: a night liturgy, begun early enough to permit a Midnight Mass.

The day starts off quietly; our Savior lies at rest in the tomb. But the quiet is not so much the hush of shock at the suffering of Good Friday as the hush of anticipation of the victory of Christ's glorious Resurrection from the dead.

The Easter Vigil divides into three sections:

A. The Light Service.

B. The Baptismal Service.

C. The Eucharistic Service.

A. **The Light Service**

Fire and light are visible symbols of Jesus Christ, the Light of the World. Both figure in the early ceremonies of the Easter Vigil:

1. Blessing the New Fire

Kindling the fire directly from a stone flint suggests the idea of Christ's new and resurrected presence among us, like a spark leaping from the flint.

2. The Paschal Candle

Lighting the large Paschal candle from the new fire carries on the symbolism of Christ, the Light of the World. In the darkness of the church with all lights extinguished the Paschal candle shines brightly. When in a few moments this Paschal light is shared with the faithful, each of whom holds his own candle, the communication of **the light of faith** and **the life of Christ's grace** is vividly represented.

- SEE how many references to this light-symbolism you can find in the Easter song "Exultet" sung by the deacon. What connection would you note between these passages and the general outline of our course as explained in the Introduction of this book?

B. The Baptismal Service

Remember that the early Christians chose this night as the perfect setting for baptizing converts into Christ's Church. What time is more fitting to receive "the new life" of Christ than on the very night when Christ accomplished man's salvation? These are the parts of the baptismal service:

1. The Reading of the Lessons

Old Testament passages are chosen which foreshadow man's salvation through baptism.

a. GENESIS 1:1-2:2. the picture of creation foreshadows a new birth, a kind of second creation after Adam's sin.

b. EXODUS 14:24-15:1. the account of the Exodus and the crossing of the Reed Sea prefigure man's deliverance from the slavery of sin by passing through the waters of baptism.

c. ISAIA 4:2-6. in speaking of "the New Jerusalem" at the end of all time, the prophet tells of the blessed state to be enjoyed by all who prove faithful to Yahweh.

d. DEUTERONOMY 31:22-30. a reminder that even God's chosen ones can fall into sin. The unfaithfulness of the Chosen People points up a warning to all members of Christ's Church, the New People of God.

2. BLESSING OF THE BAPTISMAL WATER

After the first part of the litanies in honor of the saints, the solemn blessing of the baptismal water prepares for the baptism of the converts. The climax of the blessing is reached when the Paschal candle symbolizing Christ and His power is lowered into the water. Precious oils are mixed in, both the baptismal oils of catechumens and sacred chrism.

3. THE BAPTISMS

After their long training, the new converts finally come to share "the new life" of Christ, thus becoming children of God. They are welcomed into the Christian community by all the faithful, who in turn repeat their own baptismal vows in a stirring manifestation of community faith. The priest, going up and down the aisles, sprinkles all with the newly blessed water, thus repeating the sacramental sign of their own baptisms long ago. The second part of the litanies are sung, imploring Christ's blessing upon all the members of His mystical body, both new and old.

C. The Eucharistic Service

No other Mass of the liturgical year is so significant as this one of the Easter Vigil. We celebrate here the high point of the Christian Pasch, Christ's glorious Resurrection. The bells ring out triumphantly at the Gloria and the choir exults with songs of praise and joy at Christ's victory. The faithful who have remained close to Christ in His Passion now share the fruits of His victory.

- READ the Collect prayer and the Epistle and pick out the words which you think best express the deepest meaning of our joy. Develop your thoughts in a brief essay.

The joyous "Alleluias" re-echo in the ears of the faithful as they retire from the church and return to their homes.

"Christ is risen: risen as he said."

"He is not here, for he has risen . . ." MT. 28:6

VII. EASTER SUNDAY

Within the framework of another beautiful Mass heralding Christ's triumph to all the world, the Church adds a special "Sequence" following the Gradual and Epistle, "Victimae paschali laudes":

To the Paschal Victim (Christ) let Christians bring their sacrifice of praise.

. . . Christ the Sinless One has reconciled sinners to the Father. We know that Christ truly has risen from the dead. Have mercy upon us, O King of Victory. Amen, Alleluia.

God's Plan for man's salvation has reached its crowning moment in the festal joy of Easter. The centuries of Hebrew expectation have reached fulfillment in the triumph of Christ, the Lord of History. The Messianic Age so long a dream is now a reality, and the first fruits of God's promises to the patriarchs and prophets are poured out upon mankind. With a joyful heart we can pray with all our brethren:

Pour out upon us, O Lord, the spirit of your love, so that in your goodness you may make all whom you have nourished with these Easter sacraments harmoniously one. (Post-communion Prayer for Easter Sunday.)

Part Three
CHRIST LIVING ON

CHAPTER XV

THE NEW PEOPLE OF GOD: CHRIST'S CHURCH

We have come a long way from Adam's fall from grace. God kept His promise; He sent the Savior. Christ died for men's sins, but died as a king in triumph. His love conquered sin on Good Friday, but the victory burst out in all its glory on Easter Sunday morning. The splendor of Easter illumines the total span of history, as we saw earlier, but the brightest rays streamed through the days following the Resurrection. The Church calls this period of the liturgical year Eastertide.

Section 1 of this chapter covers three phases of Christ's Paschal Victory:

I. The Risen Christ among His friends.

II. Christ's return to His Father.

III. Christ's special sending of the Spirit.

Section 2 will treat of the role of the Spirit in Christ's Church.

Section 1. CHRIST'S PASCHAL VICTORY UNFOLDS

I. THE RISEN CHRIST AMONG HIS FRIENDS

We have already noted that the Risen Savior returned to His Father in His Easter triumph. At His Father's side Christ took possession of His Kingdom. We shall see more of this Paschal Victory a little further on.

It was also true to Christ's character to show concern for His friends. The traditions of our Faith record a further unfolding of the Paschal Victory in a series of friendly encounters, each of which was charged with joy.

A. With His Mother Mary

The Gospels tell us nothing of the risen Christ's meeting with His mother. True, since her strong faith never wavered, she hardly needed a face-to-face proof to convince her of the Resurrection. And yet it is hard to picture our Lord not visiting the person who above all others cooperated so closely with Him in the Redemption. This belief has been found in the Church rather constantly all through the ages. By omitting mention of the visit, the evangelists seem to respect the intimacy of a meeting between mother and son.

Liturgy: To someone searching the Easter octave Masses, the Mother of God seems strangely absent. The truth is that her inspiration permeates each day of the liturgy. Just as she was the guiding spirit which kept the apostles together after Christ's death, so she becomes for us the perfect model of Paschal joy. In her we see the Christ-formed personality, fully transformed as we hope to be by the Paschal Victory of her son.

B. With Mary Magdalene

When the women had hastened back and broken the news of their astounding discovery to the apostles, Peter and John ran to the tomb at once to see for themselves. Mary Magdalene rushed back again, and after Peter and John had departed, remained at the spot nearest where her Lord had been. She was undoubtedly too excited and too startled to think straight, even to register joy at the angel's message. All she knew was the separation from her Lord, and so she wept. The risen Christ came to her in the quiet of the garden.

- READ the touching account of their meeting in John 20:11-18.

Liturgy: See the Gospel for Easter Thursday. Note in the Epistle of the same Mass how the liturgy introduces an early baptism of a Gentile. The message of the Mass seems to emphasize **the universality of the Church** in welcoming sinner and Gentile alike into the community of Christians.

C. With the Disciples Returning to Emmaus

It was morning when these two friends of Jesus were walking to a town just outside of Jerusalem. They were disillusioned and discouraged. They "had hoped" that this was the Messiah, who would restore the glory of Israel. They would hardly seem deserving candidates for the grace they would receive, a personal meeting with the risen Christ.

- READ the account of this meeting in Luke 24:13-35. What was the deeper meaning drawn from this episode in our book's Introduction?

Liturgy: See the Gospel for Easter Monday. Do you see any connection of thought with Peter's sermon as recorded in the Epistle of the same Mass? Note especially the second half of the Epistle.

D. With the Apostles

1. WE CAN be sure that the two disciples from Emmaus returned to Jerusalem to tell the rest how they had seen the Lord and recognized Him in "the breaking of the bread." They mentioned that Simon Peter had also seen the risen Savior. (See Luke 24:34) Did the other apostles finally put their faith in Christ's Resurrection? We can't be sure, but our Lord did not leave them much time for prolonged doubts. In a split second on that first Easter Sunday night He passed through the closed doors and stood before them.

- READ the two accounts as recorded in Luke 24:36-47 and in John 20:19-23.

- WHY do you think Luke records Christ's eating of the fish?

- IN JOHN's eyewitness account, what is the significance of verses 21-23? How do you explain the fact that Christ on this Easter Sunday night gave the Spirit to the apostles even *before* the special sending of the Spirit on Pentecost? You will see the answer more clearly by the end of this chapter.

Liturgy: See the Gospel for Easter Tuesday where Luke's account is read in the liturgy of the Mass. Why do you think the Epistle of this same Mass records the message of Christianity as preached by St. Paul? Was there any special association between Luke and Paul?

2. OUR LORD appeared to the apostles a second time, but on this

occasion Thomas, absent during the last visit, was present. Thomas' doubts about our Lord's Resurrection showed how deep was the disillusionment which the apostles suffered after our Lord's death. Christ was wonderfully patient. The incident gives us another rich insight into the Heart of Christ.

- READ about Thomas' education in John 20:24-29. Do you think that you would have believed if you had been in Thomas' situation? even before this second appearance? Why? Is it reasonable to doubt a group of eye witnesses just because we haven't seen something with our own eyes? Note *verse 29* carefully.

Liturgy: See the Gospel for the Sunday within the octave of Easter where St. John's account is highlighted. Note that this Gospel brings both visits together in order to point up Thomas' story. What virtue is stressed in the Epistle of the same Mass? Do you see any resulting connection between the Gospel and the Epistle?

3. As CHRIST had instructed them (See Mark 16:7), the apostles headed north to their native Galilee. Peter and some of the others took up fishing again as their livelihood. One day, in a miraculous sign which they had seen before, that of nets bursting with fish, the apostles recognized their Lord. Even at the distance they could make out Christ hailing them from the shore. In his typically impetuous way, Peter dived into the lake, outdistancing the heavily burdened boat to shore. Jesus was already preparing a fire for their meal, a thoughtful gesture of friendship. As they ate around the fire, he put the apostles at their ease. He had a momentous announcement to make.

- READ the incident in full from the pen of our eyewitness John in his Gospel 21:1-14. Note here again, as we saw in an earlier chapter, how God uses miracles as *signs of His presence.*

Liturgy: See the Gospel of Easter Wednesday. Note the tie-in with Peter in the Epistle, where it is Peter's preaching that is highlighted. What connection could be made between the Epistle's call to action, "Repent and be converted," and Peter's miraculous catch of fish as recorded in the Gospel?

The picnic supper on the lakeshore was finished. Christ turned to Peter beside Him and the eyes and ears of all focused upon the two. The apostles sensed that something momentous was in the air.

- READ John's reporting of the conversation between our Lord and Peter in John 21:15-17. Listen as the other apostles did. Do you understand any better than they the full significance of Christ's words? Why does Christ speak in the imagery of shepherds and flocks of sheep? Look back over "The Heart of Christ" chapter and review how this shepherd-theme developed in the writings of the prophet Ezechiel and how our Lord applied the image of the shepherd to Himself. Why do you think He now applied the same image to Peter? Do the pope and bishops of our Catholic Church wear or carry anything symbolic of this shepherd-theme? Explain the symbolism.

Liturgy: See the Mass for the Second Sunday after Easter. You might call this Peter's special Mass. What our Lord said of Himself in the Gospel, He asked of Peter as the first pope of His Church. Note in the Epistle of the same Mass that Peter himself used the image of shepherd and sheep.

II. CHRIST'S RETURN TO THE FATHER

We must be careful to note that Christ came into the **full** glory of His Paschal Victory on Easter Sunday. Satan was completely vanquished, and the conquering Lord returned **that very day** to the Father in triumph. The Father, in our human way of reckoning things, gave His approval again to the Savior's Redemptive Mission, just as He had done at the Jordan Baptism. But now the Father did more: **He enthroned our Savior "at His right hand" in full majesty and power.**

> *Therefore God also has exalted him and has bestowed upon him the name that is above every name, so that at the name of Jesus every knee should bend of those in heaven, on earth and under the earth, and every tongue should confess that* **the Lord Jesus Christ is in the glory of God the Father.** *(Phil. 2:9-11)*

- SEE also our Lord's expression of these ideas in the Gospel for the Vigil of Ascension Thursday.

A. Christ's Farewell Ascension

While recognizing Christ's complete triumph "at the right hand of God" on Easter Sunday, Catholics are sometimes confused

about the meaning of Ascension Thursday, **forty days after Easter.**
If Christ entered God's Kingdom and was enthroned in majesty on
Easter Sunday, then what event is it that we celebrate on Ascension
Thursday? The answer is recorded in the Acts of the Apostles (Acts
1:11) .

IN A WORD: Ascension Thursday marks **the farewell departure**
of Christ from His friends.

We should not, therefore, picture our Risen Savior wandering
around the earth in between visits to His choice friends. Rather
it was from "the right hand of God," that Hebrew term that refers
to heaven, where He had already been enthroned in glory, that
Christ periodically returned to earth. He chose to impress this
farewell departure above all upon His apostles and at the same time
give them **a visible manifestation** of His Easter return to the Father.
At the Transfiguration only Peter, James, and John were present; now
all the apostles and many disciples saw Christ in a moment of special
glory as He ascended visibly to the Father.

- READ St. Luke's account of Ascension Thursday's departure as
  recorded in Acts 1:9-11. Does the fact that our Lord seemed
  "to ascend" mean that heaven is above us?

- WILL the glorious Christ ever come again? When?

Liturgy: The early Christians in their liturgy celebrated the total
victory of Christ on the feast of the Resurrection, and rightly so.
But the full triumph is too rich, too complex for commemoration
on one day alone. In the fourth century, therefore, the feasts we call
Ascension Thursday and Pentecost Sunday were separated from
Easter. On each of these holy days a different aspect of the one,
total Paschal Victory was highlighted. The dates for the holy days
were ready-made in the Acts of the Apostles, where St. Luke records
the occurrence of two important events on the fortieth and fiftieth
days after Easter. The two events were the **farewell** Ascension into
heaven (but remember that Christ had returned there immediately
on Easter) and the **special** sending of the Holy Spirit before the
birth of the Church (but remember that the Spirit had already
been at work since Easter) .

IN BRIEF: (Read across and down)

ONE PASCHAL VICTORY ON EASTER

With a Triple Aspect	Connected to a Triple Event	RESULT: Three liturgical feasts:
1. Victory over death	the Resurrection itself	The Resurrection – Easter Sunday
2. Glorification at the Father's side	the farewell Ascension	The Ascension – 40 days after Easter
3. Sending of the Holy Spirit	the *special* sending of the Holy Spirit at the birth of the Church	Pentecost – 50 days after Easter

- CONSULT the Mass of Ascension Thursday in the Missal. How would you express *the two main themes* of the Mass?

  Look for Theme 1 in the Gospel, the Introit, the Alleluia, the Offertory, and the Communion.

  Look for Theme 2 in the Collect, Secret, and Post-communion prayers, and above all the special Ascension Preface.

B. Waiting for the Special Coming of the Spirit

For the "forty days" of His visits, Christ perfected the formation of the apostles for their important posts in the early Church. Even as early as Easter Sunday night, He had the Holy Spirit to help Him, as St. John brings out so well in his account of Christ's visit to the upper room:

> *"Peace be to you! As the Father has sent me, I also send you." When he had said this, he breathed upon them, and said to them,* **"Receive the Holy Spirit:** *whose sins you shall forgive, they are forgiven them: and whose sins you shall retain, they are retained." (John 20:21-23)*

- WHY do we feel no surprise that the risen Christ has already sent the Holy Spirit from heaven as early as this Easter Sunday night?

Neither were the apostles downhearted at the seeming loss of their Lord. St. Luke tells us very clearly that immediately after the farewell departure which we know as Ascension Thursday, the Apostles experienced great joy:

*And they worshipped him (Christ), and returned to Jerusalem
with great joy. (Luke 24:52)*

The Message of the Kingdom which Christ had labored to teach
them is beginning to clarify at long last. That is why they are joyful.
Now that they had all shared the exhilarating experience of contact
with the risen Christ, the Baptist's happy announcement heard long
ago began to have meaning:

". . . the kingdom of heaven is at hand." (Mt. 3:2)

The apostles were anxious about the Kingdom. Surely the coming
of the Kingdom must be very close; so they asked our Lord about it:

*"Lord, wilt thou at this time restore the kingdom to Israel?"
(Acts 1:6)*

- READ Christ's answer in Acts 1:7-8. Note that He did not deny
  the coming of the Kingdom, but He told them in so many
  words that they had much work to do before they could think
  about any hour of glory.

*"**You shall be witnesses for me** in Jerusalem and in all Judea
and Samaria and even to the very ends of the earth." (Acts 1:8)*

With a challenge like that ringing in their ears, they hurried
back to the upper room, as our Lord had directed. They awaited
there the next manifestation of the Spirit's power, the next set of
events leading up to what they with their Hebrew mentality called
"the great Day of Yahweh," the final triumph of the Lord. But
we shall see more of this ultimate fulfillment of Christ's victory in
our next chapter. To be sure, at this early date the apostles' notions
of Judgment Day and the final triumph of their Lord were still
earth-ridden and far from the reality of which Christ had spoken
in prophecy.

III. CHRIST'S SPECIAL SENDING OF THE SPIRIT

For nine days the apostles remained together in constant prayer
and expectation, until "the fiftieth day," the day of the Hebrew
Pentecost, a great feast closing the harvest and the Paschal season,
dawned over the Holy City. Under the symbols of "a violent wind"
and "parted tongues as of fire," the Holy Spirit descended again
upon the apostles in the upper room.

● READ the brief account in Acts 2:1-4.

The speciality of this Pentecost visitation by the Spirit becomes strikingly evident in the immediate aftermath. From their refuge the apostles strode forth as fearless spokesmen for their resurrected Lord. Peter, Christ-appointed leader of the twelve (including the elected Matthias of Acts 1:15-26), braved the ridicule of the crowds in Jerusalem's streets and proclaimed the authoritative Christian Message:

> ". . . let all the house of Israel know most assuredly that God has made Lord and Christ, this Jesus whom you crucified." (Acts 2:36)

● READ again with some new realization the message of the first pope as recorded in Acts 2:22-24 and 32-36. Note the key words, "Lord and Christ" (v. 36), and also "exalted at the right hand of God" (v. 33). What does Peter mean by applying these words, so sacred to the Hebrews, to Jesus of Nazareth?

Liturgy: The Mass for Pentecost Sunday brings us news of "a new creation." The Book of Genesis in its account of the first creation had recorded that "in the beginning . . . **the spirit of God was stirring among the waters.**" (Gen. 1:2). The Church's liturgy has seen in these words some vague foreshadowing of a new and greater creation, the work which the Holy Spirit would undertake after the world's Redemption by Christ. Adam's sin had driven the Spirit from God's created world; Christ's Redemption would bring the Spirit back again. The great task began, to **re-create** the world the way God intended it to be.

The spirit of the Lord fills the world, Alleluia . . . . Introit of Pentecost.

● IN REFLECTING upon the words of the prayer, "Come, Holy Spirit," do you note any reference to the Spirit's work of re-creation?

● LOOK UP the special Preface for Pentecost and see if you can find there *the triple aspect* of Christ's Paschal Victory.

● WHAT truth of our Catholic faith do you find in the Gospel of the Pentecost Mass? Does it have a feastday of its own? When?

The Meaning of Sunday for a Catholic: With Easter and Pentecost both happening on Sunday, it is easy to see why the early Christians shifted their day of rest from the Hebrew Sabbath to the first day of the week. Each Sunday became for them **"a little Easter"** and **"a little Pentecost."** This was the fullest meaning of the expression "The Lord's Day."

With deep spiritual insight, the early Christians looked on their Lord less as crucified or even risen gloriously **in the past,** than as the triumphant Christ ruling with power and majesty **in the present.** Sunday meant the triumphant Lord's impact upon their lives **today,** with the blessings of the Spirit pouring into their hearts **right now as they need them.** It was not a question of "What **I** am able to do, or what temptation **I** can overcome," but rather "What **Christ** is able to do in me, or what temptations **Christ** can overcome with me."

- RELATE these ideas to the diagram of Christocentric history which we studied earlier in the Introduction.

Section 2. THE SPIRIT IN CHRIST'S CHURCH

I. THE CHURCH, A CREATION OF THE SPIRIT: Its Early Growth

"The New Creation" accomplished by the Holy Spirit reached its climax in the formation of Christ's Church. On Pentecost Sunday the Spirit gifted the apostles with new understanding, new energies, new courage. St. Luke records in the Acts of the Apostles that the first missionary effort of St. Peter netted "three thousand souls" (Acts 2:41) for Christ's Church.

- ARE YOU reminded of any picture that our Lord employed to foreshadow this mass reception of converts into the Church? How did Peter fit into the picture our Lord used?

And so the Acts of the Apostles continues recording apostolic preaching and the resulting catch of converts to faith in Jesus of Nazareth. The pattern repeated itself:

1. **The apostles preached** Christ crucified, but gloriously risen, reigning now "at the Father's right hand."

2. **The crowds,** "pierced to the heart," **pleaded:** "Brethren, what shall we do?" (Acts 2:37)

3. **The apostles replied:** "Repent and be baptized every one of you in the name of Jesus Christ . . ." (Acts 2:38-39)

The Acts of the Apostles, therefore, is really a historical sketch of growth in the early Church under the inspiration of the Spirit.

- NOTE in the Apostles' Creed that the work of man's salvation did not end with the sending of the Savior and the accomplishment of His Redemptive Mission. The Holy Spirit carries out man's salvation within Christ's Church.

- WHERE would you mark off divisions in the Apostles' Creed according to the role in God's Plan attributed to each member of the Trinity? Does that mean that in each one's attributed work the other two had no part? Discuss.

We can conclude this section on the Church as the creation of the Holy Spirit by summing it up in another Old Testament image:

With the birth of the Church is born "A NEW PEOPLE OF GOD."

- DISCUSS the typology of the "New People of God." What was its "type" in the Old Testament? Is the "New People of God" in its final stage, or is it to undergo another change still? Explain.

II. THE CHURCH, GUIDED AND STRENGTHENED BY THE SPIRIT: Persecution

The Spirit's guidance stands out unmistakably through the early history of the Church community; first, in the rapid growth of membership, but just as much in the heroic response to fierce persecution. The Spirit breathed His strength into Christian hearts. Loyal friends of Christ never expected easy times. Christ Himself had warned them:

> *"If the world hates you, know that it has hated me before you . . . If they have persecuted me,* **they will persecute you also."** *(John 15:18, 20)*

Persecution struck first from the Sanhedrin which had condemned Christ. The Jewish leaders felt that they could not stand by idle while thousands rallied around these Galileans, fanatic followers of the Nazarene of whom they thought themselves rid. But when brought to trial, when thrown into chains, when solemnly warned at the cost of their lives not to preach the Message of Christ's Kingdom, the apostles held fast:

> *"Whether it is right in the sight of God to listen to you rather than to God, decide for yourselves. For we cannot but speak what we have seen and heard." (Acts 4:19-30)*

- READ Mark 13:9-11 and discover the real reason for the apostles' courage and confidence.

But strangely enough, the first Christian to earn a martyr's crown was not an apostle, not even a Jew of Israel or Juda. He was the deacon Stephen, born to Jewish parents who had migrated from Palestine and who, therefore, were despised by the proud inhabitants of the Promised Land. Stephen ratified his profession of faith with blood, and in a special vision saw the Triumphant Lord accept his offering:

> *"Behold, I see the heavens opened, and the Son of Man standing at the right hand of God." (Acts 7:56)*

- READ the account of Stephen's martyrdom which St. Luke gives us in Acts 7:54-60. Note the name of Saul entering the story, Saul "who approved of Stephen's death." God had wondrous plans for this savage persecutor of the Church.

- READ "the vision of Saul" in Acts 9 and see how God's Providence through the Holy Spirit launched Paul's great missionary crusade among the Gentiles. The life of St. Paul merits fuller development in another year of our high school Religion program.

III. THE CHURCH, LIVING BY THE SPIRIT: the Mystical Body of Christ

When Saul was struck down on the road to Damascus, he heard a voice, "Saul, Saul, why dost thou persecute me?" To Saul's astonished cry, "Who art thou, Lord?" the answer came right back:

> *"I am Jesus, whom you are persecuting." (Acts 9:5)*

But Saul was not persecuting Jesus; he was persecuting **the followers of Jesus.** And yet our Lord meant just what He said. In some way, therefore, in persecuting Jesus' friends, Saul persecuted **Christ Himself.** We are here at the very heart of our Catholic faith, the union of Christ with His Church, **He in us and we in Him.** This is the revealed truth which we call "the Mystical Body of Christ."

St. Paul himself will tell us more about it throughout the letters he wrote in later years.

- READ Paul's development of the mystical body in I Corinthians 12:12-26. Note that the unifying and sanctifying force in the Body of Christ *is the Holy Spirit* (Verse 13). That is why the Spirit is sometimes called "the soul of the Church."

- DID our Lord ever use another picture to teach the same idea, i.e. of "He in us and we in Him"? Refresh your memories by rereading John 15:1-6.

- SHOW how each of these two pictures, that given us by St. Paul and that by Christ Himself, helps illustrate each of the following:

  1. The idea of unity in the Church.

  2. The idea of dependence upon Christ.

  3. The idea of mutual cooperation among members.

  4. The idea of success and failure.

A. **Brothers of Christ:** Divine Adoption

If we are united to Christ by sharing the same life of grace, then indeed we are brothers of Christ, brothers in the unity of the Holy Spirit. But if we are brothers of Christ, then we are in some way sons of God, too; not sons by nature, as is Christ alone, but **sons by adoption.** St. Paul reveals God's boundless generosity:

*For whoever are led by the Spirit of God, **they are the sons of God.** Now you have not received a spirit of bondage so as to be again in fear, but you have received a spirit of adoption as sons, by virtue of which we cry, **"Abba! Father!"** (Rom. 8:14-15)*

- WHEN was man first raised to the dignity of God's adopted son? Is this sonship the same as any legal adoption, or is it something more? What is the supernatural gift which enables us to live the life of our Father in heaven?

B. **Personal Contacts with Christ:** the Sacraments

It was our Lord's redemptive triumph that merited for men the precious gift of divine adoption. It is through the sacraments of the Christian Community that man has access to this Paschal Victory of Christ.

The Sacraments are personal contacts with the Glorious Christ who is ever-present to men within the Christian Community:

1. IN BAPTISM

Christ raises man from the death of sin to the resurrected life of God's grace.

2. IN CONFIRMATION

Christ fills out the graces of baptism with a fresh communication of the Spirit, particularly of new strength and maturity.

3. IN HOLY EUCHARIST

Christ joins man to Himself in the sacrifice offered by the Christian Community.

4. IN PENANCE

Christ forgives the repentant sinner and welcomes him back into the family of God.

5. IN ANOINTING OF THE SICK

Christ readies man's body and soul for a return to health, or eases the passing to Himself.

6. IN HOLY ORDERS

Christ forms ordinary men to the pattern of His priesthood so that they may offer sacrifice and care for the faithful in the People of God.

7. IN MATRIMONY

Christ unites with a man and woman in building up His mystical body with new members.

C. **Living the Life of Christ:** the Commandments

The man who values his privilege as Christ's brother and a son in God's family values also the ways to live this life of Christ. They go together. We are fortunate to know what we must do to live up to our privileged position. Otherwise, we might be groping about without any idea of what God expected of us; life would be futile and meaningless. That is why the Commandments are **blessings,** not burdens. They are something like the directions of a roadmap. If we made up our minds to get to a town out west, we would certainly value the roadmap that would get us there.

St. Paul suffered agonies because of his keen realization of what it meant to be a son of God, especially when he found such corruption among the people of Corinth in the Greece of his time:

> *Do you not know that **your bodies are members of Christ?**
> Shall I then take the members of Christ and make them members of a harlot? . . . Or do you not know that **your members
> are the temple of the Holy Spirit,** who is in you, whom you
> have from God, and that **you are not your own? For you have
> been bought at a great price. Glorify God and bear him in
> your body.** (1 Cor. 6:15, 19-20)*

- DISCUSS what you think St. Paul means by the emphasized words.
  Enumerate the truths of our Catholic faith which you can draw
  from this brief passage.

St. Paul lashed out at every sin against God's holy will, not just impurity. Sin can have no part in men who:

1. Are redeemed by the Blood of Christ.

2. Partake of the same life with Christ.

3. Share with Christ the glorious destiny of God's Kingdom.

IV. THE CHURCH, AND THE KINGDOM TO COME: the New Jerusalem

We have seen that John the Baptist and our Lord Himself both emphasized that the Kingdom of God was already among men. With Christ and His Church the era of the Kingdom has indeed begun: we are redeemed; we make contact with the Savior within His Church; and we share His life in the sacraments. And yet, it is also true to say that the Kingdom of God has not as yet reached its **ultimate** fulfillment. That is why we pray: "Our Father, who art in heaven . . . **Thy Kingdom come.**"

As one looks about in the world today, it is evident that God does not reign over the earth as He reigns in heaven. But how can this be? Only because God allows man his own free decisions, even when those decisions strike at God's own dominion over the world He created. It is in this sense that God's Kingdom is yet to come. We await the final transformation of the world, the definitive triumph when Jesus Christ will be Victor and Judge. Sinners will not want to think about this day of justice, but they must await its

East greets West. PHOTOGRAPH BY ERNST HERB

coming with fear and trembling. Christ's friends, however, like the Christians of old, should await the Lord's coming with joy and anticipation. His triumph will mean their triumph, too.

Recall again the exhilarating passage which we saw earlier from St. Paul:

> *But if we are sons, we are heirs also; heirs indeed of God and joint heirs with Christ, provided, however, we suffer with him* **that we may also be glorified with him.** *(Rom. 8:17)*

It would be well at this point to review the diagram for the Plan of God:

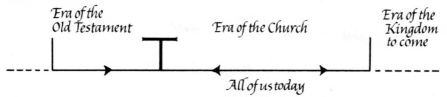

- WITHIN this framework of God's Plan identify what is meant by these biblical themes:

  1. The New Israel.

  2. The New People of God.

  3. The New Jerusalem.

- WHICH one of these three is usually applied to the "Kingdom to come"?

We shall see more about this "Kingdom to come" in the next and final chapter of this year's course.

SOME MEMORY HELPS:

1. **The Resurrection** is the triumph of Christ over death, the accomplishment of His Paschal Victory, and the pledge of our own glorification with Him.

2. **The Ascension** is Christ's farewell departure from His friends.

3. **"At the right hand of God"** is a Hebrew expression denoting participation in the power and majesty of God.

4. **Pentecost** is the feast of the special coming of the Holy Spirit and the birth of the Church.

5. **The Church** is Christ living on in the world, both in the supernatural unity of the mystical body and in the jurisdiction of the pope and bishops within this New People of God.

6. **The Sacraments** are signs effecting personal contacts with the glorious Christ through which Christ shares the benefits of His redemptive triumph with the Christian Community.

7. **The Commandments** are guidelines by which to live according to the life of Christ within us.

SUMMARY OF OUR BELIEF IN THE CHURCH

The Church is
Jesus of Nazareth,
God and man
gathering
within the People of God

1. All Christians,

2. All bishops,

3. The pope,

thus forming one total unit.

THEREFORE: Jesus + all of us Christians = the Church. As head of the mystical body, Christ unites all new generations to Himself till the end of time.

SUMMARY

Christ's triumph on Easter Sunday was complete. He rose from the dead and returned in glory to "the right hand of God." Enthroned in majesty, He could send the Holy Spirit immediately upon the apostles and His choicest friends. This He did, visiting many of them personally, particularly His Mother Mary.

On Ascension Thursday, with a special visible manifestation He made His farewell departure from His friends. Then on the Hebrew feast of Pentecost, He sent the Spirit again on the special mission of launching the Church.

The Church by God's design is the special creation of the Holy Spirit. Under the Spirit's special care, the New People of God grows rapidly, even amid persecution. Above all, through the presence of the Holy Spirit, the Church lives on as the mystical body of Christ. St. Paul also explains our privileged state as brothers of Christ and adopted sons in God's family. We share this life of Christ by our contacts with Him in the sacraments of the Christian Community. Anyone conscious of what he is by God's grace will live up to the life of Christ within him. The commandments show us how.

The Church, already sharing in God's gifts, will reach its ultimate fulfillment in "the Kingdom to come" when Christ will reign as Victor and Judge.

QUESTIONS

1. What did Christ achieve when He "descended into hell" after His Resurrection?

2. What are the reasons for presuming Christ's visit to His Mother Mary shortly after His Resurrection?

3. Contrast Thomas' attitudes before and after Christ's second visit.

4. What is the importance of Christ's conversation with Peter at the lakeshore?

5. Explain what you mean by the total Paschal Victory as it took place on Easter Sunday.

6. What event took place on what we know as "Ascension Thursday"?

7. Explain the liturgical development of the three feasts within the one Paschal Victory.

8. Did the first sending of the Holy Spirit occur on Pentecost?

9. What is special about the Holy Spirit's mission on Pentecost Sunday?

10. What do you mean when you pray the Holy Spirit "to renew the face of the earth"?

11. What did Sunday, "The Lord's Day," mean for the early Christians?

12. What is the pattern of the Church's growth in the Acts of the Apostles?

13. From what direction did persecution first strike and who was the first martyr of the Christian faith?

14. What are we to understand from Christ's vision to St. Paul in Acts 9:4-5?

15. In what sense are we brothers of Christ and sons of God?

16. How does each of the sacraments bring about a personal meeting with Jesus Christ within the Christian Community?

17. Why are the commandments really gifts of God, blessings to be gratefully accepted?

18. In what sense is the Kingdom of God already among us, and in what sense is it still to come?

Part Four
CHRIST TRIUMPHANT

CHAPTER XVI

THE DAY OF THE LORD: CHRIST'S FINAL VICTORY

The spread of our first-year course has ranged from the Garden of Paradise to the City of God, "the New Jerusalem," from **what might have been** for all of us to **what will be.** St. John's Book of the Apocalypse, which we will take in hand during this final chapter, gives the answers to questions raised in Genesis. Thus the last book of the Bible will balance off against the first as the epilogue and prologue respectively to the great Plan of God for man's salvation.

From the beginning of our course we have emphasized that the history of man has meaning, that it has carefully planned direction. At the center of His Plan God had placed His only Son made man, Jesus Christ. As the **Light of the World,** Christ illumined the time before His birth, but threw His shafts of light into the future, too. In that light, therefore, we saw that the Old Testament unfolded with a clear sense of direction and purpose, and that the New Testament took on momentous meaning in fulfillment of past promises. All of human history, in a word, is **Christocentric,** that is, revolving around the great events of the Incarnation and Redemption.

But a more significant title still is Jesus Christ, **Lord of History.** Christ does not merely illumine history; He is its Lord and King. He rules the universe, and all of creation is subject to Him. The Jews of the Old Testament had reserved the name of "Lord" for Yahweh alone, but Peter, after the mission of the Spirit on Pentecost, proclaimed to all the world that God has made **"both Lord and Christ,** this Jesus whom you crucified" (Acts 2:36). Thus today the resurrected Christ reigns in all power and majesty "at the right hand of God," and the earth awaits the great "Day of the Lord." On that day of final victory, He will come again, this time to establish the Kingdom of God forever. He will unite the People of God for all eternity.

In the first part of this chapter we shall focus attention upon

311

this "second coming of Christ," with its meaning for the People of God and for our own destiny as members thereof. The second part will spotlight the Book of the Apocalypse, with its penetrating vision of **the future that will be.**

Section 1. THE SECOND COMING OF CHRIST

I. THE DAY OF THE LORD

A. **Foreshadowing in the Old Testament**

From the time of the promises to Abraham, the Exodus from Egypt and the Covenant with Moses on Sinai, Yahweh had always been Israel's hope and deliverance. When in the turmoil of history Israel's enemies crushed God's People, the Hebrews turned to Yahweh for deliverance, and from Him they hoped for vengeance. On the great "Day of Yahweh," all wrongs would be made right; the Hebrews, as God's favored children, would crush their enemies and rule the world. Such was the Hebrew ambition and their future hope. One day the People of God would conquer.

- TRACE this "Day of Yahweh" theme back through some of the Prophets. Try these:
  1. Joel 3:14-17.
  2. Sophonia 1:14-16.
  3. Daniel 7:13-14 and 12:1-3.

B. **New Testament Fulfillment and Further Prophecy**

When John the Baptist arrived at the Jordan and preached that "the kingdom of heaven **is at hand**" (Matthew 3:2), to a religiously informed Hebrew he meant only one thing: The "Day of Yahweh" was imminent.

It was against the background of earthly ambitions for the political triumph of Israel, therefore, that Jesus Christ began to preach His Message. He labored for months and months to teach the apostles the real meaning of the Kingdom of God, to make them realize that His kingdom "was not of this world" (John 18:36). And yet, it was only with the coming of the Spirit's fuller light that they grasped His Message. With the Spirit's help, our Lord's words and the images He used, long dormant in their memories, came alive with fresh meaning. Since we are blessed with the Spirit ourselves, we too can look back with some understanding over the foreshadowings of "the Day of the Lord":

1. IN THE PARABLES

The parables were Christ's way of conveying significant spiritual truths to uneducated people. We would expect to find in them frequent references to the important question of the final destiny for the People of God; we are not disappointed.

One of the favorite images our Lord employed to picture life in the "Kingdom to come" was that of a wedding-feast. The Church, the New People of God, is the bride and Christ Himself is the bridegroom. Christ and His bride will be united in heaven forever. God will enthrone His Son at His side and welcome the bride to His Kingdom. Their happiness will be without end as they enjoy "new heavens and a new earth." In the book of Isaia these words are attributed to Yahweh:

> *Lo, I am about to create **new heavens and a new earth;** the things of the past shall not be remembered or come to mind. Instead, there shall always be rejoicing and happiness in what I create; for I create Jerusalem to be a joy and its people to be a delight; I will rejoice in Jerusalem and exult in my people. (Is. 65:17-19)*

- WHY do you think the author speaks of Jerusalem in this context? Is there some typology here?

- READ the entire parable of the wedding feast in Mt. 22:1-14. Discuss the picture it gives of "the Kingdom to come".

Another favorite parable picturing the "Day of the Lord" and the "Kingdom to come" was that of the Ten Virgins. Each of the ten had been invited to a wedding feast. They were supposed to meet the bridegroom and his bride at the entrance and enter with them for the festivities. When some of the foolish virgins missed the arrival of the wedding party, they pleaded to be let in. The reply from the bridegroom within contains some of the most tragic words in all scripture:

> *"I do not know you . . . ." (Mt. 25:12)*

- READ the entire parable of the Ten Virgins in Mt. 25:1-13. Reflect prayerfully upon the final words: "Watch, therefore, for you know neither the day nor the hour."

2. In Conversation

The Gospels have a way of making a few words expose the kernel of truth, even in ordinary conversation. Take, for example, the quick exchange with the Pharisees reported in St. Luke's Gospel:

> And on being asked by the Pharisees, "When is the kingdom of God coming?" he answered and said to them "The kingdom of God comes unawares." (Luke 17:20)

But to His closer friends Christ seems to have expanded His answer to the Pharisees' question, though still veiling it in some shadow.

- READ this somewhat perplexing passage as recorded in Luke 17:20-35, and then fill out its meaning by reading Luke 21:25-28. Notice our Lord's preference for the "Son of Man" title which we first found in the Prophet Daniel. (See Dan. 7:13)

3. In Prophecy

Christ spoke out most clearly of all about the great "Day of the Lord" in the prophecies recorded in Chapters 24 and 25 of St. Matthew. Although the evangelist links this prophetic account of the last day with the destruction of Jerusalem in a way which makes it difficult for us to separate the two events, still, the essential point comes through clearly enough: **You know not the hour; be ready!**

- READ Chapter 24:23-35 of St. Matthew's Gospel. Where in the liturgical year would you expect to find this Gospel used at Mass? Check in your Missals.

For a still clearer picture of the extraordinary events prophesied for the last day, our Lord in symbolic language pictured the Final Judgment itself:

> "But when the Son of Man shall come in his majesty, and all the angels with him, then he will sit on the throne of his glory; and before him will be gathered all the nations, and he will separate them one from another, as the shepherd separates **the sheep** from **the goats**; and he will set the sheep on his right hand, but the goats on the left." (Mt. 25:31-33)

It is significant that Christ uses the image of flocks of sheep and goats. Shepherds and flocks had always been among his favorite pictures for teaching the people. He applied to Himself the figure from the prophet Ezechiel of "the shepherd of his people" (see Ezechiel 34:5-6). Christ is "the Good Shepherd" who "lays down his life for his sheep" (Jo. 10:11). His sheep "follow him because they know his voice" (Jo. 10:4). And in another place Christ compares Himself to "a door" by which all men shall "enter (heaven)" and shall find pasture (Jo. 10:9). At that time of final peace and happiness, there shall be "one fold and one shepherd" (Jo. 10:16). But the shepherd is also the vigilant master of his flock. It is his task to separate the goats from the sheep and to remove them from his flock. Christ too must be judge. On the day of His final triumph, the "Day of the Lord," He will separate the sinners from the saints.

- READ the rest of the passage on Judgment Day in Mt. 25:34-46. What virtue provides one yardstick for measuring the goodness or failings of men? Why would you expect that such should be the norm of judgment? Review the chapter on the Kingdom for your answer.

With this picture of the sheep and goats Christ gives us an insight into the destinies of men as they will work out on the last day.

II. MAN'S LOT FOR ETERNITY: Heaven or Hell

A. **The Sheep on Christ's Right Hand:** Heaven

As a consequence of His Paschal Victory, Christ entered His Father's Kingdom in triumph. As Christ's brothers and members of His mystical body, we are meant to do the same. This is man's true destiny as intended for the People of God.

Heaven, therefore, is our home, our country, simply because it is the home and country of our Father. It is His Kingdom and we in the People of God are His heirs. (See again Romans 8:17). That was why our brother, Jesus Christ, told the apostles, and through them all of us too, that they should not fret and worry:

> "*In my Father's house there are many mansions. Were it not so, I should have told you, because **I go to prepare a place for you**. And if I go and prepare a place for you, **I am coming again, and I will take you to myself; that where I am, there you also may be**.*" (John 14:2-3)

In the light of our Lord's promise to the apostles and thus to all of us too, the true meaning of death comes into clearer focus. Death is a passage to new life. Man passes from this brief life to a life with the God who made him. Even earlier than these assurances to the apostles at the Last Supper, our Lord had spoken forcefully of man's life beyond the doors of death. Recall the assurances He gave to Martha and Mary at the death of their brother, Lazarus:

"I am the resurrection and the life: **he who believes in me,** **even if he die, shall live;** *and whoever lives and believes in me, shall never die." (Jo. 11:25-26)*

And when our Lord posed the question of faith to Martha, she answered for all men and women of faith:

"Yes, Lord, I believe that thou art the Christ, the Son of God, who hast come into the world." (Jo. 11:27)

- CONSULT the liturgy of the Mass for the Dead on the day of burial as presented in your Missals. Do you think the readings for the Epistle and Gospel are well chosen? Discuss.

St. Paul helped to shape the thinking of the early Christians by telling them to take to heart these assurances from their Master:

But we would not, brethren, have you ignorant concerning those who are asleep, lest you should grieve, even as others who have no hope. For if we believe that Jesus died and rose again, **so with him God will bring those also who have fallen asleep through Jesus.** *(1 Thess. 4:13-14)*

And, in another uplifting passage, St. Paul exults in the triumph of Jesus Christ and all who love Him:

O death, where is thy victory? O death, where is thy sting? (1 Cor. 15:55)

There are only a few things we can now know about the heaven that awaits us beyond death:

1. WE SHALL see God **face to face.** We shall live with God and come to know Him well. He will be our greatest joy, the source of our total happiness. Even the deepest of human loves, that of a husband for wife or of a mother for son, are only pale figures of the love of God for His People and the happiness it brings. As we saw earlier (see Chapter II) God loves most deeply when He gives Himself to men. St. John in his vision of the New Jerusalem re-echoes the same beautiful themes that are found in the prophets:

Behold the dwelling of God with men, and he will dwell with them. **And they will be his people, and God himself will be with them as their God.** *(Apoc. 21:3)*

- SEE Ezechiel 37:26-28 for God's wonderful promises in behalf of His People, as recorded in the Old Testament.

2. WE SHALL know **perfect happiness.** We shall join Christ, Mary, the apostles and saints, our relatives and friends; together with them we shall live with God, and in Him all our desires shall be fulfilled. Our glorified bodies, much like Christ's resurrected body, will join our glorified souls in heaven so that our happiness will be complete. St. John expresses this happiness in another way:

And God will wipe away every tear from their eyes.

And death shall be no more;

neither shall there be mourning, nor crying, nor pain any more,

For the former things have passed away. (Apoc. 21:4)

- SEE Isaia 25:8 for these same themes.

3. BUT NEITHER should we picture ourselves walking on clouds in some great beyond. Revelation tells us that **the earth too will be part of the New Creation** which we call heaven. The earth must be transformed by its own kind of resurrection. It must be liberated from every grip of evil and death, from every hold that sin may have had over it. As a result there will be no floods, earthquakes, or famine. Nothing will disrupt the perfect order and contentment in the New Paradise. In his vision of heaven St. John tells us:

And I saw **a new heaven and a new earth.** *For the first heaven and the first earth passed away. . . . (Apoc. 21:1)*

NOTE: Every man is surely conscious of his own shortcomings. He wonders how with all his faults he can hope to live in heaven with the all-perfect God. Our faith gives us the answer. Before man joins the company of God in heaven, he must first complete the growth and purification which will prepare him to take his place in God's Kingdom. We call this state of growth and purification, **purgatory,** from the Latin verb purgare, meaning "to cleanse."

In this purifying process associated with purgatory, suffering plays a part. After seeing the redemptive use which Christ made of suffering in His passion and death, we should not be surprised that suffering can achieve so much for departed souls awaiting entrance into God's Kingdom. The forced separation from God and loved ones, although only temporary, is surely one source of the suffering, but what other pain the souls in purgatory must undergo we are not sure. One thing is clear: purgatory is **not** a chamber of torture and horrors to torment good souls who have offended God however slightly. It is above all **a means of liberation,** a freeing of the departed soul from the shackles of sin, from the traces of selfishness which make contact with the all-holy God impossible. Paying the debts of temporal punishment is necessary in purgatory too, but not nearly so important.

- WHAT do you think is the actual attitude of souls in purgatory toward this redemptive kind of suffering? Do they hate it? fear it? desire it? Discuss.

- TRY TO find out how early Christians of catacomb days felt they could help the souls in purgatory? Can we help our own beloved dead? How?

Liturgy: The anticipation of the New Paradise inspires much of the liturgy of the Pentecost season. This is the season of Christian hope, as symbolized by the color of the vestments for Sunday Mass, green.

Liturgy
of the Sundays after Pentecost

The season of Pentecost lasts twenty-four Sundays and is really a living of the Spirit of Easter. Each Sunday's liturgy offers us another encouragement to live our Christian faith and to strive for the fullness of Pascal Victory that is our eternal destiny. Just as we can be confident of Christ's aid in the day-by-day struggle to reach this goal, so too when serving Him honestly we need have no fears at His coming on the "Day of the Lord." This is the message of these Sundays after Pentecost.

The spirit of the Pentecost season may be summed up:

1. **Joy and gratitude** for Christ's Paschal Victory.

2. **Courage** to fight the spiritual battles essential for sharing Christ's victory.

3. **Being alert and eager** for Christ's final triumph as the Lord and King.

- LOOK UP the Mass for the final Sunday after Pentecost. The fitting conclusion to the liturgical year pictures trumpeting angels in the Gospel, as all the world echoes to the triumph of the•Christ.

B. **The Goats on Christ's Left Hand:** Hell

The more a man realizes God's great plans, the more he comes to fear the consequences of failure. The distressing fact is that man can throw it all away. Man is always free to accept or reject God's gifts, just as we saw in the Garden of Eden. Free will is a risky business, because with it man can sin; but far more significant still is the power it gives man to love God as He should be loved, freely and wholeheartedly. Man returns God's free act of love by a free act of his own. Love means nothing if it is not free.

As we saw in the Moses chapter, sin is the refusal to love God,

319

"And they were all filled with the Holy Spirit . . ." ACTS 2:4

even though He is our father. Hell is the state of all those who die in such serious sin. The wills of sinners, like broken machinery, jam for good in an eternal act of defiance against God.

Our Lord did not mince words on the subject of hell. Recall those tragic words addressed in the parable to the foolish virgins. As to damned souls pleading for entrance into heaven, Christ replies:

". . . I do not know you." (Mt. 25:13)

- READ some of our Lord's other references to hell:

Matthew 5:22 – "the fire of Gehenna."

Matthew 22:11-14 – "the darkness outside . . . the weeping and gnashing of teeth."

John 15:6 – "cast them into the fire, and they shall burn."

Matthew 13:40-43 – "cast them into the furnace of fire, where there will be the weeping and the gnashing of teeth."

Matthew 25:41 – "Depart from me, accursed ones, into the everlasting fire which was prepared for the devil and his angels."

Mark well the recurrence of four ideas which gave Christ's hearers some insight into hell:

1. **Fire:** Man shrinks from fire as from no other pain.

2. **Darkness:** Man was made for light to see by; in darkness he suffers agonies of fear.

3. **Weeping:** Man's outlet for ordinary sorrow is tears, but this is the weeping of black despair.

4. **Gnashing of Teeth:** Man grinds his teeth in the realization of what he has thrown away, and for what? hell-fire!

NOTE: Did the Jews have any idea of what our Lord was talking about? Yes, they did. Early Jewish belief had been limited to a vague place for the dead called "Sheol," something like a huge graveyard, but later Jewish traditions record an abode of the damned also, which was called "Gehenna." Our Lord used Gehenna as a substitute term for hell. Actually, Gehenna really was the ravine which dropped sharply from the cliff at the southwest corner of Jerusalem. This was the spot where King Achaz hurled to their death human victims of sacrifice in the worship of the pagan god Moloch. You can see how this abominable place, piled high with corpses, easily came to give its evil name to the abode of the damned.

IN BRIEF: The horror of hell is two-fold:

    1. **Pain of Loss:** This means separation from God, in whose company man was destined to live as a son in His Father's house. In hell there is complete isolation from loved ones. Love or companionship is non-existent.

    2. **Pain of Sense:** Every human sense suffers punishment.. Torture of fire seems certain, but it is a peculiar type of fire. It does not consume anything, nor does it ever die out; yet it penetrates to the core of the soul as well as through the body.

Of these two horrors, the more terrible is the first, because it is a complete contradiction of everything man is and everything man is made for.

SOME MEMORY HELPS:

    1. **The "Day of the Lord"** is Christ's Triumphant Coming on the last day, when He will come in glory to take final possession of His Kingdom and to judge the world.

    2. **Heaven** is the state of perfect happiness within God's Kingdom for all the People of God who die in His love.

    3. **Hell** is the state of eternal torment and separation from God for all who die unrepentant sinners.

    4. **Purgatory** is the state of growth and purification needed to enter heaven for all who die in venial sin or still in debt for the temporal punishment due to forgiven sins.

    5. **The Communion of Saints** is the union in Christ of the faithful on earth, the blessed in heaven, and the suffering souls in purgatory.

The three classes just mentioned are often called, respectively, the Church Militant, the Church Triumphant, and the Church Suffering.

Section 2. BOOK OF THE LORD AND KING:
the Apocalypse

If we were to choose any one book of the Bible as the preeminent book of Christ as Lord and King, it would be the Book of the Apocalypse. St. John the Evangelist wrote this book of prophecy more than sixty years after Christ's Resurrection, but the thrill of His triumph vibrates through every word.

Persecution had struck and scattered his flocks; John himself was in exile on the isle of Patmos. Just like another Daniel writing to bolster the courage of his people amid persecution, John sent messages back to his friends **of hope and prophecies of final victory.** They must hold on with all confidence in their Lord and King. Truly, the victory already has been won: Christ reigns "King of kings, Lord of lords" (Apoc. 19:16).

The Book of the Apocalypse is difficult reading because of its special "literary form." We are unaccustomed to this type of writing, dense with symbolism and compact in expression. Besides, the symbolism is strongly Hebraic, as we should expect from this Galilean fisherman. But how else could John speak of "the Kingdom to come" except through symbols, representations which throw some light but which leave the mystery, too? The Kingdom of God will always remain a mystery until we pass through its gates.

THEREFORE: Do not read the Apocalypse trying to understand every symbol and every word. This is not necessary for our introduction to the book.

Read for the principal themes with which you are already familiar:

1. **The Lord reigns** triumphant and all-powerful; He will come again.

- READ 1:7-8, and 19:11-14.

2. **Saints and angels** give glory to the Lamb of God.

- READ 7:9-10, and 19:6-10.

3. **Satan is crushed** first by Michael the Archangel, then by Christ.

- READ 12:7-9, and 20:9-10.

4. **Vision of the Final Judgment** by the Son of Man.

- READ 14:14-16, and 20:11-15.

5. **The New Creation** for all the blessed of the Lord whose names are written in the Book of Life.

- READ 21:1-8, and 21:22-27.

At the very end of the Apocalypse — at the end, therefore, of the Bible itself — Christ the Lord proclaims to all generations:

"I am the Alpha and the Omega, the first and the last, the beginning and the end! Blessed are they who wash their robes that they may have the right to the tree of life, and that by the gates they may enter into the city." (Apoc. 22:13-14)

The "Alpha and the Omega," "the beginning and the end," that is another way of putting the basic truth of our Catholic faith: **Jesus Christ as "the Light of the World" illumines all history; all history takes its meaning from Him.**

Jesus Christ is the Lord of History.

The early Christians were as alive as we are to the meaning of Christ in their lives. That is why they made their constant prayer the verse of the Apocalypse:

"Come, Lord Jesus!" (Apoc. 22:21)

SUMMARY

Christ is the "Light of the World" and the "Lord of History." He will come again in glory on the great "Day of the Lord," foreshadowed in the Old Testament and prophesied again in the New. Christ Himself told us of this "Day of the Lord" in His parables, His conversations, but most of all in His prophecies about the end of the world.

On this day of days the final destiny of all mankind will be sealed. Christ the Judge will separate "the sheep" from "the goats," and all men will know the eternity of either heaven or hell. Purgatory is the purification preparing men for life with God. Perfect happiness awaits the blessed in God's Kingdom; in hell the pain of this loss will surpass even the pain of sense from hell-fire.

The Apocalypse is preeminently the Book of Christ as Lord and King. Though difficult to understand, it gives us a message of bright hope and prophesies our final triumph with God.

QUESTIONS

1. Summarize the total view of our first-year course, clustering your ideas around the double title applied to our Lord.

2. What was the Jewish interpretation of the great "Day of Yahweh?"

3. What means did Christ use to explain the "Day of the Lord" as it will be at the end of the world?

4. Describe the Final Judgment in the symbolic details given us by Christ Himself.

5. What do we know about heaven?

6. What is the purpose of purgatory?

7. What is the spirit of the post-Pentecost season?

8. Why is free will such a wonderful power of the soul; why is it risky too?

9. With what ideas did Christ give us a picture of hell?

10. What is the double horror of hell?

11. What is the general content of the Apocalypse?

12. What is the final message recorded in the Apocalypse, and therefore, in the whole Bible?

APPENDIX

THE BOOKS OF THE BIBLE

Old Testament

I. THE PENTATEUCH

GENESIS: traditional stories to teach religious truths concerning the creation of the world and God's favored creature, man; also, a sketchy history of the patriarchs Abraham, Isaac, Jacob, and Jacob's twelve sons.

EXODUS: account of the Hebrew liberation from Egyptian slavery and of the journey to the Promised Land; God ratified the Covenant with His People and gave Moses the Ten Commandments as the Covenant's charter.

LEVITICUS: a code of religious and civil laws.

NUMBERS: a report of incidents during the forty years in the desert.

DEUTERONOMY: a collection of religious messages to the Hebrew people, terminated by the account of the death of Moses.

NOTE: These five books are called the Pentateuch, from the Greek word meaning "composed of five books." They are attributed to the great Hebrew leader Moses, though Scriptural scholars believe he gave the original impetus only, while later editors prepared the final version. The Pentateuch is sometimes called the Torah or Books of the Law.

II. THE HISTORICAL BOOKS

THE BOOK OF JOSUE: tells of the entry into the Promised Land, the conquest of the hostile inhabitants, and the division of land among the twelve tribes.

326

THE BOOK OF JUDGES: narrates events centering around the chiefs whom God raised at critical points in Hebrew history, especially when the people mixed with pagan neighbors and forgot the Covenant.

THE BOOK OF RUTH: contains a little narrative about a Moabite woman who, as a symbol of the kingdom's universality, is mentioned among the early ancestors of Christ Himself.

THE FOUR BOOKS OF KINGS AND

TWO BOOKS OF PARALIPOMENON: are devoted to the royal period of Hebrew history, in particular the reign of David, of Solomon, and of their successors. Paralipomenon means "the parts omitted" in the previous four books and therefore, added in the two following. These six historical books continue to the time when the kingdom of Juda fell to Nabuchodonosor, and the inhabitants of Jerusalem were dragged away into captivity.

THE FIRST BOOK OF ESDRAS AND

THE BOOK OF NEHEMIA (sometimes called Second Esdras): report the construction of Jerusalem by the repatriated Jews after their captivity in Babylon; a spiritual revival ensues.

A Special Classification:

Listed among the historical books are three which by literary form resemble edifying religious stories, though many historical details are mixed in.

THE BOOK OF TOBIA: tells the story of two captives at Ninive, a father and son, who strikingly exemplify charity and filial devotion.

THE BOOK OF JUDITH: highlights in story form the heroism of a Hebrew woman in behalf of her nation's liberty.

THE TWO BOOKS OF THE MACHABEES: record the religious revolt against paganism under the leadership of the Machabee brothers during the second century before Christ's birth.

III. THE BOOKS OF WISDOM

THE BOOK OF JOB: a probing of the problem of pain and suffering in the world, as seen in the life of a good man.

THE PSALMS: prayers and liturgical songs, a good number of which are attributed to David. They were sung and recited in adoration, praise, and gratitude to God, with faith and hope in the golden era of the Messiah.

PROVERBS: a collection of moral sayings, bits of advice particularly for the young.

ECCLESIASTES: a series of meditations on life and death.

CANTICLE OF CANTICLES: a wedding song symbolizing the love of God for His People.

WISDOM: writings in praise of traditional Jewish values.

SIRACH OR ECCLESIASTICUS: a book of moral training and religious education, with special praise for God's Wisdom in history.

NOTE: The Wisdom Literature demonstrates how the Hebrew people shared many oriental ideas and traditions with their neighbors in the Orient. These were preserved, however, in a way distinctively Hebrew.

IV. THE PROPHETIC BOOKS

THE GREAT PROPHETS:

Isaia	Lamentations	Ezechiel
Jeremia	Baruch	Daniel

THE TWELVE MINOR PROPHETS:

Osee	Jona	Sophonia
Joel	Michea	Aggai
Amos	Nahum	Zacharia
Abdia	Habacuc	Malachia

New Testament

THE GOSPELS: each of the four Gospels in its own distinctive way collects sections of the preaching and catechesis of the early Church; thus are recalled some of the many things which Jesus said and did.

St. Matthew   St. Mark   St. Luke   St. John

THE ACTS OF THE APOSTLES: recounts the early growth and persecutions of the Church, especially marking the roles of Peter
as pope and Paul as the missionary to the Gentile world.

THE EPISTLES: include a number of the letters addressed to the
early Christian communities to clarify and strengthen their faith.

St. Paul to the Romans

Corinthians, 1-2	Thessalonians, 1-2
Galatians	Timothy, 1-2
Ephesians	Titus
Philippians	Philemon
Colossians	Hebrews

St. James
St. Peter, 1-2
St. John, 1-2-3
St. Jude

THE APOCALYPSE: was composed by St. John the Evangelist in a
highly symbolic style in order to affirm and represent the final
triumph of the Lord.

INDEX

INDEX

3 5282 00174 6224